Women's Spirituality

Resources for Christian Development

edited by
Joann Wolski Conn

Paulist Press ♦ New York ♦ Mahwah

In memory of my mother,
Gladys Strand Wolski,
and for my father,
Joseph Bernard Wolski

Library of Congress
Catalog Card Number: 85-62869

ISBN: 0-8091-2752-0

Published by Paulist Press
997 Macarthur Boulevard
Mahwah, New Jersey 07430

Printed and bound in the
United States of America

Contents

Acknowledgements

"Women's Spirituality: Restriction and Reconstruction" by Joann Wolski Conn from *Cross Currents* (Fall 1980): 293–308. Reprinted by permission.

"The Effects of Women's Experience on Their Spirituality" by Sandra M. Schneiders from *Spirituality Today* (Summer 1983): 100–116. Reprinted by permission.

"On Feminist Spirituality" by Anne Carr from *Horizons* (Spring 1982): 96–103. Reprinted by permission.

"In a Different Voice: Visions of Maturity" from *In a Different Voice: Psychological Theory and Women's Development* by Carol Gilligan, Cambridge, Mass.: Harvard University Press. Copyright © 1982 by Carol Gilligan. Reprinted by permission.

"The Evolving Self" from *The Evolving Self: Problem and Process in Human Development* by Robert Kegan, Cambridge, Mass.: Harvard University Press. Copyright © 1982 by the President and Fellows of Harvard College. Reprinted by permission.

Selection from *Toward a New Psychology of Women* by Jean Baker Miller. Reprinted by permission of Beacon Press and the author. Copyright © 1976 by Jean Baker Miller.

"The Construction of Femininity" from *Understanding Women: A Feminist Psychoanalytic Approach* by Luise Eichenbaum and Susie Orbach, copyright © 1983 by the authors. Reprinted by permission of Basic Books, Inc., Publishers.

"A Feminist Critique of Jung" by Naomi R. Goldenberg from *Signs: 2/2* (1976): 443–449. Reprinted by permission of the University of Chicago Press.

"A Feminist Perspective on Jung's Concept of the Archetype" by Demaris S. Wehr from *Feminist Archetypal Theory: Interdisciplinary Re-Visions of Jungian Thought* by Lauter and Rupprecht. Copyright © 1985 by The University of Tennessee Press. Reprinted by permission.

Selection from *Catherine of Siena: The Dialogue* translated by Suzanne Noffke, O.P. and preface by Giuliana Cavallini, New Jersey: Paulist Press. Copyright © 1980 by The Missionary Society of St. Paul the Apostle in the State of New York.

Selection from *The Collected Works of St. Teresa of Avila* translated by Kieran Kavanaugh, O.C.D. and Otilio Rodriguez, O.C.D. Copyright © 1976 by Washington Province of Discalced Carmelites, Inc. Reprinted by permission of ICS Publications.

Selection from *The Collected Works of St. John of the Cross* translated by Kieran Kavanaugh, O.C.D. and Otilio Rodriguez, O.C.D. Copyright © 1964 by Washington Province of Discalced Carmelites, Inc. Reprinted by permission of ICS Publications.

Selection from *A Commentary on Saint Ignatius' Rules for the Discernment of Spirits* translated by Jules J. Toner, S.J. Copyright © 1982. Reprinted by permission of The Institute of Jesuit Sources.

"An Inclusive-Language Translation of the Ignatian Rules for Discernment" translated by Elisabeth M. Tetlow. Copyright © 1984. Reprinted by permission of Elisabeth M. Tetlow and the College Theology Society, co-publisher with The University Press of America.

Summaries of "Stages of Faith" pages 133, 149, 172, 182, 197 from *Stages of Faith: The Psychology of Human Development and the Quest for Meaning* by James W. Fowler. Copyright © 1981 by James W. Fowler. Reprinted by permission of Harper & Row, Publishers, Inc.

Selection from *The Passionate God* by Rosemary Haughton. First published by Darton Longman & Todd Ltd., London Copyright © 1982 by Darton, Longman & Todd, Ltd. Published in the U.S.A. by Paulist Press. Copyright © 1982 by Rosemary Haughton. Reprinted by permission.

Selection from "The Incomprehensibility of God and the Image of God Male and Female" by Elizabeth A. Johnson from *Theological Studies* 45 (September 1984). Copyright © 1984. Reprinted by permission.

"The Sophia-God of Jesus and the Discipleship of Women" from *In Memory of Her* by Elisabeth Schüssler Fiorenza. Copyright © 1983 by Elisabeth Schüssler Fiorenza. Reprinted by permission of The Crossroad Publishing Company.

"Non-Patriarchal Salvation" by Bernard Cooke from *Horizons* (Spring 1983): 22–31. Reprinted by permission.

"Impasse and Dark Night" by Constance FitzGerald from *Living with Apocalypse: Spiritual Resources for Social Compassion* edited by Tilden H. Edwards. Copyright © 1984 by Shalem Institute for Spiritual Formation, Inc. Reprinted by permission of Harper & Row, Publishers, Inc.

"Revisioning the Ignatian Rules for Discernment" by Joann Wolski Conn, first printed in this collection of essays.

"Thérèse of Lisieux from a Feminist Perspective" by Joann Wolski Conn, first appeared in *Spiritual Life* (Winter 1982): 233–239.

Appreciations

For helping me to understand and appreciate the consolation and desolation of women's spirituality I am grateful to my companions for many years in the Sisters, Servants of the Immaculate Heart of Mary (Monroe, Michigan), and to my supportive colleagues and friends Constance FitzGerald, Sandra Schneiders, Mary Jo Weaver, Denise Lardner Carmody, Margaret Gorman, Barbara Charlesworth Gelpi, Anne Carr, Mary Ann Hinsdale, Demaris Wehr, Elizabeth Dreyer, Elizabeth Koenig, and Felicidad Oberholzer.

A generous Neumann College Faculty Development Grant from the Pew Foundation supported the initial research for this book. I appreciate the interest and support shown by all the administration, faculty, staff, and students at Neumann College. Those in the Neumann Graduate Program in Pastoral Counseling deserve my special thanks.

I would like to thank my editors, Lawrence Boadt, for his advice about the original design, and Jean Marie Hiesberger and Georgia Mandakas, for their assistance at each stage of the project. I would also like to thank John and Denise Carmody for their help with my original proposal for this book.

Most of all, I would like to thank my husband Walt for suggesting the idea of this book in the first place, and for being *the* great resource for this woman's spirituality.

Introduction

Joann Wolski Conn

I once agreed to give a workshop on women's spirituality and later found it publicized as "Feminine Spirituality." For me this was a case of false advertising. So I began the workshop by explaining why we would be dealing with women's spirituality and not feminine spirituality. I am doing the same thing in this anthology; thus a few words about the title are important.

This book is not called "Feminine Spirituality" because feminine often refers to a set of abstract qualities that are assumed to be unchanging and universal. These qualities have been defined by men, projected onto women, then reclaimed by men as the complement to their masculine qualities. This book, on the other hand, aims to be concrete, historical, and particular, and to work with categories defined by women for women. Feminine, insofar as it refers to qualities such as sensitivity and passivity which are assumed to be natural to women and unnatural for men, perpetuates a false stereotype. Finally, feminine is often negatively construed to mean wheedling and manipulative. This book aims to examine and criticize these very assumptions. "The feminine" is a socially constructed ideal attitude. Women are taught to accept and conform to this "natural" dimension of their nature. This book, on the other hand, encourages women to examine socially conditioned beliefs and feelings with an eye to accepting what promotes maturity and rejecting what inhibits it. The norm, therefore, is not feminine nature but women's critical evaluation of standards for maturity.

The book is not called "Feminist Spirituality" because, for many people whom I teach and counsel, this term is counter-productive. It makes them suspicious or angry. Unfortunately, they associate it with exclusion of men or with "doing to men what they have done to us." For me, feminism means an affirmation of women's full equality with men, an awareness of the history of women's experience in our male-centered culture, an inclusive movement of women and men who build a society and church which eliminate all forms of domination. As such, it is the truest expression of the gospel of Jesus, an opinion which will become clearer as one moves through this book. As a title, however, it could be a barrier to teachers, pastoral counselors, spiritual directors, preachers, or others who might otherwise consider using this book to promote women's Christian development. I hope this anthology will be useful for women and men who do not yet identify themselves as feminist. It gives psychological and spiritual resources for appreciating the feminist perspective as the most helpful framework for promoting authentic religious maturity.

This book is for and about women: it addresses concrete persons whose biological sexuality and historical situation have occasioned a certain type of socialization. For example, society teaches women to view only certain roles, attitudes and feelings as appropriate for them. Women are educated to roles which are called "separate but equal," yet are really separate and subordinate, often only auxiliary to a male-centered culture. Self-sacrifice motifs and attitudes of dependence are promoted for women as expected virtues, yet for men are regarded as unique heroism or even as weakness. Understanding this socialization and its consequences for women's spirituality is the focus of this book.

My own socialization as a white, middle-class, Western Christian woman gives me only a limited perspective on these issues. While I cannot claim to be offering resources for black women's spirituality, there may be something here that black women might wish to use; only they can say, however, what that might be and how they might modify it to suit their lives. When the word women appears in this text, therefore, it should be understood to reflect predominantly the experience of white, middle-class, Western women.

Spirituality is a term often distorted by dualism or naive religious assumptions. When spirit is taken to mean "the opposite of matter," then spirituality is only associated with invisible thoughts or feelings. When spirit is defined as "what God is," then spirituality becomes a narrowly religious term. When spirituality is understood as a contemporary philosophical and psychological as well as religious term, however, these distortions are corrected. Philosophers speak of our human spirituality as our capacity for self-transcendence, a capacity demonstrated in our ability to know the truth, to relate to others lovingly, and to commit ourselves freely to persons and ideals. Psychologists sometimes use the term for that aspect of personal essence that gives a person power, energy, and motive force. Religious persons speak of spirituality as the actualization of human self-transcendence by whatever is acknowledged as the ultimate or the Holy, that is, by whatever is considered religious. Within religious spirituality one can find specific spiritualities such as Jewish, Christian, Hindu.

Christian spirituality involves the human capacity of self-transcending knowledge, love, and commitment as it is actualized through the experience of God, in Jesus, the Christ, by the gift of the Spirit. Because God's Spirit comes to us only through experience and symbols inseparable from human community and history, Christian spirituality includes every dimension of human life.

Christian spiritual development, therefore, cannot legitimately be identified as soul development, or be associated exclusively with development in prayer and virtue. To be experienced and studied adequately, it should be viewed as total human development. Once this view is accepted, however, the problematic nature of women's spiritual development begins to be recognized.

Women's spiritual development is perplexing and difficult for three reasons.

(1) For women the possibilities for mature humanity/spirituality are restricted. Models of human development universally recognize that movement away from conformity and predetermined role expectations and toward greater autonomy (i.e., self-direction, self-affirmation, self-reliance) is necessary for maturity. Yet women's experience shows that most women are socialized into conformity to subordinate roles or are arrested at the threshold of autonomy. To make matters worse, the most prevalent psychological models of human development stop at autonomy, at a notion of maturity as differentiation from others, as independence, as taking control of one's life. Yet women's experience convinces them that maturity must include not only autonomy but also relationship. It must value

not only independence but also belonging. That is, women's experience makes them suspicious of autonomy as the goal of human maturity, while it makes them struggle against social pressures even to reach as far as that ambiguous goal.

(2) Christian teaching and practice, instead of promoting women's maturity, has significantly contributed to its restriction. Women have consistently been taught to value only one type of religious development—self-denial and sacrifice of one's own needs for the sake of others. Whereas men have been taught to couple self-denial with prophetic courage to resist unjust authority, women have been taught to see all male authority as God-given and to judge that assertion of their own desires was a sign of selfishness and pride. The problem lies not so much with the model of religious development as with its application. For example, to encourage self-denial without attention to the way women are prevented from having a self (i.e., sufficient self-direction, autonomy) is, in effect, simply to promote conformity to a male-approved role.

Although spiritual directors might encourage women to follow their own desires so that they can give adult self-surrender to God, they often neglect the particular difficulty and complexity of that task for women. Because women are socialized to notice and respond to everyone else's desires, they frequently repress their own desires so much that they do not or cannot easily contact them. Or they cannot admit the adult longing for autonomy because they assume it means selfishness. On the other hand, women sometimes resist autonomy because they wisely suspect that it is not the appropriate goal of human maturity. To compound the difficulty, they are also suspicious of self-surrender as a religious goal because it has so often been used by men as a tool for women's domination. Because of the complexity and significance of these issues women need and deserve special resources for their Christian development.

(3) Women's spirituality is problematic because some women judge that the Christian spiritual tradition is so sexist that it is no longer usable for mature women. Other women conclude that their spiritual development demands that women and men become creatively involved in the challenging and long-range task of reconstructing the commonly accepted, male-dominated Christian tradition. Because this work of reconstruction has only just begun, and has yet to become part of the mainstream of counseling, teach-

ing, and spiritual direction, women are in need of special resources for their Christian development.

This book presents resources for women and men to use in discerning appropriate ways to support women as they struggle with each of these problematic areas. In Section I, my essay explains these problematic areas in more detail and gives additional examples of their implications for women's lives. The other essays also explain women's spirituality and the challenge of moving toward a feminist spirituality. Section II presents models of women's psychological development that spring from explicit attention to three concerns: the male-centered bias of prevailing developmental models, the need for a new model of human maturity based on equal examination of both women's and men's experience, and the need for a whole new psychology of women. Section III presents both classical and contemporary models of religious development. These models were chosen for the way they stress characteristics of development which are particularly well suited to women's situation today. The models come equally from women's as well as men's religious experience. Section IV offers essays from women and men who are now revisioning Christian tradition in order to address the third problematic area of women's spirituality: the need to reconstruct the entire tradition so that it gives equal affirmation to women's experience.

I have used all the material in this anthology in undergraduate and graduate courses in spirituality, women's studies, and pastoral counseling. These authors have influenced my own prayer and ministry of spiritual direction. Therefore, the final editing of these selections is based on my own practical appreciation of these resources for my own and other women's Christian development.

Section I

Issues in Women's Spirituality

The three essays in this section set forth the basic issues and establish the tone of this book. The first issue, the inseparability of human development and religious development, is addressed by each essay giving examples of the practical implications of this fact. The second issue is the unique and problematic situation of women's spirituality today. My essay prompted a male graduate student to declare, "Until I read this essay I thought Christian spirituality was basically the same for everybody. Now I see there is only this person's spirituality, with all the complexities of that experience. If women have experiences in common, then they have a spirituality common to women and different from mine." Sandra Schneiders' essay develops this theme. The third issue is the relationship between women's spirituality and feminist spirituality. When women become explicitly conscious of the way a male-centered society and church affects their spirituality, they may accept the challenge and rewards of moving toward a feminist spirituality. Anne Carr's essay explains this challenge and some rewards.

The tone of the book is positive, constructive, inclusive of men's as well as women's experience. The essays are suggestive rather than dogmatic, yet are firm in their affirmation of the compatibility of feminism and Christianity. That is, from within the male-centered Christian community they represent a certain "loyal opposition."

Women's Spirituality: Restriction and Reconstruction

Joann Wolski Conn

At the heart of the problem of women's spirituality is a subtle but devastating twist on the Patristic theme: "The glory of God is humanity fully alive." Women in the Christian tradition have unfortunately been led to believe that God is glorified by their humanity only partially alive, because they have been restricted to roles that limit their capacities for self-direction and restrict their ability to experience self-esteem.

This article will examine three aspects of women's self-direction and self-esteem. First, how is this an issue in spirituality? Second, what are the central reasons why women's spirituality continues to be problematic? Third, what is being done now, and what can be done in the future to deal with this issue?

WHAT IS SPIRITUALITY?

Spirituality as life-experience and as a field of study is no longer identified simply with asceticism and mysticism, or with the practice of virtue and methods of prayer. From the perspective of the actualization of the human capacity to be spiritual, to be self-transcending—that is, relational and freely committed spirituality encompasses all of life. In general, religious spirituality is a matter of the experience and/or study of the actualization of human self-transcendence by the Holy, by Ultimate Concern—that is, by what is acknowledged as "religious." Specifically, Christian spirituality

involves the actualization of this human capacity through the experience of God, in Jesus the Christ, through the gift of the Spirit.
Because this God, Jesus, and the Spirit are experienced through
body-community-history-influenced human life and symbols,
Christian spirituality includes *every* dimension of human life. Thus,
Christian spiritual development cannot legitimately be identified as
soul development, nor be exclusively associated with development
in prayer and virtue. To be adequately experienced and studied, it
should be viewed as total human development. When this view is
accepted, however, the problematic nature of women's spiritual development begins to be recognized.

PROBLEMATIC NATURE OF WOMEN'S SPIRITUALITY

Realizing that spiritual development is human development,
however, makes women's spirituality problematic for three central
reasons. First, for women the possibilities for mature humanity/
spirituality are restricted. Models of human development universally recognize that movement away from conformity and predetermined role expectations and toward greater autonomy (i.e. self-
direction, self-affirmation, self-reliance)[1] is necessary for maturity.
Yet, women's experience shows that most women are socialized into
conformity to a passive role or are arrested at the threshold of autonomy.[2] Second, Christian teaching and practice, instead of promoting women's maturity, has significantly contributed to this
restriction. Especially sad is the fact that so many women are estranged from themselves by absorption of the Christian tradition's
most common God-images. Third, women's spirituality is problematic because some women judge that religious maturity can really
only be accomplished by rejecting biblical tradition, while other
women conclude that their spiritual development demands that
women and men become creatively involved in the challenging and
long-range task of reconstructing the commonly accepted, male-
dominated Christian tradition.

Women's Humanity/Spirituality Is Restricted

Most patterns of family and education continue to reinforce two
roles for women. Women are socialized into being desirable objects

who dress, think, and act in order to receive acceptance and adulation, especially from males. Living for "another" is the second pervasive role expectation set for women. "Living for" can usually be simply translated: submerge yourself in the other's identity, needs, interests. Thus, a woman's self-actualizing potential is often anesthetized. She is taught to wait for someone to find her, and then life will take on purpose and worth. Even career women and members of religious communities do not escape this conditioning. Junior executive women can become an "office wife" to the boss, taking care of all his detail work and envisioning their purpose in the business as "smoothing the way" so that he can be absorbed in important decisions. For religious women, their community can function as a surrogate identity. They can be encouraged to take on a new work because of "community needs" rather than because they have discerned that this is what they really want and are suited for.[3]

Because women are often thought to be naturally self-effacing and dedicated, the deeply problematic effects of the way women are conditioned to this behavior are overlooked. Recent studies show that women's behavior that is praised as virtuous (i.e., loving) and mature (i.e., other directed) is actually often behavior symptomatic of severe immaturity. Women spending themselves on their family, their students, patients, or members of their religious community often have low self-esteem, and thus their emotional dependency makes them subtly very demanding on others for appreciation and adulation. Their inability to be assertive and their lack of self-worth can result in covert manipulation, pretended helplessness, evasion of conflict situations. Their desire for peace at any price has a high cost: repression of anger can result in bouts of depression. On the other hand, behavior that is criticized as not virtuous, as selfish or immature (e.g., a mother leaving small children in the care of others so that she can pursue an interesting job even though there is no severe financial need, or a member of a religious community questioning her superior's judgment about the appropriateness of an assignment) can be the behavior of a woman whose self-worth is more secure, who is less emotionally dependent and, thus, less demanding and less manipulative in her relationships.[4]

Because spiritual growth demands movement from an orientation toward heteronomy through autonomy in order to reach an ultimately mature, free relationship to God, women's conditioning toward conformity to a passive "merger self" rather than a "seeker self" is an especially cruel seduction.[5] Women are led to believe they are virtuous when actually they have not yet taken the necessary possession of their lives to have an authentic "self" to give in self-donating love. They are often praised as holy when they are still spiritually dwarfed!

The central issues of the women's movement focus on women's growing awareness of their need for autonomy in order to be truly human: desire for equality and mutuality in female-male relationship; the need to evaluate critically one's mother-daughter relationships; demands for symmetrical family patterns of work and parenting; conviction that woman-to-woman relations are as life-sustaining as conjugal relations.[6] Christian women need networks of assistance which will help them to realize that these are also central issues in the development of their spirituality—that is, of their basic capacities for self-transcending human and God relationships. The sound assertiveness training that is a common component of programs to help women in transition from traditional roles to more self-directive lives might just as appropriately be a component of spiritual formation programs. An empirical approach to spiritual direction maintains that growth in prayer involves the ability to heighten awareness of what one *really wants* in life and how one *really feels* in God's presence.[7] Women conditioned to role conformity, to self-doubt, and to dependency may find it quite difficult to get in touch with their own deepest desires or to be peacefully present to a God who respects their adult freedom and calls them friend not servant. Freedom and friendship involve making significant decisions and owning up to the consequences; they involve risk and struggle with ambiguity which insecure women find very difficult, if not impossible, to face.

Christian Tradition Has Legitimated
a Restrictive Spirituality for Women

Christian teaching and treatment of women has been one of the most effective means of legitimating and even promoting restrictive heteronomy rather than mature autonomy for women. Recent research has so carefully documented the sexism which permeates

Christian churches that a few representative examples are sufficient to focus the issue.

Jesus' complete acceptance of women's equal dignity and his calling women to full discipleship are clearly, though sometimes reluctantly, recorded in the Gospels.[8] However, the Pastoral letters show that early Church practice and attitudes often were not in continuity with the gospel vision in which women were valued in themselves rather than as subordinate wives or mothers or as unobtrusive virgins.[9]

From Patristic times to the present women have been presumed to be the image of God only or especially when conformed to male-approved roles which restrict women's self-esteem and self-actualization.[10]

Why did women support this religious vision so faithfully, and why do many women continue to support it? One of the main reasons is that ministers/priests and women identified religious with domestic values. For example, obedience to God became obedience to one's husband or to children's needs. Domestic virtues of humility and selfless devotion were cited as evidence that women are naturally more religious than men. When women have no other experiential source for rival values or symbols, they find religion a central means to define themselves and to find community. Religion provided social involvement outside the home in maternal associations and moral reform societies. These had the effect of organizing women and promoting gender-group consciousness. However, these effects were quite ambiguous for women. For although voluntary associations encourage some independence and self-definition, they also encourage women to fit into limited, clerically defined roles centered on family and subordinated to male authorities. Thus women's emergence, in these situations, is not necessarily an indication of personal autonomy but rather a continuation of conformity to socially-religiously defined "female responsibility."[11] When women's emergence is not accompanied by possibilities for public teaching and governing roles in the Church it is clear that heteronomy continues.

Recent Vatican documents continue to project an inconsistent attitude toward women. Statements about women's equality and ability to direct their own lives stand alongside presuppositions about women's appropriateness for serving in auxiliary, nurturing ministerial roles. The often repeated phrase, "women's different yet complementary role in ministry," is translated into action in almost every case as a subordinate role.[12] Hierarchical resistance to canon law revisions that admit women to full participation in church leadership[13] leaves no doubt about the way ecclesiastical practice continues to restrict women's spiritual development.

Detrimental Effects of Prevailing God-images

Women's mature humanity is also restricted by their absorption of the dominant God-images perpetuated by the fact that Church tradition often ignores or misinterprets basic biblical teaching.

What is ignored is the clear affirmation of both the Hebrew and Christian Scriptures that God is spirit and, thus, totally transcends sex which is rooted in matter. Such an abstract theological statement is absolutely central to biblical revelation, yet is not often explicitly repeated in Scripture. Thus it can easily be obscured by the abundance of anthropomorphic language which, coming from a patriarchal culture, is dominated by the use of masculine pronouns for this spirit God. This male language is in practice often misinterpreted as, in some way, accurately expressing a revelation of God as a male being. There are scattered examples of feminine anthropomorphic language which could balance the picture, reinforcing that God is neither female nor male, but that feminine language is seldom used in liturgical texts or Church documents. Jesus' understandable use of masculine parental language for this spirit God is mistakenly taken as a revelation that God is a male being. Consequently, most women absorb a totally masculine God-image and, thus, can mistakenly presume that men are more like God and women are rightly dependent on men for liturgical mediation of God's presence.[14]

Women's spirituality is severely damaged by this distortion of biblical revelation. It prevents a woman from valuing and affirming herself as authentically an image of God. It restricts a woman's ability to utilize her own experience as a revelation of God's qualities and activities. It can actually alienate a woman from her own experience when she presumes that "the Holy" is not at all like herself.

Just how personally damaging this distortion is, and therefore how problematic the consequent lack of self-esteem can be for women's spirituality, is suggested by the research of Dr. Ana-Maria Rizzuto, professor of psychiatry at Tufts Medical School. In *The Birth of the Living God*, through clinical studies of women's and men's attitudes toward God, Rizzuto both explains how a person's God-image is formed and developed and demonstrates its potential for generating belief or unbelief. The principal research was done with Dr. Rizzuto's patients. However, at later stages of research, she studied persons on her staff at Tufts and found no difference of any significance between her staff members and patients in their way of relating to God.[15]

It is Rizzuto's central thesis that no child in the Western world brought up in ordinary circumstances reaches school age without forming at least a rudimentary God representation which she/he may use for belief or unbelief. Challenging Freud, Rizzuto makes two key points: 1) belief is not a symptom of pathology; 2) the God-image is more than an "exalted" father; it draws its components from other early objects: mother, grandparents, or even an early aggrandized self-representation. The rest of developmental life may leave the God-image untouched as the person continues to revise parent- and self-representations during the life cycle. Developmentally, a crucial moment for revision of the God-image is late adolescence. At this stage there is a need to integrate a more cohesive, unified self-representation which will support major decisions about life, career, marriage. This reshuffling brings about new encounters between self-images and God representations. If the God representation is not revised to keep pace with changes in self-representation, it soon becomes experienced as ridiculous or irrelevant or, on the contrary, threatening or dangerous.[16]

Rizzuto's empirical studies show that "*belief in God* or its absence depends upon whether or not a *conscious 'identity of experience'* can be established between the God representation of a given developmental moment and the object and self-representations needed to maintain a sense of self which provides at least a minimum of relatedness and hope."[17]

Implications for women's mature spirituality are profound. On the one hand, if women retain a God-image that implies a denial or denigration of women's worth or potential for self-direction and full ministry, this is probably an indicator of unresolved developmental issues. For example, after studying misinterpretations of biblical language, some of my women students will say, "I don't mind that God is pictured only as a man or that we aren't allowed to do the same things men do in the Church." These women, almost without exception, are experiencing male resistance to their desire to be self-directing, or are very insecure and only beginning to sense their own potential. On the other hand, a woman experiencing a shift in self-representation from being dependent and conforming to being more self-directive, more willing to risk making significant decisions, can be expected to feel a strain in her relation to her God-image if such a woman's God-image works to reinforce a lack of self-esteem and to restrict hope. Such a woman, in order to maintain her spiritual development, must drop that God-image; she must cease to believe in that God.

Some women authors who have come to the judgment that they must reject the Jewish-Christian tradition about God explain their decision in a way consonant with Rizzuto's thesis. Everything these women experienced and knew of Christianity, they say, involved accepting God as ultimately present in male authority figures. Thus, when their self-understanding evolved to the point where they moved away from a heteronomous conformity to roles insisted upon by male authorities, they realized that consistency in their life demanded that they renounce belief in the God that legitimated this male domination. These women are convinced that the Christian tradition will support no other God-image and, therefore, they must reject Christianity as a significant source for sustaining their spiritual development.[18]

Other self-affirming women agree that a solely male God-image must be set aside, yet they find flaws in the position just mentioned. These women pose a series of penetrating questions to those who reject Christianity on this ground. Since you can appreciate and even reconstruct such intrinsically patriarchal traditions like that of Freud and Jung, why can you not do the same with biblical religion? Is it because religious authorities are still too intimidating? Rejection can function as unresolved dependency, as an indication that one is still responding to Jesus and God as oppressive fathers rather than encountering them as God-images which might have some liberating things to say as well as some severe cultural limitations. In addition, are you not sometimes writing about the Jewish-Christian tradition in such a simplistic way that, if this same method were applied to Buddhism or Hinduism you would be inclined to characterize the writers as very poorly educated in that tradition or even as bigots?[19]

Such challenging criticism is a demonstration that women religious scholars have "come of age." As adults they can deal with conflicting opinions and need not repress disagreement in order to project the illusory picture of a united front which actually hides insecurity. They are secure enough to raise difficult issues. What is more, they are courageous enough to face the full implications of renouncing a patriarchal Christianity while still hoping to find in Christianity resources for a mature spirituality. They are facing the call to reconstruct that tradition.

RECONSTRUCTING A TRADITION TO SUPPORT WOMEN'S SPIRITUALITY

A reconstructed Christian tradition is slowly emerging as women and men become aware of the detrimental effects of patriarchy on everyone and especially on women. Women's spirituality can be supported if all of us, both women and men, make progress in a twofold process. To begin, we must reexamine presuppositions about human development, discover the history of women's experience and leadership that has never been told, and explicate the women-liberating insights implicit in biblical teaching about God. As soon as we have these resources available we must begin to incorporate them into every aspect of life and ministry: teaching, writing, celebrating, praying, counseling, reconciling, befriending, protesting. As long as this process remains "frontier territory," experienced as the unknown and fraught with risk, women's spirituality will continue to be especially problematic.

Examining Models of Human Development

Of the growing number of studies in this area the contributions of two women can serve as examples of significant new viewpoints.

Carol Gilligan has examined the limitations of the developmental models constructed by Kohlberg and Erikson. These limitations result from their reliance on a predominantly male data base for their theorizing.[20]

Kohlberg describes the most mature level of moral development in terms of a person living according to universal principles of justice and respect for individual rights. For the men Kohlberg studied, the moral imperative is expressed as an injunction to respect the rights of others and to protect from interference the right to life and self-fulfillment. However, for the women Gilligan interviewed the moral imperative repeatedly emerged as an injunction to care, a responsibility to discern and alleviate the world's trouble. In Kohlberg's view these women are judged to be developmentally immature, not yet to have moved beyond the interpersonal level and followed the path toward independent, principled judgment he found in the research on men from which his stages were derived.[21] Gilligan suggests that Kohlberg's repeated finding of developmental inferiority in women may have more to do with the standard used for measurement than with the quality of women's moral thinking.[22] A more adequate standard, says Gilligan, would be one which incorporates the "moral voices" of both women and men. Development for both sexes then would involve an integration of rights and responsibilities through a principled understanding of the complementarity of these male and female views. For the women Gilligan studied, this integration of rights and responsibilities appears to take place through a principled understanding of equality and reciprocity. For the men Kohlberg studied, it appears to be the recognition through experience of the need for a more active responsibility in taking care that corrects the potential indifference of a morality of noninterference. Aware of the fact that social conventions now lend a particular shape to women's and men's moral experience, Gilligan envisions a general standard which could admit this diversity and promote genuine complementarity. Using such a standard, Gilligan concludes that in the development of mature morality women come to see the violence generated by inequitable relationships, while men come to realize the limitations of a conception of justice blinded to the real inequities of human life.[23]

Although Erikson's life-cycle research recognizes the differences in women's and men's experience, Gilligan notes the limitation caused by the fact that Erikson does not incorporate women's experience into the normative model. Erikson observes: while for men identity precedes intimacy and generativity in the ideal cycle of differentiation, separation, and later attachment, for women these tasks seem, rather, to be fused. Intimacy goes along with identity as a woman comes to know herself through relationships with others. Erikson presumes this is a matter of meeting a man by whose name she will be known and by whose status she will be defined. In any case, the cycle-stages are admittedly different for women and men. Nevertheless, Gilligan observes, Erikson charts the life-cycle stages using only male experience to define development: identity continues to precede intimacy in his conception. Consequently, given Erikson's scheme, in the life cycle there is little preparation for the intimacy of the first adult stage. Only the initial stage of trust versus mistrust suggests the kind of mutuality Erikson means by intimacy and generativity. Other stages emphasize separation and differentiation.[24] However, women's development, as Gilligan's research demonstates, is marked by a recognition of the way interdependence can create strength, build resources, and motivate giving in the mature feminine style. The elusive element in women's development lies in its admission of the continuing importance of attachment in the human life cycle. Gilligan maintains that only when life-cycle theorists divide their attention equally and begin to understand women's experience as well as they have understood men's experience will their vision be adequate and their theories become correspondingly more fertile.[25]

A second new viewpoint is Georgia Sassen's recent reexamination of women's response to our commonly held model of human success. It has led her to suggest that we reconstruct our basic institutions.[26]

Martina Horner's research in 1968 concluded that 65% of the women studied showed anxiety over success because they anticipated that success in competitive achievement activity, especially against men, produced social rejection and loss of femininity. These results were so widely accepted that "fear of success" became a common expectation in research on women.[27]

Sassen took another look at that research and came to a different conclusion. Defining anxiety as a sense of disintegration occurring when a person is unable to make meaning,[28] Sassen judges that the women in the original research were not simply afraid. They were, rather, unable to take competitive success and construct a vision to which they could personally be committed. Their knowing structure was oriented more to preserving and fostering relation-

ships than toward winning. What should be done about these results? Some people favor teaching women how to "succeed in a
man's world." Sassen suggests, on the contrary, that society affirm
the structures and values women bring to the issue of competition
versus relationship and reconstruct institutions according to these
values and structures.[29]

How does this affect women's spirituality? Women are especially committed to replace the emphasis on clericalism and hierarchical leadership in institutions which embody Christian ministry.
Speaking from their own experience of attempting to live out com-
munitarian, mutual workstyles which affirm gifts of ministry in all
persons, they admit their scruples about being identified with a
Church whose hierarchical response to women's desire for complete
equality often treats that desire as an inappropriate desire to compete
with men.[30] Priests' refusal to relate to women in liturgical settings
with an invitation to full participation creates a widening gap between liturgy and women's spirituality.[31]

Of course, there are also some men who are uncomfortable
about defining success as competition. Since Vatican II priests commonly say that successful authority and leadership can only be service, not competitive domination. The deliberate need to renounce
power is a growing concern.[32] Thus it is especially anguishing to
women that they are systematically excluded from an equal share in
areas which demand nurturing qualities they have "specialized in"
for years.

Women must and do admit their collaboration in perpetuating
this unhealthy model of human success by often encouraging men
in their competitive ideal of history making, rather than criticizing
that ideal.[33] The challenge now is to grow together in fostering a re-
newed model of humanity.

Recovering Women's Experience and Leadership

Christian women's spiritual growth, in addition to models of
human development which explicitly include their experience, requires satisfaction of the basic need for meaning and identity. In-
dispensable here is the need to recover the general history of
women's religious experience. Urgent also is the need to tell the
story of women's leadership. Because meaning requires imagina-

tion,[34] women need to picture their own past and have role models to support their vision for the future.

Although the field of women's history is young it has already developed through three phases or approaches. As in human growth, tasks of earlier stages remain significant even when later tasks emerge.

Compensatory history was naturally the first phase. Because so many notable women are missing from traditional history, especially from religious history, this continues to be a long-term undertaking. Whereas the first phase documented oppression—handicapped sometimes by acceptance of these women as exceptional or even deviant (i.e. deviant from male-defined history and norms)—scholars have now moved to investigating how women operated in a male-defined world *on their own terms*.[35]

Phase two recovers women's experience expressed in their own words and, among many issues, investigates the extent to which women's religious experience indicates that a struggle for self-affirmation, self-definition, and autonomous self-donation are intrinsic to their conversion and progress in holiness.

For example, Penelope Washbourn's cross-cultural research on pre-contemporary women shows how that particular tradition of female spirituality centers on the affirmation of female sexuality in its many seasons of change. Drawing from songs, prayers, liturgies, prose and poetry composed by women, Washbourn demonstrates that the symbols and forms of women's worship, prayer and celebration express women's bodily experience: menstruation, passionate love and longing, motherhood or barrenness, and aging. The question for her modern readers is not how we can duplicate the past, but how we can discover in our new roles—which are defined in terms wider than fertility—a sense of worship which appropriately incorporates bodily experience in the many seasons of life.[36]

Studies of Teresa of Avila's spiritual development are nothing new. However, studies which incorporate the concerns of the present article are seeing Teresa's experience from a quite new angle of vision. Catherine Cress Romano has examined the struggles through which Teresa eventually found her own way to integrate passionate love and history-making work, given Teresa's erotic personality in her patriarchal Spanish culture. Romano interprets Teresa's conversion struggle as rooted in an unresolved adolescent identity crisis, or as assumption of a sick identity incapable of integrating body, early adolescent feelings of competence, and capacity for leadership and love of challenge, with the female roles permitted in her male-dominated culture. Her will to change was hampered by her immature pattern: excessive dependence, neurotic need for love, unexpressed anger turned instead toward herself.[37]

Exhaustion of old defenses and, eventually, autonomous self-surrender to another force was Teresa's way, at mid-life, out of her old pattern. Teresa surrendered to a force (a faith-interpretation sees God working through this force) coming through her experience of contemplating the wounded Christ suffering for her, accepting and loving her. This experience enabled Teresa to recognize and accept her anger at restrictions placed on her competence, to accept her own humanity and erotic feelings, and to reenter the world and create a new Teresa and a new environment of activity in which she plays a leading role.[38]

However, according to Romano, to handle the conflicts this leadership generated in her culture, Teresa's socialization led her to develop a new neurosis: she projected her wishes entirely onto Christ rather than accept them as genuinely her own. That is, Teresa could accept leadership only as an act of obedience to Christ who commanded it.[39]

Nevertheless, as Teresa consciously surrendered to her new states of ecstasy, she grew more confident of her new relationship to Christ as being *her own* relationship. In later life she admitted only one true authority in her life and that was the Christ of her visions.[40] Romano thus explores a theme of particular interest to women: Teresa's progress in holiness necessitated a struggle for autonomy and self-affirmation.

Other pioneering research in women's history has uncovered the way women's own ideals of holiness integrated love and intellect, and empowered women to challenge family and social expectations and to esteem a self-chosen life.[41]

Because the spiritual tradition of women is often carried on in recent times outside the official context of religion, studies of women's fiction offer helpful resources for women's spirituality.

This literature demonstrates how women's spiritual quest concerns women's awakening to forces of energy larger than the self, to powers of connection with nature and with other women, and to acceptance of body. For women, conversion is not so much giving up egocentric notions of power as passing through an experience of nothingness finally to gain power over their own lives.[42]

In summary, this second phase of women's history has already recovered sufficient evidence about women's experience to challenge basic assumptions about women's natural passivity or innate possession of religious virtue. Most important of all, though, it provides women today with resources for praise, pride, and power to affirm their own unique spirituality.

A third phase is emerging in which women view themselves not as another minority but, more accurately, as the majority of humanity. Now the question becomes: what would history itself look like if seen through women's eyes and values? Let me give just one example of the consequent shift in basic patterns of meaning. Elisabeth Schüssler Fiorenza reconstructs early Christian history according to a new interpretive model which sees the early Christian movement basically as a conflict movement struggling with acceptance of egalitarian leadership relations rather than as an intrinsically patriarchal society trying to restrain heresy and preserve orthodoxy.[43]

Because all historical reconstructions, including the New Testament, are not facts but interpretations, we must evaluate the interpretive model through which references to persons and events are already filtered. That Western culture is interpreted through a systematic androcentrism is evident in the fact that nobody questions the historical role of men as agents in the Church. Only the leadership role of women is problematic because maleness is the norm. Given her command of the sources, Fiorenza has no trouble showing how the Lukan Easter narrative omits other material favorable to women's full apostleship and how the Pastoral letters require that the structures of leadership be patterned after the patriarchal family structure. But was this an inevitable development?[44]

Any insistence that it was inevitable overlooks the fact that these patriarchal structures were not the only institutional options available to and realized by Christians. Since women such as Phoebe were founders and leaders of house churches (Rom 16:1–3), the missionary house churches seem to have been patterned after egalitarian private associations and not after the patriarchal household.[45]

What is even more significant is the evidence that patriarchal structures are not normative because the Jesus traditions promote egalitarian impulses; they are not patriarchally defined. They record that, although women in ancient culture were socially marginal and religiously inferior, Jesus included women as disciples and primary witnesses of the resurrection. Since discipleship replaced traditional family bonds (Mk 3:35), women disciples are no longer defined by the patriarchal order of marriage and family. It is not natural motherhood but being Jesus' disciple that is decisive. Why? A sevenfold transmission of the synoptic tradition proclaiming that the first and the leaders should be last and slaves, demonstrates that Jesus radically criticized social and religious hierarchical and patriarchal relationship of dependence and domination. God's fatherhood prohibits any ecclesial patriarchial self-definition. Christ's lordship rules out any relationship of dominance within the Christian community.[46]

When this egalitarian impulse becomes the defining element in the interpretive model for reconstructing early Christian history we can do justice to all the New Testament traditions and need not eliminate or downplay women's discipleship and leadership.[47] Women's and men's spirituality can thus be nourished and challenged by the radical call to egalitarian relationship to Jesus ("I have not called you servants but friends.") which could be the pattern for all our relationships, and the inspiration for new theology.

The Leadership Conference of Women Religious has already begun to incorporate implications of this reconstruction in its suggestions for a contemporary theology of the vows, particularly the vow of obedience.

> If to vow obedience meant to commit oneself to a personal quest for freedom and holiness in a community context and to involve oneself in a broader human quest for the liberation of all people both by a prophetic challenge to structures of domination and by a constructive participation in the evolution of new models of community the vow would make sense not only to religious but to their contemporaries.[48]

Reinterpreting Familiar God-images

The importance of symbolism for spirituality cannot be overestimated. The experience of grace cannot be accurately recognized or correctly interpreted without the help of symbols derived from the world of ordinary sensory experience. Any image or analogy naturally has limited ability to express symbolically God's self-communication, to be revelation.[49] However, it is the common interpretation of symbols, as we saw earlier in this article, that has been particularly limiting for women's spirituality. Therefore, attention to recent reinterpretations of familiar God-images and to their liberating and challenging implications will conclude this article.

For centuries, interpreters of scripture have explored the male language of faith. Now, like the housekeeper of Luke 15:8, Phyllis Trible, among other scholars, has lit a lamp and once more swept the house of biblical tradition to find the lost coin: female imagery and motifs.[50]

Scripture itself, in the formal parallelism between the phrases "male and female" and "in the image of God" (Gen 1:27) provides the metaphor which Trible uses as the basic clue in her search. This metaphorical language carefully preserves the otherness of God. The Hebrew term *the-image-of* stresses the difference between Creator and creature. God is neither male nor female, nor any combination of the two. Yet Genesis teaches that to understand the basic metaphor, male and female, is to have a human clue for detecting divine reality.[51]

According to Trible, this metaphor functions in two ways. First, it directs attention to partial expressions of the image of God-male: the father (Ps 103:13), the husband (Hos 2:16), the king (Ps 98:6). In the same way, images of God the pregnant woman (Isa 42:4), the mother (Isa 66:13), the midwife (Ps 22:9) are partial expressions of God-female. However, precisely because the metaphor presents a *balanced* image while biblical language is imbalanced in favor of male metaphors, it provides Trible with an impetus to seek out female language for God. Using literary tools which demonstrate the inseparability of biblical form and content, Trible examines a term which saturates scripture: the root word *rahamim* which in the singular form means "womb" and in the plural expands to mean "compassion, mercy, love"—the most persistent biblical description of God. Trible sketches a cumulative poetic picture of Yahweh as a deity who conceived, was pregnant, writhed in labor pains, brought forth a child, and nursed it.[52]

If religious education and homilies would consistently proclaim

these powerful metaphors perhaps more women (and men) could
identify with Arlene Swidler's liberating experience.

> I find that retiring to my room at a quiet hour . . . and putting
> myself in the presence of God who is my Mother is the most re-
> laxing and invigorating spiritual experience I know.[53]

In *How Do I Pray?* eight other women and nineteen men joined Arlene Swidler in answering the title question. This booklet provides
some clear evidence that female language, though just as appropriate
for God as male language, is not yet used with equal comfort even
by persons with good theological training. All the men used exclusively masculine God-language. Of the women, four used only masculine God-language, four used neutral language (i.e., no personal
pronouns), and only one explicitly voiced comfort with feminine
language. The only male theologians I know of whose books use
feminine God-language in equal measure with masculine are Matthew Fox and John Carmody.[54]

Besides directing attention to female language for the deity, the
image of God, male and female, guides Trible's research in a second
way. It directs attention to three scriptural traditions which embody
male and female within the common context of the goodness of creation.

First, Trible explains, in a way that non-biblical scholars can
easily understand, that Genesis 2 is a life story that culminates in a
poem to sexuality as man and woman become one flesh of mutuality
and harmony. However, this equality disintegrates through disobedience; subordination is the consequence of sin; the curse is upon
the serpent, not the woman, in Genesis 3. The Song of Songs, on
the other hand, recovers the grace of sexuality, not the sin of sexism.
In this love poetry, so widely commented upon by mystics and
Church fathers, there is no male dominance, no female subordination, and no stereotyping of either sex. Trible demonstrates how the
portrayal of the woman actually defies the connotations of the "second sex." She works, keeps vineyards and flocks. Throughout the
Song she is independent and fully the man's equal. Although he
sometimes approaches her, she most often initiates their meetings.
Her movements are bold and open; she describes love with revealing
images. Never is she called a wife nor required to bear children.

Love for the sake of love is the Song's message, and the portrayal of the female delineates this message best. Third, Trible shows that the tradition in the book of Ruth actively challenges and transforms the male culture that it reflects. It has a happy ending because the brave, bold decisions of women embody and bring to pass the blessings of God. Strong women make a new beginning with a strong man who reacts to their initiative. At the end, having suffered and struggled, the image of God, male and female, rejoices in the goodness of life.[55]

If, as Trible demonstrates, the image of God-female can be strong, initiating, brave, self-defining, what about the image of God-male? Are the male qualities which patriarchy emphasizes and legitimates really the central qualities of God the father in Jesus' religious heritage or in his own teaching about God? Robert Hammerton-Kelly, explicitly acknowledging women's legitimate concerns with this question, explores the way Hebrew and Christian scriptures depict God's fatherhood as directly challenging the patriarchal family as normative for mediating God's presence. When God rules, only free, reciprocal love is praised or promoted.[56]

One of the most persistent themes of Scripture is the call to leave the familiar and risk going into the unknown, with trust that God is present in the new situation. I believe this call echoes in the issues raised in the present article. One strand of Christian tradition has consistently taught that God's glory is humanity fully alive. Now, however, I believe many women and men are being called to respond to the challenge of a new Christian anthropology—new because it explicitly acknowledges and affirms women's experience. I believe that God is only glorified when this inclusive humanity is fully alive!

NOTES

1. Jane Loevinger, "Stages of Ego Development," in *Adolescents' Development and Education*, ed. Ralph L. Mosher (Berkeley, California: McCutchan, 1979), pp. 110–123.

2. Men also conform to social roles. However, whereas male roles stress self-affirmation and differentiation from others, women's roles reinforce passivity and submersion in others' needs. Men's spirituality has its

own problematic aspects which are implied here but are not the focus of this article.

3. Madonna Kolbenschlag, *Kiss Sleeping Beauty Good-Bye* (New York: Doubleday, 1979), pp. 10–40.

4. *Ibid.*

5. The concepts of "merger self" and "seeker self" are developed in Gail Sheehy, *Passages* (New York: E.P. Dutton, 1976), pp. 110, 287.

6. Kolbenschlag, *Sleeping Beauty*, pp. 41–67; 119–156.

7. William A. Barry, "Spiritual Direction: the Empirical Approach," *America*, 24 April 1976, pp. 356–358.

8. See, for example, Raymond E. Brown, "Roles of Women in the Fourth Gospel," *Theological Studies* 36 (December 1975): 688–699.

9. Elisabeth Schüssler Fiorenza, "You are not to be called Father," *Cross Currents*, Fall 1979, pp. 312–315.

10. Rosemary Radford Ruether, ed., *Religion and Sexism* (New York: Simon and Schuster, 1974).

11. Nancy F. Cott, *The Bonds of Womanhood* (New Haven: Yale University Press, 1977); Ann Douglas, *The Feminization of American Culture* (New York: Alfred A. Knopf, 1977).

12. James A. Coriden, ed., *Sexism and Church Law* (New York: Paulist, 1977).

13. Thomas J. Green, "The Revision of Canon Law: Theological Implications," *Theological Studies* 40 (December 1979): 593–679, at 666.

14. Sandra M. Schneiders, "Christian Tradition on Women," *SIDIC* 9 (Fall 1976): 8–13. Forty autobiographical essays written last semester by my women undergraduate students, as well as my discussions with many other women—students and colleagues—confirm Schneiders' conclusions.

15. Ana-Maria Rizzuto, M.D., *The Birth of the Living God* (Chicago: University of Chicago Press, 1979), p. 181.

16. *Ibid.*, pp.180–200.

17. *Ibid.*, p. 202.

18. See, for example, Naomi R. Goldenberg, *Changing of the Gods* (Boston: Beacon Press, 1979); Carol Christ and Judith Plaskow, eds., *Womanspirit Rising* (San Francisco: Harper & Row, 1979), pp. 193–286.

19. Rosemary Ruether, "A Religion for Women: Sources and Strategies," *Christianity and Crisis*, 10 December 1979, pp. 307–311, at 309.

20. Carol Gilligan, "In a Different Voice: Women's Conceptions of Self And Morality," *Harvard Educational Review* 47 (November 1977): 481–517. I realize that there are many different interpretations and evaluations of Kohlberg and Erikson, but for the sake of focus here I will simply present Gilligan's own view.

21. *Ibid.*, p. 484.

22. *Ibid.*, p. 489. Gilligan is not attempting to answer the problem of women's lack of encouragement to develop full maturity by redefining maturity. Rather, she maintains that Kohlberg's definition of maturity is too narrow and gives disproportionate emphasis to the rational dimensions of morality.

23. *Ibid.*, p. 511.

24. Carol Gilligan, "Woman's Place in Man's Life Cycle," *Harvard Educational Review* 49 (November 1979): 431–446, at 437. Gilligan makes no mention of Erikson's position that each life task is somehow influential at every stage in the life cycle. Her bibliography does not cite the essay on women: Erik Erikson, "Once More the Inner Space," in *Life History and the Historical Moment* (New York: Norton, 1975), pp. 225–242.

25. Gilligan, "Woman's Place," p. 445. Erikson seems to agree in *Life History*, p. 241.

26. Georgia Sassen, "Success Anxiety in Woman: A Constructivist Interpretation of its Source and its Significance," *Harvard Educational Review* 50 (February 1980): 13–24.

27. *Ibid.*, pp. 13–15.

28. Sassen is using the definition of anxiety explained by Robert Graham Kegan in "The Evolving Self: A Process Conception for Ego Psychology," *The Counseling Psychologist* 8 (Spring, 1979): 5–34.

29. Sassen, "Success Anxiety," pp. 20–24.

30. See, for example, Mary Hunt, "Women Ministering in Mutuality: The Real Connections," *Sisters Today*, August/September 1979, pp. 35–43.

31. See, for example, Sandra M. Schneiders, "Liturgy and Spirituality—The Widening Gap," *Spirituality Today*, September 1978, pp. 196–210.

32. See, for example, Henri Nouwen, "The Monk and the Cripple: Toward a Spirituality of Ministry," *America*, 15 March 1980, pp. 205–210.

33. Dorothy Dinnerstein, *The Mermaid and the Minotaur* (New York: Harper & Row, 1976).

34. Elizabeth Leonie Simpson, "A Holistic Approach to Moral Development and Behavior," in *Moral Development and Behavior*, ed. Thomas Lickona (New York: Holt, Rinehart and Winston, 1976), pp. 159–170, at 163.

35. Gerda Lerner, *The Majority Finds Its Past* (New York: Oxford University Press, 1979), pp. 145–159.

36. Penelope Washbourn, *Seasons of Woman* (San Francisco: Harper & Row, 1979).

37. Catherine Cress Romano, "A Psycho-Spiritual History of Teresa of Avila: A Woman's Perspective," in *Western Spirituality: Historical Roots, Ecumenical Routes*, ed. Matthew Fox (Notre Dame, Indiana: Fides/Claretian, 1979), pp. 261–295, at 286.

38. *Ibid.*

39. *Ibid.* p. 288.

40. *Ibid.*, pp. 294–295.

41. See, for example, Rosemary Ruether and Eleanor McLaughlin, *Women of Spirit* (New York: Simon and Schuster, 1979). For an anthology which includes the experience of slave and urban black women, see Nancy F. Cott and Elizabeth H. Pleck, *A Heritage of Her Own* (New York: Simon and Schuster, 1979).

42. See, for example, Carol Christ, *Diving Deep and Surfacing* (Boston: Beacon, 1980).

43. Elisabeth Schüssler Fiorenza, "You are not to be called Father," *Cross Currents*, Fall 1979, pp. 301–323.

44. *Ibid.*, p. 314.

45. *Ibid.*, p. 315.

46. *Ibid.*, p. 317.

47. *Ibid.*, pp. 315–318.

48. Sandra M. Schneiders, "A Contemporary Theology of the Vows," in *Journeying . . . Resources* (Washington, D.C.: Leadership Conference of Women Religious, 1977), pp. 14–27, at 24.

49. See, for example, Avery Dulles, S.J., "The Symbolic Structure of Revelation," *Theological Studies* 41 (March 1980): 51–73.

50. Phyllis Trible, *God and the Rhetoric of Sexuality* (Philadelphia: Fortress, 1978).

51. *Ibid.*, pp. 200–201; 21–23.

52. *Ibid.*, pp. 36–56.

53. Arlene Swidler, "In the presence of God my Mother," in *How Do I Pray?*, ed. Robert Heyer (New York: Paulist, 1978), p. 33.

54. See, for example, Matthew Fox, *Whee! We, wee All the Way Home* (Wilmington, North Carolina: Consortium Books, 1976); John Carmody, *The Progressive Pilgrim* (Notre Dame, Ind.: Fides/Claretian, 1980).

55. Trible, *Rhetoric of Sexuality*, pp. 72–196.

56. Robert Hamerton-Kelly, *God the Father* (Philadelphia: Fortress, 1979).

The Effects of Women's Experience on Their Spirituality

Sandra M. Schneiders

Whatever else the feminist movement may have accomplished, it has established the fact that Western society, including the Christian church, is male-dominated.[1] Some are convinced that this state of affairs corresponds to the divine plan of God.[2] Others, both men and women, are convinced that the God of Judeo-Christian revelation calls us to liberate ourselves and one another from what can only be called the shackles of sexism, as we are to liberate ourselves from racism, anti-Semitism, and every other form of human oppression.[3]

In this article I am not concerned primarily with the fact of this male dominance, nor with its injustice, nor with strategies for overcoming it. Rather, I want to investigate the effect of the experience of male dominance, whether welcomed or rejected, on the religious experience or spirituality of women. In particular, I am interested in how their experience of religious marginalization, exclusion, and subordination has affected women's ministry and their sense of themselves in relation to God.[4]

No one will be surprised by the assertion that the overt effects of male dominance on women's spirituality have been largely negative. But I am more concerned with another aspect of these effects, an aspect that I do not think has received very much attention and that I feel has great potential for the spiritual development of women, namely, what I might call the "flip-side" of these negative effects, the seeds of new life in an experience of death.

Let us turn first to the more easily observable dimension of women's spirituality, namely, the ministerial dimension. It is only within the last ten to twenty years that women Catholics have even used the term *ministry* in relation to themselves. In general, nonordained Catholics, male or female, did not see themselves as active participants in the church's mission except through a generalized good example in the faithful performance of the duties of their state in life.[5] But women's experience had two characteristics which lay male experience did not.

First, unlike men, women *could* not be ordained, and thus the real possibility of participation in the official ministry of the church did not function in the shaping of the religious imagination and self-understanding of Catholic girls as they grew to maturity in the church. While boys experienced ministry as a viable option for themselves and freely situated themselves in relation to this possibility, girls experienced themselves as completely excluded from this dimension of Christian experience. Only recently, as women who feel called to ordained ministry share their stories with the community, have we begun to realize how humanly destructive and spiritually traumatic this early experience of ecclesial rejection has been for female Catholics.[6]

Secondly, women in general, even in their secular lives, rarely functioned in public or independent roles. There were, in secular spheres, always notable exceptions: women writers, teachers, doctors, politicians, and lawyers. But they were considered anomalies. Most women were socialized in the church, as well as in the secular sphere, to nonpublic roles. In the public spheres the normal woman appeared, to herself and to others, as male-dependent. She was the daughter of, the mother of, the sister of, the wife of someone who had a name in a way that she never would. Just as she supported the significant males in her life as they graduated from professional school, ran for office, made policy, declared and fought wars, and made the money that supported their families, so women in the church supported significant males as they advanced to ordination, made the rules Catholics lived by, administered the sacraments, and governed the church.

EFFECTS OF EXCLUSION FROM MINISTRY

What effects did women's exclusion from ordained ministry have on their self-understanding as Christians? It is fairly easy to list a number of negative effects. First, women seldom considered themselves as called to ministry. What we would today refer to as ministry, women considered as "auxiliary services," perhaps a form of lay apostolate, or just neighborly kindness. Visiting the sick, singing in the choir, teaching CCD, raising a Christian family, nursing and teaching and social work were not considered part of the official ministry of the church but, as lay activities, ways of helping the clergy in ministry that properly belonged only to them.

Secondly, women early in life developed a fairly pronounced and much emphasized sense of sacral unworthiness. Not only could they not be ordained; they were not even to be in the sanctuary while divine service was taking place. They were not to touch the sacred vessels nor read the word of God in public. Even functions that a six-year-old boy could perform, such as serving Mass or bearing the processional cross, were forbidden to even the most spiritually mature and experienced woman Christian.[7]

A corollary of their sacral unworthiness was their total sacramental dependence on men. The approach to God in the characteristically Catholic way, that is through the sacraments of penance and Eucharist, was totally male-controlled and women thus totally male-dependent. Although most women surely experienced this dependence as simply "the way things are," there were occasions when the painfulness of their inferior sacramental position rose to consciousness. This occurred, for example, when mothers had to explain to their little daughters why they could not be altar servers, when sisters had to submit to weekly experiences of confession to chaplains appointed without the sisters' advice or consent and who were often appointed to the "good sisters" because they were unsuitable for other ministries, and when sacraments were denied women who found divorce and remarriage the only solution to desertion or domestic violence.

Women's exclusion from orders reinforced their subordination in all spheres because it divinized maleness and conversely excluded femininity from the sphere of the divine.[8] The priest was seen as the very representative of God, "another Christ." This divine status, in principle open to all men, was closed to women who not only could not accede to divine status but could not have any access to the divinity except through the mediation of men. We have perhaps not even begun to fathom the extent to which a priori exclusion of women, solely because they are women, from ordained ministry has limited, distorted, and subverted the Christian identity of women. This rejection of women, however, has a "flip side," a set of effects that we have perhaps not properly evaluated nor maximized. Indeed, they are effects that could only be seen as positive potentialities in the light of the kinds of realizations that feminist thought has so recently brought to the level of consciousness.

First is the fact that the ministry of women, which has been no less real for the fact of being unrecognized and unnamed, has never been "ritualized." From one point of view this is unfortunate. But from another point of view it is a blessing. There is an inverse ratio between ritualization and personalization. It belongs to the very nature of ritual that it largely subsumes the individuality of the ritualist. Women's ministry has never been anything other than the personal service of one human being to another in the name of Christ. It is fairly easy to ritualize personal service; but as anyone who has tried to implement the liturgical reforms of Vatican II knows well, it is not nearly so easy to repersonalize ministries that have been almost totally ritualized. Women have initiated children into the Christian experience at every level; they have heard the anguished avowals of the guilty and loved them to reconciliation; they have made mealtimes experiences of Christian unity; they have consoled the sick and assisted the dying into the arms of God. None of this ministerial activity, even though it is the substance of the sacraments, is ritualized when carried out by women. It has never lost its entirely personal and interpersonal character. Such ministry, in the hands of women, has rarely been an exercise of power or a mode of social control and discipline. The nonritualized ministry of women has contributed very little to the pervasive image of the Christian God as a stern, even violent, father-figure bent on exact justice and retribution. Indeed, experienced spiritual directors know that, when a person's violent God image begins to be healed, that healing is very often effected by, and expressed in, a recognition in God of the qualities one has experienced in the women in one's life—mother, sister, wife, or lover.

It is not surprising that women ministers in general have had, as a group, far less difficulty in understanding and practicing their ministries as service rather than as exercises of power. And a corollary of this "power-less" experience of ministry is that women ministers in the postconciliar church have been quickest to revise their institutional commitments in order to respond to unconventional but very real needs. Women ministers have led the way in identification with the oppressed and in real commitment of personal and communal resources to the promotion of social justice here and abroad.[9]

I would not want to be understood as suggesting that the exclusion of women from ordination and the nonrecognition of their ministry is justifiable or good. But it is a fact. It is also a fact that those who have been persecuted, humiliated, undervalued, and denied their rightful place in the society of the church are singularly well equipped for identification with the great Minister, Jesus, who was himself a simple layman persecuted and disowned by the religious authorities of his day, and who found in his solidarity with the poor and the unrecognized the basis for a nonritualized ministry of personal service characterized by a gentleness and a powerlessness that were singularly revelatory of the true God.[10]

EFFECTS OF SOCIALIZATION

The effects on women's ministerial consciousness of their socialization into private, male-dependent roles in the church has also been largely negative in ways analogous to the effects of their exclusion from ordained ministry. First, women have been virtually excluded from any participation in the shaping of the church's internal and external policy. The church's laws regarding marriage, which apply in their burdensome dimensions disproportionately to women, have been formulated without the contribution of the women whose experience is in question. Canon law regarding religious, of whom three out of every four in the church are women, has been formulated by men without the input of the women whose lives it governs[11] and, in most respects, it is also enforced by men. Official church documents on every kind of social problem—poverty, war, economics, labor, medical ethics, political involvement—have been formulated without the contribution of women who constitute the vast majority of the poor and the starving throughout the world, who make fifty-nine cents to every dollar made by men for comparable work in this country, who experience in their bodies as mothers a disproportionate number of the medical problems that raise moral issues, who almost always find themselves the sole support of dependent children when marriages collapse.[12]

Secondly, women's socialization to private, male-dependent roles in the church has kept most women from exercising religious leadership. Not only has this deprived the church of vast resources of creative leadership; it has deprived women of a sense of themselves and of other women as leaders and limited their imagination in regard to what services they might render. Women religious have constituted something of a counteracting force in the sphere of leadership, but it is only very recently that religious women have reclaimed their leadership from a kind of pseudoclericalization and have begun to use it to empower, and be empowered by, their lay sisters.

A third effect is the tendency of most women to accept as normal and unquestionable the monopoly of leadership and authority by the men with whom they work. Women who experience themselves as always subordinate to men, and who depend on men for affirmation and approval, are very threatened by the emergence of leadership potential in other women. Indeed, many women actually mistrust women in ministerial situations and prefer to work for men. Such women attribute to themselves and to other women the stereotypical traits of flightiness, lack of confidentiality, poor judgment, sentimentality, and lack of intelligence that they have been socialized to regard as characteristic of women whose appropriate role is in the private sphere and in subordination to men.

At this point I would again like to investigate the "flip side," the positive potential hidden in this base coin of women's male-dependent socialization in the church. One effect of women's rarely functioning in ministry except in subordination to men is that women, in general, have more experience of men in ministry than men do of women. Women have never carried on exclusively feminine ministries. They have always had to involve men at some level or other and find ways to work with or around them. Men have rarely had to deal with women as equals and virtually never, until very recently, as superiors. The result, which is becoming very evident in the contemporary church, is that women are far better prepared, in most cases, for partnership with men in ministry than men are for working with women.

A second, and closely related effect, is that women's adjustment to their new more public roles is, by comparison, far easier than men's corresponding adjustment to nonpublic roles. Public skills, for example, conducting meetings, speaking in public, and administration, are relatively easy for an intelligent adult person to master. But skill in the private sphere, skill in interpersonal relationships, empathy, a sense of the feeling tone of a complicated situation, sensitivity to others—the skills in which most women have been exercised from their earliest years and in which they have received endless practice in their private and subordinate roles as adults—are much more difficult to master when one starts late in life.

Although it is unfortunate that women have borne much more than their share of responsibility for fostering the human and personal qualities of interaction, it is indeed fortunate that someone has preserved these qualities, and the ministry of the church will surely be enriched in years to come as women's experience more deeply influences the ministerial activity of the church. We can expect ever more emphasis on mutuality, shared responsibility, nonauthoritarian policies and procedures, and basic humaneness in operation as concern for persons catches up with our overly developed concern for institutions.[13]

A third effect of women's private socialization in the church is that women have usually been the victims of hierarchical organization, seldom participants in it. Although the effect of victimization by power structures is sometimes, indeed often, to motivate the victims to seize that power for themselves when they get the chance and use it to similarly victimize others, it can also happen that the victims repudiate for others that from which they themselves have suffered so much.[14] It is sadly true that there are some women in the church who seek power in order to do to others what has been done to them. But what is much more obvious, especially in women's religious communities, is that women find it easy to imagine and create nonhierarchical community structures. They talk much more easily than most men do of participative government, shared authority, noncoercive discipline, empowerment, and mutuality.[15] Women in ministerial situations, especially those in which they have some degree of leadership, are introducing these same nondominative values and patterns into the church's service.

Again, I have no intention of denying or white-washing the distortion of women's ministerial consciousness that their socialization to exclusively private, male-dependent roles has brought about; nor do I wish to pretend that all women have profited by their painful experience and that none have become alienated, angry, or vengeful. But women's suffering has rarely been without fruit, even when it was unjustly caused and violent in nature. Recent studies of women ministers in the church and of women who feel called to ordained ministry, for example, show patterns of remarkable psychological maturity, commitment, tolerance of hardship, and developed ministerial consciousness that comparable studies of male ordained ministers do not show.[16]

MASCULINIZING RELIGIOUS EXPERIENCE

Let us turn now to the less public sphere of women's spirituality, namely, their experience of God. I want to look at two factors that have conditioned that experience and at the effects, again both negative and positive, of that conditioning. First is what I have called the "masculinizing" of Christian religious experience. As the history of spirituality shows, the vast majority of (though certainly not all) spiritual directors and authors of spiritual books have been men. Virtually all theologians have been men. All confessors and most counselors have been men. Even in women's religious orders most of the instruction and formation was either done by men or out of the books and rules written by men. The effects of this predominance of masculine experience on women's spiritual formation is quite evident and much of it is unfortunate.

First, men have been largely ignorant of the existence of a feminine approach to the spiritual life that might be quite different from their own. Male spiritual directors, retreat directors, and preachers habitually propose for women a combination of masculine spiritual practice and the ideal of the "eternal feminine" which, in Jungian terms, is more a projection of the male "anima" than a real ideal for women.[17] Men have taught women to beware of specifically male vices: pride, aggression, disobedience to lawful hierarchical authority, homosexuality, lust, and the like. Women have rarely been alerted to those vices to which their socialization prompts them, for example, weak submissiveness, fear, self-hatred, jealousy, timidity, self-absorption, small-mindedness, submersion of personal identity, and manipulation.[18]

Secondly, the predominance of the intellectual over the affective approach to the knowledge of God, of method over intuition in prayer, of Christian warfare over friendship as the model of the spiritual life, of asceticism over mysticism, of submission to authority over personal initiative in the apostolate have all expressed the concerns of men and the experiences of men. Women down through the ages have been urged by women as well as by men to be "virile" in their spiritual lives, to conquer themselves, to be soldiers of Christ in the spiritual army of God, to acquire by force the "manly" virtues.[19]

A third and particularly lamentable effect of male dominance in the area of spirituality has been the partial eclipse of the feminine experience and feminine models in Scripture and in the history of spirituality. Women have rarely been encouraged to imitate the great women of salvation history. Rarely is a eucharistic president, even at a liturgy celebrated by a preponderantly female community, sufficiently sensitive to modify the Eucharistic Prayer's retracing of salvation history in order to call to mind not only Adam but Eve, not only Abraham and Isaac and Jacob but also Sara and Rebeccah and Rachel, not only Moses but Miriam, not only David but Ruth, not only Peter but Mary Magdalene. The only feminine model who has been invoked with real fervor and consistency in the male church has been Mary, the Mother of Jesus, and that invocation has been badly misused in many periods of church history to reinforce and sacralize the subordination and passivity of women.[20] We have fewer records of women saints, partly because men set the criteria for sanctity and wrote the hagiographies. Even those women who have been canonized have rarely had the same type of official prominence that male saints have enjoyed. There was, after all, little they could be except "virgins" or "martyrs," or "neither virgin nor martyr." Until our own day no woman was ever recognized as a doctor of the

church,[21] despite the array of women theologians and spiritual giants
such as Juliana of Norwich, Catherine of Genoa, Teresa of Avila,
Hadewijch of Antwerp, Mechtilde of Magdeburg, the Gertrudes,
the Brigids, Catherine of Siena, Marie of the Incarnation, Angela of
Foligno, and all the others.

Finally, women have been largely conditioned to evaluate anything in their spiritual experience that seemed especially feminine as
questionable or negative. Even Teresa of Avila laments continually
the weak and womanly (virtually equivalent terms) traits of herself
and her sisters.[22] Passivity in prayer has been suspect; compassion
is too likely to be weakness; gentleness with oneself is probably tepidity; and gentleness with others a compromise of values. It is only
in our own day, as more and more spiritual seekers have turned to
the spiritualities of the East, that we have come to look critically at
our body-denying, overly methodical, highly verbal and intellectual,
muscular, vertical, conquering model of the spiritual life.[23] Suddenly interior silence, passivity, body-centered prayer, patience
with oneself, compassion for others, and intuition, all stereotypically feminine elements, are emerging as desirable aspects of the
spirituality of everyone, men and women alike.

While it is certainly true that feminine religious experience has
never been lacking in the church, it is equally true that it has been
undervalued and underutilized and that the spiritual lives of women
have been much impoverished by the masculinizing of religious experience throughout history.

But once again I would like to attend to the "flip side" of this
impoverishment. As Carl Jung has so convincingly explained, individuation, or the process of human self-actualization that is the
characteristic developmental task of the middle years if a person is
to reach maturity in the second half of life, is a function of the integration of our conscious ego with the material of the unconscious.
In particular, Jungian psychological theory has made us aware of the
necessity for a person to integrate the contrasexual side of his or her
personality if he or she is to achieve wholeness. The woman must
bring to consciousness and integrate the masculine in herself and the
man must do the same with the feminine in himself.[24] I think that
women have a large head start on this project as it realizes itself in
the area of spirituality.

First, women have always been taught to value the masculine

in themselves, to seek to acquire masculine virtues and to think and pray in masculine ways. The God they seek to imitate has been imaged in masculine terms. On the contrary, men have been spiritually trained to repress as shameful the feminine in themselves, to deny it and disguise it.[25] Women may well have to work to appreciate to the full the feminine in themselves, but it is, after all, their own identity. Men have the more difficult task of reversing the negative judgment on the feminine in general and especially in themselves and then incorporating it. In one sense, women have accomplished the more difficult task, the appropriation of the opposite. Women often need to come home to themselves in their femininity in the spiritual life.[26] But that is often the less strenuous of the two tasks.

A second effect of the masculinizing of women's spiritual experience is that women often understand men's spiritual experience better than men understand women's. In one sense, women have "been there," have undertaken the same modes and procedures, embraced the same ideals and models, striven for the same goals in the spiritual life and suffered from the same kinds of fears and failures that men have. It is not at all surprising to me that the vast increase in the number of spiritual directors in this country has been among women. Not only do women have a variety and depth of interpersonal experience often lacking to men that well fits them for one-to-one ministry, developed skills in the private sphere, and a nonhierarchical approach to ministry that many people welcome; but many women also have a much more whole, that is both masculine and feminine, approach to spiritual experience.[27]

EFFECTS OF EXCLUSIVELY MALE GOD

Now let us turn to a second factor that has conditioned women's experience of God, namely, the presentation of God in almost exclusively male terms. I am not speaking here of the masculinity of Jesus, which is a separate topic too extensive to handle in this article, but of God, the creator of all things and the source of life upon whom all human beings depend. Let me say at the outset that Scripture does not present God in exclusively male terms.[28] As the well-known biblical scholar, Phyllis Trible, has shown in her remarkable book *God and the Rhetoric of Sexuality*,[29] God is presented from the moment of creation as one whose true image is humanity as male-and-female, and that the feminine dimension of God is repeatedly highlighted in the Old Testament. It is also true that the Spirit of God is personified in the Old Testament as the feminine figure Wisdom[30] and it is she who appears in the New Testament as the Spirit of Jesus. Nevertheless, largely because all rabbis, priests, Scripture scholars, and preachers have been men, neither the feminine dimension of God nor the feminine presentation of the Spirit has been adverted to in our religious training or liturgical experience. Many Catholics are genuinely shocked the first time they hear a professor or homilist refer to God our Mother or to the Holy Spirit as "she."

The negative effects of this exclusively masculine presentation of God on the religious experience of women are not hard to identify. Perhaps the most profoundly destructive is the deep sense of exclusion from the divine that women imbibe as part of their sense of who they are. God, to women, is man "writ large." Men are God "writ small." God and man belong to the same order of things and from that order women are excluded. How else can we explain the fact that women, for so long, considered it a matter of divine institution that only men could "represent God" as family head or ordained minister?[31] Indeed, many women are still profoundly uncomfortable even in receiving Communion from a woman and utterly incapable of conceiving of a woman as eucharistic president. Women's sense of the inappropriateness of women's participating in the sphere of the divine is a projection onto their sisters of their own sense of themselves as alienated from the divine. Much healing of sacralized self-repudiation is necessary before women, taught from infancy that God is malelike and males are Godlike, can appropriate their own real and equal participation in the divine nature.[32]

A second negative effect on women's spirituality of the masculine presentation of God is that women (and men as well) have most often experienced God the way they have experienced men. They admire, depend upon, and defer to God. But they can also be dominated, used, undervalued, and basically despised by God. They are ever guilty, a nuisance, and can justify themselves only by unrelenting service, continual performance, and lowly self-efface-ment. For a woman to come to any real appreciation of what she means to God, not for what she does but for who she is, not in spite of her sins but because of her beauty, often requires immense effort in prayer and the wise support of a mature and liberated spiritual guide.

A third and closely related negative effect on women's spirituality of the masculine presentation of God is the sense many women instinctively have that they must go to God through and by the permission of men. Just as women have had to present themselves, until quite recently, to the secular world as "Mrs."—that is, an extension of a named male—or as "Miss"—that is, not yet fully adult because not yet named and claimed by a man—so women have related to God rather exclusively through men by whom they were baptized and confirmed, from whom alone they could receive the Eucharist, to whom they had to go with every secret sin, who presided over their marriage or religious vows, and will anoint them at the moment of death. The word of God was preached to them by men and, as women, they were excluded from the study of theology which would give them independent access to the meaning of that word. Marriage problems, vocational crises, and the religious doubts of women were all handled by men. Even a religious congregation composed entirely of women could not open or close a chapter, elect a major superior, amend its own constitutions, or receive the vows of its new members without the empowering presence of a man. In short, any matter which was even remotely related to the realm of the sacred was mediated to women by men.

There can be no doubt that this experience of God as male with its logical conclusions has been negative in the extreme. But, once again, there is a "flip side" to this base coin to which we do well to attend in order that we might appreciate and maximize it.

First, women's sense of being not among the truly Godlike has preserved in women, much more than in men, the sense of the utter "otherness" and noncontrollability of God. Women have little tendency to assimilate themselves to God, to attempt to present themselves as God's vicar on earth, or to speak in God's name.[33] Women are frequently much more sensitive to the reality of God's actual and free intervention in their lives, less ready to explain it away or attribute it to their own talent or luck. Women are often more ready to appeal to God for help and believe that God can and will respond. It is often said that women carry the faith and pass it on to the next generation. There is no doubt that the majority of churchgoers, as

well as of religious, are women. Real religion is born of a profound
sense of the otherness and transcendence of God and, although
women have been shortchanged on the specifically Christian experience of God's likeness to us by the Incarnation, they are perhaps
the chosen bearers of the sense of God's transcendence, a sense that
alone can keep us from annihilating our race in an orgy of techno-
logical and military hubris.

Secondly, because women have not experienced themselves as
representatives of God, they have almost never taken it upon themselves in the course of history to persecute others in the name of God.
Women have been hounded as witches, condemned and branded,
imprisoned and executed by the males of the religious establishment, but they have very rarely condemned others in the name of
God or fought holy wars to destroy God's enemies. As women enter
various ministries to the so-called sinners—to the divorced and re-
married, to homosexuals and lesbians, to prostitutes and alcoholics
and addicts—they seldom feel called upon to threaten people with
divine wrath. Women ministers often choose to circumvent or ignore questions of excommunication and of who can and cannot receive the sacraments, and to offer people what they need rather than
what they "deserve."

Thirdly, the fact—undoubtedly deplorable in itself—that
women have always been totally dependent on men for official religious participation has led women to specialize in the only religious
activity they could engage in without male permission or help—
namely, personal prayer. Anyone with much experience in the ministry of spiritual direction can testify to the fact that women, by and
large, have much better developed personal prayer lives than men.
One finds that even among the clergy a distressing number of men
have never learned to do real *lectio divina* that does not degenerate
into study, to meditate in such a way as to pass beyond the rational
to the affective, or to enter even the lower reaches of contemplation.
For many men, at least until quite recently, their prayer life has con-
sisted in "saying Mass" and/or "reading the office." Women, on the
contrary, often through their restriction to devotional prayers and
their exclusion from the public sphere of ministerial activity, have
frequently found their way through to genuine affective prayer,
often of a high order.

I hope that it is evident that I do not condone in any way, nor wish to perpetuate for one minute longer, the marginalization or oppression of women in the church. But I do think that women's unique experience as Christians, structured as it is by the paschal mystery of Jesus, in which life eternal issues from the death inflicted on him by human evil, instructs us always to stir the ashes of human violence in the expectation that the phoenix of new life will rise before our eyes. The religious experience of women has been limited and distorted in many ways while their ministry has gone unnamed and their vocation to ordination denied. But their suffering, inexcusable as it is, has also been a fire in which much gold has been refined. That gold belongs to women, but it has been given to them by the same God who entrusted the message of the resurrection to a woman, Mary Magdalene, who instructs us as he instructed her, to take this good news of salvation to our brothers as well as to our sisters. The good news is that the night of oppression and inferiority is dying and that a new day is dawning—a day in which the religious experience and ministry of women will be fully at the service of the church for the liberation of men as well as of women. It is the privilege of our generation to greet this new day with the song of Miriam, who led the sons and daughters of Israel in worship after they had crossed over from slavery to the freedom of the children of God.

NOTES

1. The findings concerning the universal oppression of women by the representatives at the United Nations International Women's Year meeting in 1975 were so devastating that the decade 1975–85 was declared the Decade of Women. When the mid-decade meeting was held in 1980 to evaluate the progress made so far, it was found that the situation of women throughout the world had actually deteriorated since 1975.

2. The most recent full scale presentation and defense of this position is S. B. Clark, *Man and Woman in Christ: An Examination of the Roles of Men and Women in Light of Scripture and the Social Sciences* (Ann Arbor: Servant, 1980).

3. In the document summarizing the dialogues between representatives of the Women's Ordination Conference and of the National Con-

ference of Catholic Bishops of the U.S., released by the NCCB on May 28, 1981, there is a section summarizing areas of agreement and of disagreement between WOC and episcopal participants. The first area of disagreement was formulated as follows: "Patriarchy is understood as divinely derived because it reflects the natural order and thus is the order of creation" (bishops) vs. "Patriarchy is understood as a reflection of an unjust societal order and not part of God's order of creation" (WOC). "Dialogue on Women in the Church: Interim Report," *Origins* 11 (25 June 1981): 90.

4. For a particularly well-documented treatment of this subject, see J.W. Conn, "Women's Spirituality: Restriction and Reconstruction," *Cross Currents* 30 (1980): 293–308.

5. In the 1940s, '50s, and '60s the accepted definition of the "lay apostolate" was "the participation of the laity in the apostolate of the hierarchy." See Pope Pius XII, "Allocution to Italian Catholic Action" (4 September 1940), *AAS* 32 (1940): 362.

6. The *National Catholic Reporter*, 17 July 1981, devoted a good part of the issue to the question of women's desire for ordination. It included considerable firsthand testimony of women to their experience of exclusion. Similar stories emerged during the Second Women's Ordination Conference held in Baltimore, Maryland, November 10–12, 1978. The proceedings of the conference were published as *New Woman, New Church, New Priestly Ministry*, ed. Maureen Dwyer (Baltimore, 1980).

7. That the root of this exclusion of women from the realm of sacred things and actions in ritual taboos related to menstruation and childbearing is fairly generally recognized today. Despite this fact, the exclusion of women from even such minor roles as serving at the eucharistic liturgy was reiterated by the Vatican Congregation for the Sacraments and Divine Worship in a collection of norms on Eucharistic Practices, approved by Pope John Paul II on April 17, 1980 and issued May 23, 1980. The text, "*Inaestimabile Donum*," appears in *Origins* 10 (5 June 1980): 41–44; see par. 18, p. 43.

8. This divinization of maleness has led some feminists to a revival of goddess worship and/or witchcraft in an attempt to counteract its destructive effect on women's sense of self. See, for example, C. P. Christ, "Why Women Need the Goddess: Phenomenological, Psychological, and Political Reflections," *Womanspirit Rising: A Feminist Reader in Religion*, ed. C. P. Christ and J. Plaskow (San Francisco: Harper & Row, 1979), pp. 273–87; and N. R. Goldenberg, *Changing of the Gods: Feminism and the End of Traditional Religions* (Boston: Beacon, 1979), pp. 85–114.

M. Daly is perhaps the most categorical (former?) Catholic writer on this subject. She has concluded that the myth and symbols of Christianity are inherently and unredeemably sexist. See M. Daly, "The Qualitative Leap Beyond Patriarchal Religion," *Quest* 1 (1974): 21. See also her *Beyond God the Father: Toward a Philosophy of Women's Liberation* (Boston: Beacon, 1973).

9. I am referring here to the widely recognized leadership of women religious in the church's contemporary turn toward active involvement in social justice.

10. A profound and biblically very sound meditation on this aspect of Jesus' ministry is A. Nolan, *Jesus Before Christianity* (Maryknoll: Orbis, 1978).

11. See R. A. Hill, "Canon Law After Vatican II: Renewal or Retreat?" *America* 137 (1977): 298–300.

12. See M. P. Burke, *Reaching for Justice: The Women's Movement* (Washington, D.C.: Center of Concern, 1980), especially chap. 4, for documentation of the disproportionate burden of poverty borne by women.

13. See, for example, D. Donnelly, Team: *Theory and Practice of Team Ministry* (New York: Paulist, 1977).

14. The recognition on the part of women concerned with the ordination question of the dangers inherent in incorporation into the clerical caste and system has led many to the position that the clerical system must be changed before women should accept ordination. See A. Kelley and A. Walsh, "Ordination: A Questionable Goal for Women," *The Ecumenist* 11 (July-August 1973): 81–84, as well as the proceedings of the Second Women's Ordination Conference (fn. 6 above).

15. See, for example, *LCWR Recommendations: Schema of Canons on Religious Life* (Washington, D.C.: LCWR, 1977) in which the major superiors of women's congregations in the United States repeatedly criticized the hierarchical, noncollegial, and dominative principles underlying the provisions of the proposed code.

16. See F. Ferder, *Called to Break Bread?: A Psychological Investigation of 100 Women Who Feel Called to Priesthood in the Catholic Church* (Mt. Rainier, Md.: Quixote Center, 1978), especially pp. 27–32.

17. On the "anima" archetype see E. Jung, *Animus and Anima* (Dallas: Spring, 1957 and 1981), pp. 45–94; R. A. Johnson, *He: Understanding Masculine Psychology* (New York: Harper and Row, 1974); J. A. Sanford, The Invisible Partners: How the Male and Female in Each of Us Affects Our Relationships (New York: Paulist, 1980).

18. After writing this paper I discovered that virtually this same point had been made quite a while ago, and at length, by V. S. Goldstein, "The Human Situation: A Feminine Viewpoint," The Nature of Man in Theological and Psychological Perspective, ed. S. Doniger (New York: Harper and Row, 1962), pp. 151–70. My thanks to B. Waugh of the Center for

Women and Religion of the Graduate Theological Union, Berkeley, for this reference.

19. Teresa of Avila is a doctor of the church who, from time to time, gives voice to the negative spiritual stereotypes of women in her day. See, for example, *The Interior Castle*, trans. K. Kavanaugh and O. Rodriguez (New York: Paulist, 1979), IV, 3, 11, p. 83; V, 3, 10, p. 101; and elsewhere.

20. A particularly valuable study of the potentiality and the abuse of Mariology is R. R. Reuther's *Mary—The Feminine Face of the Church* (Philadelphia: Westminster, 1977).

21. P. Paul VI declared St. Teresa of Avila and St. Catherine of Siena doctors of the church on October 4, 1970.

22. See fn. 19 above.

23. M. Fox in *A Spirituality Named Compassion and the Healing of the Global Village, Humpty Dumpty and Us* (Minneapolis: Winston, 1979) gives a rather thoroughgoing criticism of "phallic" spirituality.

24. This is the project described by Sanford in *The Invisible Partners*.

25. One of the problems with Jung's theory of the archetype of the "animus," the masculine principle in women, is that he seems to construct it as a kind of mirror image of the "anima," the feminine principle in men, without attending to the basically different and unequal valuation of masculine and feminine by women as well as by men. Goldenberg in *Changing of the Gods*, pp. 46–71, gives an appreciative but very critical evaluation of Jungian archetypal theory, especially as it applies to women.

26. A. B. Ulanov, *Receiving Women: Studies in the Psychology and Theology of the Feminine* (Philadelphia: Westminster, 1981) deals specifically with this developmental task of women.

27. This phenomenon was noted years ago by J. Wintz, "Women: The Church's Newest Spiritual Guides," *St. Anthony Messenger* 83 (May 1976): 22–27.

28. S. M. Schneiders, "Christian Tradition on Women," *SIDIC* 9 (Fall 1976): 8–13.

29. (Philadelphia: Fortress, 1978).

30. See Reuther, *Mary*, pp. 25–30.

31. Cf. C. Christ, "Why Women Need the Goddess," p. 275.

32. Cf. C. Christ and J. Plaskow, "Introduction: Womanspirit Rising," *Womanspirit Rising*, pp. 2–3.

33. It is notable that the leadership of the Moral Majority is entirely male-dominated and that a major plank in the MM platform is the necessity to keep women in subordination to men by the nonratification of the Equal Rights Amendment and by so-called profamily legislation.

On Feminist Spirituality

Anne Carr

Discussion about women and spirituality can range from romanticized claims of special privilege to insistence that equality means sameness. Some typical questions focus the issues. "What is a women's spirituality?" "How is it different from male spirituality?" "What is spirituality, anyway?" And, "what is a feminist spirituality?" "Is it androgynous?" "Is it a stage on the way to something else?"[1]

SPIRITUALITY

Spirituality can be described as the whole of our deepest religious beliefs, convictions, and patterns of thought, emotion, and behavior in respect to what is ultimate, to God. Spirituality is holistic, encompassing our relationships to all of creation—to others, to society and nature, to work and recreation—in a fundamentally religious orientation. Spirituality is larger than a theology or set of values precisely because it is all-encompassing and pervasive. Unlike theology as an explicit intellectual position, spirituality reaches into our unconscious or half-conscious depths. And while it shapes behavior and attitudes, spirituality is more than a conscious moral code. In relation to God, it is who we really are, the deepest self, not entirely accessible to our comprehensive self-reflection. In a Christian context, God's love goes before us in a way we can never fully name.

49

Spirituality can be a predominantly unconscious pattern of relating seldom reflected on, activated only in certain situations, as at Sunday Mass or during a personal crisis. As such it is a dimension of life for the most part unexamined, resting on convention, upbringing, or social expectations. But spirituality can also be made conscious, explicitly reflected on, developed, changed, and understood in a context of growth and cultivation of the fundamental self in a situation of response and relationship. Christian spirituality entails the conviction that God is indeed personal and that we are in immediate personal relationship to another, an Other who "speaks" and can be spoken to, who really affects our lives.

Although it is deeply personal, spirituality is not necessarily individualistic, because within the relationship to the ultimate, to God, it touches on everything: our relations to others, to community, to politics, society, the world. Spirituality can be consciously oriented toward the inclusive social context in which we live.

Spirituality is expressed in everything we do. It is a style, unique to the self, that catches up all our attitudes: in communal and personal prayer, in behavior, bodily expressions, life choices, in what we support and affirm and what we protest and deny. As our deepest self in relation to God, to the whole, and so literally to everything, spirituality changes, grows, or diminishes in the whole context of life. Consciously cultivated, nourished, cared about, it often takes the character of struggle as we strive to integrate new perceptions or convictions. And it bears the character of grace as we are lifted beyond previous levels of integration by a power greater than our own.

Spirituality is deeply informed by family, teachers, friends, community, class, race, culture, sex, and by our time in history, just as it is influenced by beliefs, intellectual positions, and moral options. These influences may be unconscious or made explicit through reading, reflection, conversation, even conversion. And so spirituality includes and expresses our self-conscious or critical appraisal of our situation in time, in history, and in culture.

As a style of response, spirituality is individually patterned yet culturally shaped. Implicit metaphors, images, or stories drawn from our culture are embodied in a particular spiritual style; these can be made explicit through reflection, journal keeping, conversations with friends, or therapy. We each live a personal story that is part of a wider familial, cultural, racial, and sexual myth. When our myths are made conscious, we can affirm or deny them, accept parts and reject others, as we grow in relationship to God, to others, to our world. Personal, familial, religious, cultural, racial, sexual stories answer the great questions: Where do I come from? How should I live? What is the meaning of the end, of death? Making myths explicit means that we have already moved beyond them and that they become available for criticism.

WOMEN'S AND MEN'S SPIRITUALITIES

Even with affirmations of equality between women and men, of a single-nature anthropology in contrast to a dual-nature view,[2] it seems clear that there are differences between the sexes in basic style of understanding and relationship. Thus there are probably differences in women's and men's spiritualities. Recognition of difference, while admitting real equality, need not entail subversive notions of complementarity that really means subordination or inferiority of one in relation to the other. What are these differences, prescinding from the question (unanswerable, I think) of whether these are the result of nature or nurture?

In a helpful book, *Women's Reality*,[3] Anne Wilson Schaef describes the differences between what she calls the White Male System and an emergent Female System on the basis of her consultant work with both women and men. The White Male System is the dominant one in our culture. While there are other systems (Black, Native American, Hispanic) the White Male System, she argues, views itself as (1) the only one, (2) innately superior, (3) knowing and understanding everything, and (4) believing that it is possible to be totally logical, objective, and rational. Schaef lists a set of contrasts that might help us get at differences in women's and men's spiritualities. These contrasts, of course, describe abstract types; no one is completely one type or another. And some men are in fact in the Female System, while some women are in the White Male System. The following indicate some of these different gender based perspectives.

Issues	White Male System	Female System
Time	Clock	Process
Relationships	Hierarchy	Peer
Center of focus	Self and work	Relationship (self-others)
Sexuality	Central	Part in whole
Intimacy	Physical	Verbal
Friendship	Team effort	Knowing and being known
Power	Zero sum (scarcity)	Limitless
Money	Absolute, real	Relative, symbolic
Leadership	To lead	To enable
Negotiation	Fun = winning	Fun = creativity

In sum, the White Male System is analytic, concerned with definition, explanation, either/or, and is goal-centered. The Female System is synthetic, concerned with understanding, both/and, and is process-centered.

Feminist consciousness, as critical of religious and cultural ideologies which reach into our very perception, thought, and language, must be a little suspicious here. Rather than delimiting a female spirituality to one side of the list, would not a critical feminist consciousness try to hold elements of both sides together, in critical correlation with one another? Do we not need to preserve the values of traditional female characteristics while recognizing certain values in the traditional male traits?

Schaef performs an exercise with her groups (male, female, mixed) in which she asks participants to list characteristics of God (whether they believe in God or not) and of humankind; then characteristics of male and female. Invariably, she writes, the lists look like this:

God	Humankind	Male	Female
male	childlike	intelligent	emotional
omnipotent	sinful	powerful	weak
omniscient	weak	brave	fearful
omnipresent	stupid/dumb	good	sinful
eternal	mortal	strong	like children

She concludes that male is to female as God is to humankind. And this, she argues, is the mythology of the White Male System, whose basic hierarchical structure is God—men—women—children—animals—earth, in a system of dominance. Schaef says our traditional theology supports this myth. Clearly feminist theology, and other forms of contemporary theology, do not.

FEMINIST SPIRITUALITY

A feminist spirituality would be distinguished from any other as a spiritual orientation which has integrated into itself the central elements of feminist consciousness. It is the spirituality of those who have experienced feminist consciousness raising.

Feminist spirituality is thus different from women's spirituality, that is, the distinctive female relationship to the divine in contrast to the male. Women's spirituality might be studied across particular historical periods, or within particular religions, or racial or cultural groups (e.g., puritan, Muslim, Black or, as above, White, middle class, Western) and certain "female" characteristics delineated. For example, in contrast to male spirituality, women's spirituality might be described as more related to nature and natural processes than to culture; more personal and relational than objective and structural; more diffuse, concrete, and general than focused, universal, abstract; more emotional than intellectual, etc.

A specifically feminist spirituality, on the other hand, would be that mode of relating to God, and everyone and everything in relation to God, exhibited by those who are deeply aware of the historical and cultural restriction of women to a narrowly defined "place" within the wider human (male) "world." Such awareness would mean that we are self-consciously critical for the cultural and religious ideologies which deny women full opportunities for self-actualization and self-transcendence. This critical stance is both negative and positive. Negatively, it bears a healthy suspicion and vigilance toward taken-for-granted cultural and religious views that, in a variety of subtle ways, continue to limit the expectations of women to passive, subordinate, auxiliary roles and rewards. Positively, this critical stance includes a vision of the world in which genuine mutuality, reciprocity, and equality might prevail. A fully developed feminist spirituality would bear the traces of the central elements of feminist consciousness, integrated within a wider religious framework.

Such a spirituality would affirm and be deeply at home in the reality of sisterhood. It would recognize the importance of the supportive network among women of all ages, races, and classes and would espouse non-competitive, non-hierarchical, non-dominating modes of relationship among human beings. As critical, it would recognize the competitive and non-supportive ways in which women have sometimes related to one another in the past and would consciously struggle to achieve authentic, interdependent modes of relationship. As religious, and as Christian, such a spirituality would strive to integrate the model of feminist sisterhood into a wider vision of human community with men as brothers. Thus it would be open to all people and would not cease calling the brothers to task for their failings and to wider vision of human mutuality, reciprocity, and interdependence before a God who wills our unity and community.

As feminist, such a spirituality would encourage the autonomy, self-actualization, and self-transcendence of all women (and men). It would recognize the uniqueness of each individual as she tells her own story (there is no universal women's experience) and affirm each one as she strives to make her own choices. As critical, it would recognize the cultural and religious limitations placed on women in the past and present; and as self-critical, the temptation of the feminist group to impose another ideology as oppressive as the old obedience to the fathers. Feminist spirituality would consciously struggle to free itself from ideologies in favor of the authentic freedom of the individual and the group as it attempts to be faithful to its own experience. As religious, and as Christian, a feminist spirituality would strive for an ever freer, but always human, self-transcendence before a God who does not call us servants but friends.

In its encouragement of sisterhood and autonomy, feminist spirituality understands the wider dimensions of human oppression, especially the relationships of racism, classism, sexism, and elitism in our society, and affirms the liberation of all oppressed groups. As critical, it would resist limiting the women's movement to a luxury only the affluent can afford, but would embrace the plight of women of all colors and all classes, that is, be genuinely self-critical. As religious, and as Christian, such a spirituality would strive to become global in its concerns, in its prayer as in action, to become truly inclusive of the whole of God's world, to pray and to act with the inclusive mind of God, that is, to be self-transcendent.

A Christian feminist spirituality is universal in its vision and relates the struggle of the individual woman—black, brown, yellow or white, rich or poor, educated or illiterate—to the massive global problems of our day. For in recognizing the problem (the sin) of human exploitation, violence, and domination of male over female, rich over poor, white over color, in-group over out-group, strong over weak, force over freedom, man over nature, it sees the whole through the part. Such a spirituality strives to be not elitist but inclusive. It invites men, and all the other oppressor groups, to conversion. Yet it remains critical, on guard against the easy cooptation that can dim its radical vision of human mutuality and cooperation. Wise as a serpent, cunning as a dove, Christian feminist spirituality resorts to prayer as the only hope for its vision even as it struggles to act, here and now, to bring it into reality.

Given the possible scope of feminist spirituality as it views the whole through the lens of women's situation, what can be said about female and male spirituality? That each has its values and limitations. That the emergent female spirituality has strong humanistic and corrective elements for contemporary society. The feminist spirituality is, I think, new. With the exception, perhaps, of the 19th century Protestant feminists, the feminist spirituality I have described differs not only from male spirituality, past and present, but from a good deal of female spirituality as well. Clearly, it would be available for everyone, male and female. And clearly, it would be androgynous, if by the term is meant focus on the person as integrating the full range of human possibilities, with choices dependent on talents and attractions rather than the stereotypes of race, class, and sex. (The oppressors are oppressed, too, by limited horizons.) Strictly feminist spirituality, with its particular stress on female bonding in sisterhood, affirmation of the self-actualization and self-transcendence of women, and interrelationships among sexism, racism, and classism, is, one hopes, a temporary stage on the way to a fuller human spirituality.

In the present, however, it remains a stage that has only begun to be explored. Analogies with the experience of other oppressed or minority groups might be helpful. One who has worked in and with any of these groups, shared in their struggle and their prayer, even if she is not a member of the group can to some extent know what that experience is, can be "converted." So, too, any man who has identified with the struggle of women can participate in the feminist experience, share in a feminist spirituality. Given the massive distortions of both the religious and the cultural traditions, I would say that in truth any man should. All the spiritualities of liberation, notwithstanding the distinctive and never to be totally assimilated experience of the "minority," do have a convergent unity. But it is precisely through the particularities of the individual group that some purchase on the broader vision can be had.

The feminist experience is unique in that it potentially covers the world, every human group. It is this that has led some feminists to maintain that male-female domination is not only the oldest, but the source of all oppressor-oppressed relationships. And because of the close familial, personal, ethnic, and class ties involved, it is also often seen as the most difficult to deal with. And yet that very closeness of male-female, in whatever group, may offer stronger possibilities for overcoming the split, for healing the wound, particularly in the religious context that spirituality encompasses. For here, in the Christian framework at least, human beings understand themselves in relation to a God who is ultimate, yet incarnate, whose name is love, who calls us to unity, whose revelation is in the death and resurrection of Jesus, who is among us in the Spirit (our experience of spirituality) that our joy may be complete. The Spirit is advocate, comforter, clarifier of sin and of truth.

A feminist spirituality, with its sources in women's experience of friendship and sisterhood, might express the experience of joy in the divine-human relationship, as suggested by Judith Plaskow in her study of Protestant theologies of sin and grace in relation to the experience of women. This is the experience of grace or the Spirit which is neither "shattering" (Niebuhr) as by an authoritarian father-judge nor a quietistic "acceptance" as by an understanding mother (Tillich), neither "subordination nor participation which threatens the boundaries of the individual self." It is an experience of grace or the Spirit "best expressed in words using the prefix 'co'— co-creating, co-shaping, co-stewardship; and in non-objectifying process words, aliveness, changing, loving, pushing, etc."[4] The suggestion is similar to one made by Elisabeth Schüssler Fiorenza about the metaphor of friend/friendship in relation to God.[5]

What if one were to envision God as friend, even as a feminist friend, rather than father or mother? What if God is friend to humanity as a whole, and even more intimately, friend to the individual, to me? A friend whose presence is joy, ever-deepening relationship and love, ever available in direct address, in communion and presence? A friend whose person is fundamentally a mystery, inexhaustible, never fully known, always surprising? Yet a friend, familiar, comforting, at home with us: a friend who urges our freedom and autonomy in decision, yet who is present in the community of interdependence and in fact creates it? A friend who widens our perspectives daily and who deepens our passion for freedom—our own and that of others? What if? Jesus' relationship to his disciples was that of friendship, chosen friends; he was rather critical of familial ties. His friendship transformed their lives—both women and men—expanded their horizons; his Spirit pressed them forward. Can we pray to the God of Jesus, through the Spirit, as friends?

NOTES

1. An earlier version of these reflections was presented at a seminar on feminist spirituality organized by Mary Jo Weaver of Indiana University, Bloomington, in October, 1981, and supported by a grant from Lily Endowment.

2. See Research Report: *Women in Church and Society,* ed. Sara Butler, M.S.B.T. (Mahwah, NJ: Catholic Theological Society of America, 1978), pp. 32–40.

3. (Minneapolis: Winston, 1981).

4. *Sex, Sin and Grace: Women's Experience and the Theologies of Reinhold Niebuhr and Paul Tillich* (Washington, DC: University Press of America, 1980), p. 172.

5. "Why Not the Category Friend/Friendship?" *Horizons* 2/1 (Spring 1975), pp. 117–18.

Section II

Women's Psychological Development

Contrary to common expectations, my primary inspiration for this section comes not from contemporary psychology but from the classical tradition of Christian spirituality. Teresa of Avila and Catherine of Siena understood the primacy of adequate self-understanding before Carol Gilligan or Jean Baker Miller. While I regard Gilligan and Miller as valuable resources, I have been drawn to them because I was already in the school of Teresa and Catherine.

In her *Life* (Ch. 13, #15, included in Section III), Teresa advises her students: "This path of self knowledge must never be abandoned. . . . Along this path of prayer, self knowledge . . . is the bread with which all palates must be fed no matter how delicate they may be. . . ." Catherine, too, images self-knowledge as a basic food for spiritual growth. In *The Dialogue* (#10, included in Section III) Catherine pictures God as saying, "So think of the soul as a tree made for love and living only by love. . . . The circle in which this tree's root, the soul's love, must grow is true knowledge of herself. . . ."

The psychological essays in this section are resources for this self-knowledge. One could ask how feminist psychology is a resource for spiritual self-knowledge? Put another way: How can feminism, which promotes self-fulfillment, be compatible or congruent with a spirituality which fosters self-denial?

The answer to this question lies in its assumptions. First, there is no need to assume conflicting goals. Both feminist psychology and spiritual development aim at the common goal of maturity, and put a primary emphasis on the balance between relationship and independence. Both spirituality and psychology value vulnerability as a human quality capable of generating empathy for others: when vulnerability is accepted as a normal human condition one can avoid the harmful defenses against having to admit it.

The assumption that spirituality and psychology are incompatible also seems to assume that the self comes "ready-made" with needs to be either fulfilled or denied. Yet we must ask deeper questions: How is one's self constructed? How can one avoid self-deception about what gives fulfillment and what should be denied? Feminism teaches women to examine critically the way socialization in a patriarchal culture affects their self-understanding; it raises their consciousness to awareness and affirmation of themselves as authors of their own life-story. A parallel goal (maturity as authentic relationship) and process (discernment) in Christian spirituality exists, as Teresa of Avila, Ignatius of Loyola and others explain and will be presented in Section III.

In this section one should notice the similarities between the Christian goal of union with God demonstrated by loving care for all persons, and the ideal of human maturity promoted in essays by Miller, Gilligan, and Kegan. Gilligan rejects autonomy as the only appropriate goal for human maturity in moral decisions and presents instead a goal which equally values relationships. The insights in her work are not yet integrated into a full model of life-span development. That task, however, has been attempted and is the contribution of her colleague at Harvard, Robert Kegan. He explicitly intends to present a model which listens as carefully to women's experience as it does to men's. As a result, his model demonstrates how the qualities which have come to characterize men and women stereotypically—autonomy and relationship—are the focus of life-span tasks at *every* stage of everyone's development. Whereas Kegan contributes a complete developmental model, and Gilligan re-examines women's moral development, Miller presents characteristics of a whole new psychology of women. She explains that autonomy as the goal of maturity is a carry-over from men's experience and implies that one should be able to give up affiliations in order to become separate and self-directed. Women seek more than autonomy as was defined for men; indeed, they seek a fuller ability to encompass relationships *simultaneously* with the fullest development of themselves. Too often women are misinterpreted or penalized for affirming to men a basic truth: everyone's individual development proceeds only through affiliation as well as differentiation. And this development involves conflict which is an inevitable fact of life and is not necessarily harmful.

Because this is a new, uncomfortable position that women may interpret as backward or aggressive unless they find a community of correct interpretation and mutual support, selections from Miller, Gilligan, and Kegan are offered as resources which may support just such a community for women.

The Eichenbaum and Orbach essay is a resource for understanding how a woman's sense of her self is produced. They argue that "femininity" is constructed principally within mother-daughter relationships. For example, a mother's unconscious identification with her daughter can make a mother annoyed when her daughter reveals her needs and does not control herself as she (i.e., the mother) has learned she must do in order to be "feminine" in the only way that earns respect: being long-suffering and self-effacing. Women who may identify with mothering roles (e.g., teachers, counselors, spiritual directors) may also find themselves feeling this annoyance toward their students and clients.

Because Jung's psychology values religion and seems so sympathetic toward women, it is often accepted by religious women without reservation. Goldenberg's and Wehr's essays provide a necessary critique of Jung's male-centered view of women's development. While these selections will enable one to appreciate some aspects of Jung's theory of archetypes, they clearly reveal and confront the sexist assumptions which influence Jung's theory of "the feminine."

In a Different Voice:
Visions of Maturity

In a Different Voice:
Visions of Maturity

In a Different Voice:
Visions of Maturity

Carol Gilligan

Attachment and separation anchor the cycle of human life, describing the biology of human reproduction and the psychology of human development. The concepts of attachment and separation that depict the nature and sequence of infant development appear in adolescence as identity and intimacy and then in adulthood as love and work. This reiterative counterpoint in human experience, however, when molded into a developmental ordering, tends to disappear in the course of its linear reduction into the equation of development with separation. This disappearance can be traced in part to the focus on child and adolescent development, where progress can readily be charted by measuring the distance between mother and child. The limitation of this rendition is most apparent in the absence of women from accounts of adult development.

Choosing like Virgil to "sing of arms and the man," psychologists describing adulthood have focused on the development of self and work. While the apogee of separation in adolescence is presumed to be followed in adulthood by the return of attachment and care, recent depictions of adult development, in their seamless emergence from studies of men, provide scanty illumination of a life spent in intimate and generative relationships. Daniel Levinson (1978), despite his evident distress about the exclusion of women from his necessarily small sample, sets out on the basis of an all-male study "to create an overarching conception of development that could encompass the diverse biological, psychological and social changes occurring in adult life" (p. 8).

63

Levinson's conception is informed by the idea of "the Dream," which orders the seasons of a man's life in the same way that Jupiter's prophecy of a glorious destiny steers the course of Aeneas' journey. The Dream about which Levinson writes is also a vision of glorious achievement whose realization or modification will shape the character and life of the man. In the salient relationships in Levinson's analysis, the "mentor" facilitates the realization of the Dream, while the "special woman" is the helpmate who encourages the hero to shape and live out his vision: "As the novice adult tries to separate from his family and pre-adult world, and to enter an adult world, he must form significant relationships with other adults who will facilitate his work on the Dream. Two of the most important figures in this drama are the 'mentor' and the 'special woman' " (p. 93).

The significant relationships of early adulthood are thus construed as the means to an end of individual achievement, and these "transitional figures" must be cast off or reconstructed following the realization of success. If in the process, however, they become, like Dido, an impediment to the fulfillment of the Dream, then the relationship must be renounced, "to allow the developmental process" to continue. This process is defined by Levinson explicitly as one of individuation: "throughout the life cycle, but especially in the key transition periods . . . the developmental process of *individuation* is going on." The process refers "to the changes in a person's relationships to himself and to the external world," the relationships that constitute his "Life Structure" (p. 195).

If in the course of "Becoming One's Own Man," this structure is discovered to be flawed and threatens the great expectations of the Dream, then in order to avert "serious Failure or Decline," the man must "break out" to salvage his Dream. This act of breaking out is consummated by a "marker event" of separation, such as "leaving his wife, quitting his job, or moving to another region" (p. 206). Thus the road to mid-life salvation runs through either achievement or separation.

From the array of human experience, Levinson's choice is the same as Virgil's, charting the progress of adult development as an arduous struggle toward a glorious destiny. Like pious Aeneas on his way to found Rome, the men in Levinson's study steady their lives by their devotion to realizing their dream, measuring their progress in terms of their distance from the shores of its promised success. Thus in the stories that Levinson recounts, relationships, whatever their particular intensity, play a relatively subordinate role in the individual drama of adult development.

The focus on work is also apparent in George Vaillant's (1977) account of adaptation to life. The variables that correlate with adult adjustment, like the interview that generates the data, bear predominantly on occupation and call for an expansion of Erikson's stages. Filling in what he sees as "an uncharted period of development" which Erikson left "between the decades of the twenties and forties," Vaillant describes the years of the thirties as the era of "Career Consolidation," the time when the men in his sample sought, "like Shakespeare's soldier, 'the bauble Reputation' " (p. 202). With this analogy to Shakespeare's Rome, the continuity of intimacy and generativity is interrupted to make room for a stage of further individuation and achievement, realized by work and consummated by a success that brings societal recognition.

Erikson's (1950) notion of generativity, however, is changed in the process of this recasting. Conceiving generativity as "the concern in establishing and guiding the next generation," Erikson takes the "*productivity* and *creativity*" of parenthood in its literal or symbolic realization to be a metaphor for an adulthood centered on relationships and devoted to the activity of taking care (p. 267). In Erikson's account, generativity is the central stage of adult development, encompassing "man's relationship to his production as well as to his progeny" (p. 268). In Vaillant's data, this relationship is relegated instead to mid-life.

Asserting that generativity is "not just a stage for making little things grow," Vaillant argues against Erikson's metaphor of parenthood by cautioning that "the world is filled with irresponsible mothers who are marvellous at bearing and loving children up to the age of two and then despair of taking the process further." Generativity, in order to exclude such women, is uprooted from its earthy redolence and redefined as "responsibility for the growth, leadership, and well-being of one's fellow creatures, not just raising crops or children" (p. 202). Thus, the expanse of Erikson's conception is narrowed to development in mid-adulthood and in the process is made more restrictive in its definition of care.

As a result, Vaillant emphasizes the relation of self to society and minimizes attachment to others. In an interview about work, health, stress, death, and a variety of family relationships, Vaillant says to the men in his study that "the hardest question" he will ask is, "Can you describe your wife?" This prefatory caution presumably arose from his experience with this particular sample of men but points to the limits of their adaptation, or perhaps to its psychological expense.

Thus the "models for a healthy life cycle" are men who seem distant in their relationships, finding it difficult to describe their wives, whose importance in their lives they nevertheless acknowledge. The same sense of distance between self and others is evident in Levinson's conclusion that, "In our interviews, friendship was largely noticeable by its absence. As a tentative generalization we would say that close friendship with a man or a woman is rarely experienced by American men." Caught by this impression, Levinson pauses in his discussion of the three "tasks" of adulthood (Building and Modifying the Life Structure, Working on Single Components of the Life Structure, and Becoming More Individuated), to offer an elaboration: "A man may have a wide social network in which he has amicable, 'friendly' relationships with many men and perhaps a few women. In general, however, most men do not have an intimate male friend of the kind that they recall fondly from boyhood or youth. Many men have had casual dating relationships with women, and perhaps a few complex love-sex relationships, but most men have not had an intimate non-sexual friendship with a woman. We need to understand why friendship is so rare, and what consequences this deprivation has for adult life" (p. 335).

Thus, there are studies, on the one hand, that convey a view of adulthood where relationships are subordinated to the ongoing process of individuation and achievement, whose progress, however, is predicated on prior attachments and thought to enhance the capacity for intimacy. On the other hand, there is the observation that among those men whose lives have served as the model for adult development, the capacity for relationships is in some sense diminished and the men are constricted in their emotional expression. Relationships often are cast in the language of achievement, characterized by their success or failure, and impoverished in their affective range:

At forty-five, Lucky, enjoyed one of the best marriages in the Study, but probably not as perfect as he implied when he wrote, "You may not believe me when I say we've never had a disagreement, large or small."

The biography of Dr. Carson illustrates his halting passage from identity to intimacy, through career consolidation, and, finally, into the capacity to *care* in its fullest sense . . . he had gone through divorce, remarriage, and a shift from research to private practice. His personal metamorphosis had continued. The mousy researcher had become a charming clinician . . . suave, untroubled, kindly and in control . . . The vibrant energy that had characterized his adolescence had returned . . . now his depression was clearly an *affect;* and he was anything but fatigued. In the next breath he confessed, "I'm very highly sexed and that's a problem, too." He then provided me with an exciting narrative as he told me not only of recent romantic entanglements but also of his warm fatherly concern for patients (Vaillant, 1977, pp. 129, 203–206).

The notion that separation leads to attachment and that individuation eventuates in mutuality, while reiterated by both Vaillant and Levinson, is belied by the lives they put forth as support. Similarly, in Erikson's studies of Luther and Gandhi, while the relationship between self and society is achieved in magnificent articulation, both men are compromised in their capacity for intimacy and live at great personal distance from others. Thus Luther in his devotion to Faith, like Gandhi in his devotion to Truth, ignore the people most closely around them while working instead toward the glory of God. These men resemble in remarkable detail pious Aeneas in Virgil's epic, who also overcame the bonds of attachment that impeded the progress of his journey to Rome.

In all these accounts the women are silent, except for the sorrowful voice of Dido who, imploring and threatening Aeneas in vain, in the end silences herself upon his sword. Thus there seems to be a line of development missing from current depictions of adult development, a failure to describe the progression of relationships toward a maturity of interdependence. Though the truth of separation is recognized in most developmental texts, the reality of continuing connection is lost or relegated to the background where the figures of women appear. In this way, the emerging conception of adult development casts a familiar shadow on women's lives, pointing again toward the incompleteness of their separation, depicting them as mired in relationships. For women, the developmental markers of separation and attachment, allocated sequentially to adolescence and adulthood, seem in some sense to be fused. However, while this fusion leaves women at risk in a society that rewards separation, it also points to a more general truth currently obscured in psychological texts.

In young adulthood, when identity and intimacy converge in dilemmas of conflicting commitment, the relationship between self and other is exposed. That this relationship differs in the experience of men and women is a steady theme in the literature on human development and a finding of my research. From the different dynamics of separation and attachment in their gender identity formation through the divergence of identity and intimacy that marks their experience in the adolescent years, male and female voices typically speak of the importance of different truths, the former of the role of separation as it defines and empowers the self, the latter of the ongoing process of attachment that creates and sustains the human community.

Since this dialogue contains the dialectic that creates the tension of human development, the silence of women in the narrative of adult development distorts the conception of its stages and sequence. Thus, I want to restore in part the missing text of women's development, as they describe their conceptions of self and morality in the early adult years. In focusing primarily on the differences between the accounts of women and men, my aim is to enlarge developmental understanding by including the perspectives of both of the sexes. While the judgments considered come from a small and highly educated sample, they elucidate a contrast and make it possible to recognize not only what is missing in women's development but also what is there.

This problem of recognition was illustrated in a literature class at a women's college where the students were discussing the moral dilemma described in the novels of Mary McCarthy and James Joyce:

I felt caught in a dilemma that was new to me then but which since has become horribly familiar: the trap of adult life, in which you are held, wriggling, powerless to act because you can see both sides. On that occasion, as generally in the future, I compromised. (*Memories of a Catholic Girlhood*)

I will not serve that in which I no longer believe, whether it calls itself my home, my fatherland or my church: and I will try to express myself in some mode of life or art as freely as I can and as wholly as I can, using for my defense the only arms I allow myself to use—silence, exile and cunning. (*A Portrait of the Artist as a Young Man*)

Comparing the clarity of Stephen's *non serviam* with Mary McCarthy's "zigzag course," the women were unanimous in their decision that Stephen's was the better choice. Stephen was powerful in his certainty of belief and armed with strategies to avoid confrontation; the shape of his identity was clear and tied to a compelling justification. He had, in any case, taken a stand.

Wishing that they could be more like Stephen, in his clarity of decision and certainty of desire, the women saw themselves instead like Mary McCarthy, helpless, powerless, and constantly compromised. The contrasting images of helplessness and power in their explicit tie to attachment and separation caught the dilemma of the women's development, the conflict between integrity and care. In Stephen's simpler construction, separation seemed the empowering condition of free and full self-expression, while attachment appeared a paralyzing entrapment and caring an inevitable prelude to compromise. To the students, Mary McCarthy's portrayal confirmed their own endorsement of this account.

In the novels, however, contrasting descriptions of the road to adult life appear. For Stephen, leaving childhood means renouncing relationships in order to protect his freedom of self-expression. For Mary, "farewell to childhood" means relinquishing the freedom of self-expression in order to protect others and preserve relationships: "A sense of power and Caesarlike magnanimity filled me. I was going to equivocate, not for selfish reasons but in the interests of the community, like a grown-up responsible person" (p. 162). These divergent constructions of identity, in self-expression or in self-sacrifice, create different problems for further development—the former a problem of human connection, and the latter a problem of truth. These seemingly disparate problems, however, are intimately related, since the shrinking from truth creates distance in relationship, and separation removes part of the truth. In the college student study which spanned the years of early adulthood, the men's return from exile and silence parallels the women's return from equivocation, until intimacy and truth converge in the discovery of the connection between integrity and care. Then only a difference in tone reveals what men and women know from the beginning and what they only later discover through experience.

The instant choice of self-deprecation in the preference for Stephen by the women in the English class is matched by a child-like readiness for apology in the women in the college student study. The participants in this study were an unequal number of men and women, representing the distribution of males and females in the class on moral and political choice. At age twenty-seven, the five women in the study all were actively pursuing careers—two in medicine, one in law, one in graduate study, and one as an organizer of labor unions. In the five years following their graduation from college, three had married and one had a child.

When they were asked at age twenty-seven, "How would you describe yourself to yourself?" one of the women refused to reply, but the other four gave as their responses to the interviewer's question:

> This sounds sort of strange, but I think maternal, with all its connotations. I see myself in a nurturing role, maybe not right now, but whenever that might be, as a physician, as a mother . . . It's hard for me to think of myself without thinking about other people around me that I'm giving to.
>
> (Claire)

> I am fairly hard-working and fairly thorough and fairly responsible, and in terms of weaknesses, I am sometimes hesitant about making decisions and unsure of myself and afraid of doing things and taking responsibility, and I think maybe that is one of the biggest conflicts I have had . . . The other very important aspect of my life is my husband and trying to make his life easier and trying to help him out.
>
> (Leslie)

I am a hysteric. I am intense. I am warm. I am very smart about people . . . I have a lot more soft feelings than hard feelings. I am a lot easier to get to be kind than to get mad. If I had to say one word, and to me it incorporates a lot, *adopted*.

(Erica)

I have sort of changed a lot. At the point of the last interview [age twenty-two] I felt like I was the kind of person who was interested in growth and trying hard, and it seems to me that the last couple of years, the not trying is someone who is not grow- ing, and I think that is the thing that bothers me the most, the thing that I keep thinking about, that I am not growing. It's not true, I am, but what seems to be a failure partially is the way that Tom and I broke up. The thing with Tom feels to me like I am not growing . . . The thing I am running into lately is that the way I describe myself, my behavior doesn't sometimes come out that way. Like I hurt Tom a lot, and that bothers me. So I am thinking of myself as somebody who tried not to hurt people, but I ended up hurting him a lot, and so that is something that weighs on me, that I am somebody who unintentionally hurts people. Or a feeling, lately, that it is simple to sit down and say what your principles are, what your values are, and what I think about myself, but the way it sort of works out in actuality is sometimes very different. You can say you try not to hurt peo- ple, but you might because of things about yourself, or you can say this is my principle, but when the situation comes up, you don't really behave the way you would like . . . So I consider myself contradictory and confused.

(Nan)

The fusion of identity and intimacy, noted repeatedly in wom- en's development, is perhaps nowhere more clearly articulated than in these self-descriptions. In response to the request to describe themselves, all of the women describe a relationship, depicting their identity *in* the connection of future mother, present wife, adopted child, or past lover. Similarly, the standard of moral judgment that informs their assessment of self is a standard of relationship, an ethic of nurturance, responsibility, and care. Measuring their strength in the activity of attachment ("giving to," "helping out," "being kind," "not hurting"), these highly successful and achieving women do not mention their academic and professional distinction in the context of describing themselves. If anything, they regard their professional activities as jeopardizing their own sense of themselves, and the conflict they encounter between achievement and care leaves them either divided in judgment or feeling betrayed. Nan explains:

> When I first applied to medical school, my feeling was that I was a person who was concerned with other people and being able to care for them in some way or another, and I was running into problems the last few years as far as my being able to give of myself, my time, and what I am doing to other people. And medicine, even though it seems that profession is set up to do exactly that, seems to more or less interfere with your doing it. To me it felt like I wasn't really growing, that I was just treading water, trying to cope with what I was doing that made me very angry in some ways because it wasn't the way that I wanted things to go.

Thus in all of the women's descriptions, identity is defined in a context of relationship and judged by a standard of responsibility and care. Similarly, morality is seen by these women as arising from the experience of connection and conceived as a problem of inclusion rather than one of balancing claims. The underlying assumption that morality stems from attachment is explicitly stated by Claire in her response to Heinz's dilemma of whether or not to steal an overpriced drug in order to save his wife. Explaining why Heinz should steal, she elaborates the view of social reality on which her judgment is based:

> By yourself, there is little sense to things. It is like the sound of one hand clapping, the sound of one man or one woman, there is something lacking. It is the collective that is important to me, and that collective is based on certain guiding principles, one of which is that everybody belongs to it and that you all come from it. You have to love someone else, because while you may not like them, you are inseparable from them. In a way, it is like loving your right hand. *They are part of you;* that other person is part of that giant collection of people that you are connected to.

To this aspiring maternal physician, the sound of one hand clapping does not seem a miraculous transcendence but rather a human absurdity, the illusion of a person standing alone in a reality of interconnection.

For the men, the tone of identity is different, clearer, more direct, more distinct and sharp-edged. Even when disparaging the concept itself, they radiate the confidence of certain truth. Although the world of the self that men describe at times includes "people" and "deep attachments," no particular person or relationship is mentioned, nor is the activity of relationship portrayed in the context of self-description. Replacing the women's verbs of attachment are adjectives of separation—"intelligent," "logical," "imaginative," "honest," sometimes even "arrogant" and "cocky." Thus the male "I" is defined in separation, although the men speak of having "real contacts" and "deep emotions" or otherwise wishing for them.

In a randomly selected half of the sample, men who were situated similarly to the women in occupational and marital position give as their initial responses to the request for self-description:

> Logical, compromising, outwardly calm. If it seems like my statements are short and abrupt, it is because of my background and training. Architectural statements have to be very concise and short. Accepting. Those are all on an emotional level. I consider myself educated, reasonably intelligent.

> I would describe myself as an enthusiastic, passionate person who is slightly arrogant. Concerned, committed, very tired right now because I didn't get much sleep last night.

> I would describe myself as a person who is well developed intellectually and emotionally. Relatively narrow circle of friends, acquaintances, persons with whom I have real contacts as opposed to professional contacts or community contacts. And relatively proud of the intellectual skills and development, content with the emotional development as such, as a not very actively pursued goal. Desiring to broaden that one, the emotional aspect.

> Intelligent, perceptive—I am being brutally honest now—still somewhat reserved, unrealistic about a number of social situations which involve other people, particularly authorities. Improving, looser, less tense and hung up than I used to be. Somewhat lazy, although it is hard to say how much of that is tied up with other conflicts. Imaginative, sometimes too much so. A little dilletantish, interested in a lot of things without nec-

essarily going into them in depth, although I am moving toward correcting that.

I would tend to describe myself first by recounting a personal history, where I was born, grew up, and that kind of thing, but I am dissatisfied with that, having done it thousands of times. It doesn't seem to capture the essence of what I am, I would probably decide after another futile attempt, because there is no such thing as the essence of what I am, and be very bored by the whole thing . . . I don't think that there is any such thing as myself. There is myself sitting here, there is myself tomorrow, and so on.

Evolving and honest.

I guess on the surface I seem a little easy-going and laid back, but I think I am probably a bit more wound up than that. I tend to get wound up very easily. Kind of smart aleck, a little bit, or cocky maybe. Not as thorough as I should be. A little bit hard-ass, I guess, and a guy that is not swayed by emotions and feelings. I have deep emotions, but I am not a person who has a lot of different people. I have attachments to a few people, very deep attachments. Or attachments to a lot of things, at least in the demonstrable sense.

I guess I think I am kind of creative and also a little bit schizophrenic . . . A lot of it is a result of how I grew up. There is a kind of longing for the pastoral life and, at the same time, a desire for the flash, prestige, and recognition that you get by going out and hustling.

Two of the men begin more tentatively by talking about people in general, but they return in the end to great ideas or a need for distinctive achievement:

I think I am basically a decent person. I think I like people a lot and I like liking people. I like doing things with pleasure from just people, from their existence, almost. Even people I don't know well. When I said I was a decent person, I think that is almost the thing that makes me a decent person, that is a decent quality, a good quality. I think I am very bright. I think I am a little lost, not acting quite like I am inspired—whether it is just a question of lack of inspiration, I don't know—but not accomplishing things, not achieving things, and not knowing where I want to go or what I'm doing. I think most people especially doctors, have some idea of what they are going to be doing in four years. I [an intern] really have a blank . . . I have great ideas . . . but I can't imagine me in them.

I guess the things that I like to think are important to me are I am aware of what is going on around me, other people's needs around me, and the fact that I enjoy doing things for other people and I feel good about it. I suppose it's nice in my situation, but I am not sure that is true for everybody. I think some people do things for other people and it doesn't make them feel good. Once in awhile that is true of me too, for instance working around the house, and I am always doing the same old things that everyone else is doing and eventually I build up some resentment toward that.

In these men's descriptions of self, involvement with others is tied to a qualification of identity rather than to its realization. Instead of attachment, individual achievement rivets the male imagination, and great ideas or distinctive activity defines the standard of self-assessment and success.

Thus the sequential ordering of identity and intimacy in the transition from adolescence to adulthood better fits the development of men than it does the development of women. Power and separation secure the man in an identity achieved through work, but they leave him at a distance from others, who seem in some sense out of his sight. Cranly, urging Stephen Daedalus to perform his Easter duty for his mother's sake, reminds him:

Your mother must have gone through a good deal of suffering . . . Would you not try to save her from suffering more even if— or would you?
    If I could, Stephen said, that would cost me very little.

Given this distance, intimacy becomes the critical experience that brings the self back into connection with others, making it possible to see both sides—to discover the effects of actions on others as well as their cost to the self. The experience of relationship brings an end to isolation, which otherwise hardens into indifference, an absence of active concern for others, though perhaps a willingness to respect their rights. For this reason, intimacy is the transformative experience for men through which adolescent identity turns into the generativity of adult love and work. In the process, as Erikson (1964) observes, the knowledge gained through intimacy changes the ideological morality of adolescence into the adult ethic of taking care.

Since women, however, define their identity through relationships of intimacy and care, the moral problems that they encounter pertain to issues of a different sort. When relationships are secured by masking desire and conflict is avoided by equivocation, then confusion arises about the locus of responsibility and truth. McCarthy, describing her "representations" to her grandparents, explains:

> Whatever I told them was usually so blurred and glossed, in the effort to meet their approval (for, aside from anything else, I was fond of them and tried to accommodate myself to their perspective), that except when answering a direct question, I hardly knew whether what I was saying was true or false. I really tried, or so I thought, to avoid lying, but it seemed to me that they forced it on me by the difference in their vision of things, so that I was always transposing reality for them into terms they could understand. To keep matters straight with my conscience, I shrank, whenever possible, from the lie absolute, just as, from a sense of precaution, I shrank from the plain truth.

The critical experience then becomes not intimacy but choice, creating an encounter with self that clarifies the understanding of responsibility and truth.

Thus in the transition from adolescence to adulthood, the dilemma itself is the same for both sexes, a conflict between integrity and care. But approached from different perspectives, this dilemma generates the recognition of opposite truths. These different perspectives are reflected in two different moral ideologies, since separation is justified by an ethic of rights while attachment is supported by an ethic of care.

The morality of rights is predicated on equality and centered on the understanding of fairness, while the ethic of responsibility relies on the concept of equity, the recognition of differences in need. While the ethic of rights is a manifestation of equal respect, balancing the claims of other and self, the ethic of responsibility rests on an understanding that gives rise to compassion and care. Thus the counterpoint of identity and intimacy that marks the time between childhood and adulthood is articulated through two different moralities whose complementarity is the discovery of maturity.

The discovery of this complementarity is traced in the study by questions about personal experiences of moral conflict and choice. Two lawyers chosen from the sample illustrate how the divergence in judgment between the sexes is resolved through the discovery by each of the other's perspective and of the relationship between integrity and care.

The dilemma of responsibility and truth that McCarthy describes is reiterated by Hilary, a lawyer and the woman who said she found it too hard to describe herself at the end of what "really has been a rough week." She too, like McCarthy, considers self-sacrificing acts "courageous" and "praiseworthy," explaining that "if everyone on earth behaved in a way that showed care for others and courage, the world would be a much better place, you wouldn't have crime and you might not have poverty." However, this moral ideal of self-sacrifice and care ran into trouble not only in a relationship where the conflicting truths of each person's feelings made it impossible to avoid hurt, but also in court where, despite her concern for the client on the other side, she decided not to help her opponent win his case.

In both instances, she found the absolute injunction against hurting others to be an inadequate guide to resolving the actual dilemmas she faced. Her discovery of the disparity between intention and consequence and of the actual constraints of choice led her to realize that there is, in some situations, no way not to hurt. In confronting such dilemmas in both her personal and professional life, she does not abdicate responsibility for choice but rather claims the right to include herself among the people for whom she considers it moral not to hurt. Her more inclusive morality now contains the injunction to be true to herself, leaving her with two principles of judgment whose integration she cannot yet clearly envision. What she does recognize is that both integrity and care must be included in a morality that can encompass the dilemmas of love and work that arise in adult life.

The move toward tolerance that accompanies the abandonment of absolutes is considered by William Perry (1968) to chart the course of intellectual and ethical development during the early adult years. Perry describes the changes in thinking that mark the transition from a belief that knowledge is absolute and answers clearly right or wrong to an understanding of the contextual relativity of both truth and choice. This transition and its impact on moral judgment can be discerned in the changes in moral understanding that occur in both men and women during the five years following college (Gilligan and Murphy, 1979; Murphy and Gilligan, 1980). Though both sexes move away from absolutes in this time, the absolutes themselves differ for each. In women's development, the absolute of care, defined initially as not hurting others, becomes complicated through a recognition of the need for personal integrity. This recognition gives rise to the claim for equality embodied in the concept of rights, which changes the understanding of relationships and transforms the definition of care. For men, the absolutes of truth and fairness, defined by the concepts of equality and reciprocity, are called into question by experiences that demonstrate the existence of differences between other and self. Then the awareness of multiple truths leads to a relativizing of equality in the direction of equity and gives rise to an ethic of generosity and care. For both sexes the existence of two contexts for moral decision makes judgment by definition contextually relative and leads to a new understanding of responsibility and choice.

The discovery of the reality of differences and thus of the contextual nature of morality and truth is described by Alex, a lawyer in the college student study, who began in law school "to realize that you really don't know everything" and "you don't ever know that there is any absolute. I don't think that you ever know that there is an absolute right. What you do know is you have to come down one way or the other. You have got to make a decision."

The awareness that he did not know everything arose more painfully in a relationship whose ending took him completely by surprise. In his belated discovery that the woman's experience had differed from his own, he realized how distant he had been in a relationship he considered close. Then the logical hierarchy of moral values, whose absolute truth he formerly proclaimed, came to seem a barrier to intimacy rather than a fortress of personal integrity. As his conception of morality began to change, his thinking focused on issues of relationship, and his concern with injustice was complicated by a new understanding of human attachment. Describing "the principle of attachment" that began to inform his way of looking at moral problems, Alex sees the need for morality to extend beyond considerations of fairness to concern with relationships:

> People have real emotional needs to be attached to something, and equality doesn't give you attachment. Equality fractures society and places on every person the burden of standing on his own two feet.

Although "equality is a crisp thing that you could hang onto," it alone cannot adequately resolve the dilemmas of choice that arise in life. Given his new awareness of responsibility and of the actual consequences of choice, Alex says: "You don't want to look at just equality. You want to look at how people are going to be able to handle their lives." Recognizing the need for two contexts for judgment, he nevertheless finds that their integration "is hard to work through," since sometimes "no matter which way you go, somebody is going to be hurt and somebody is going to be hurt forever." Then, he says, "you have reached the point where there is an irresolvable conflict," and choice becomes a matter of "choosing the victim" rather than enacting the good. With the recognition of the responsibility that such choices entail, his judgment becomes more attuned to the psychological and social consequences of action, to the reality of people's lives in an historical world.

Thus, starting from very different points, from the different ideologies of justice and care, the men and women in the study come, in the course of becoming adult, to a greater understanding of both points of view and thus to a greater convergence in judgment. Recognizing the dual contexts of justice and care, they realize that judgment depends on the way in which the problem is framed.

But in this light, the conception of development itself also depends on the context in which it is framed, and the vision of maturity can be seen to shift when adulthood is portrayed by women rather than men. When women construct the adult domain, the world of relationships emerges and becomes the focus of attention and concern. McClelland (1975), noting this shift in women's fantasies of power, observes that "women are more concerned than men with both sides of an interdependent relationship" and are "quicker to recognize their own interdependence" (pp. 85–86). This focus on interdependence is manifest in fantasies that equate power with giving and care. McClelland reports that while men represent powerful activity as assertion and aggression, women in contrast portray acts of nurturance as acts of strength. Considering his research on power to deal "in particular with the characteristics of maturity," he suggests that mature women and men may relate to the world in a different style.

That women differ in their orientation to power is also the theme of Jean Baker Miller's analysis. Focusing on relationships of dominance and subordination, she finds women's situation in these relationships to provide "a crucial key to understanding the psychological order." This order arises from the relationships of difference, between man and woman and parent and child, that create "the milieu—the family—in which the human mind as we know it has been formed" (1976, p. 1). Because these relationships of difference contain, in most instances, a factor of inequality, they assume a moral dimension pertaining to the way in which power is used. On this basis, Miller distinguishes between relationships of temporary and permanent inequality, the former representing the context of human development, the latter, the condition of oppression. In relationships of temporary inequality, such as parent and child or teacher and student, power ideally is used to foster the development that removes the initial disparity. In relationships of permanent inequality, power cements dominance and subordination, and oppression is rationalized by theories that "explain" the need for its continuation.

Miller, focusing in this way on the dimension of inequality in human life, identifies the distinctive psychology of women as arising from the combination of their positions in relationships of temporary and permanent inequality. Dominant in temporary relationships of nurturance that dissolve with the dissolution of inequality, women are subservient in relationships of permanently unequal social status and power. In addition, though subordinate in social position to men, women are at the same time centrally entwined with them in the intimate and intense relationships of adult sexuality and family life. Thus women's psychology reflects both sides of relationships of interdependence and the range of moral possibilities to which such relationships give rise. Women, therefore, are ideally situated to observe the potential in human connection both for care and for oppression.

This distinct observational perspective informs the work of Carol Stack (1975) and Lillian Rubin (1976) who, entering worlds previously known through men's eyes, return to give a different report. In the urban black ghetto, where others have seen social disorder and family disarray, Stack finds networks of domestic exchange that describe the organization of the black family in poverty. Rubin, observing the families of the white working class, dispels the myth of "the affluent and happy worker" by charting the "worlds of pain" that it costs to raise a family in conditions of social and economic disadvantage. Both women describe an adulthood of relationships that sustain the family functions of protection and care, but also a social system of relationships that sustain economic dependence and social subordination. Thus they indicate how class, race, and ethnicity are used to justify and rationalize the continuing inequality of an economic system that benefits some at others' expense.

In their separate spheres of analysis, these women find order where others saw chaos—in the psychology of women, the urban black family, and the reproduction of social class. These discoveries required new modes of analysis and a more ethnographic approach in order to derive constructs that could give order and meaning to the adult life they saw. Until Stack redefined "family" as "the smallest organized, durable network of kin and non-kin who interact daily, providing the domestic needs of children and assuring their survival," she could not find "families" in the world of "The Flats." Only the "culturally specific definitions of certain concepts such as family, kin, parent, and friend that emerged during this study made much of the subsequent analysis possible . . . An arbitrary imposition of widely accepted definitions of the family . . . blocks the way to understanding how people in The Flats describe and order the world in which they live" (p. 31).

Similarly, Miller calls for "a new psychology of women" that recognizes the different starting point for women's development, the fact that "women stay with, build on, and develop in a context of attachment and affiliation with others," that "women's sense of self becomes very much organized around being able to make, and then to maintain, affiliations and relationships," and that "eventually, for many women, the threat of disruption of an affiliation is perceived not just as a loss of a relationship but as something closer to a total loss of self." Although this psychic structuring is by now familiar from descriptions of women's psychopathology, it has not been recognized that "this psychic starting point contains the possibilities for an entirely different (and more advanced) approach to living and functioning . . . [in which] affiliation is valued as highly as, or more highly than, self-enhancement" (p. 83). Thus, Miller points to a psychology of adulthood which recognizes that development does not displace the value of ongoing attachment and the continuing importance of care in relationships.

The limitations of previous standards of measurement and the need for a more contextual mode of interpretation are evident as well in Rubin's approach. Rubin dispels the illusion that family life is everywhere the same or that subcultural differences can be assessed independently of the socioeconomic realities of class. Thus, working-class families "reproduce themselves not because they are somehow deficient or their culture aberrant, but because there are no alternatives for most of their children," despite "the mobility myth we cherish so dearly" (pp. 210–211). The temporary inequality of the working-class child thus turns into the permanent inequality of the working-class adult, caught in an ebb-tide of social mobility that erodes the quality of family life.

Like the stories that delineate women's fantasies of power, women's descriptions of adulthood convey a different sense of its social reality. In their portrayal of relationships, women replace the bias of men toward separation with a representation of the interdependence of self and other, both in love and in work. By changing the lens of developmental observation from individual achievement to relationships of care, women depict ongoing attachment as the path that leads to maturity. Thus the parameters of development shift toward marking the progress of affiliative relationship.

The implications of this shift are evident in considering the situation of women at mid-life. Given the tendency to chart the unfamiliar waters of adult development with the familiar markers of adolescent separation and growth, the middle years of women's lives readily appear as a time of return to the unfinished business of adolescence. This interpretation has been particularly compelling since life-cycle descriptions, derived primarily from studies of men, have generated a perspective from which women, insofar as they differ, appear deficient in their development. The deviance of female development has been especially marked in the adolescent years when girls appear to confuse identity with intimacy by defining themselves through relationships with others. The legacy left from this mode of identity definition is considered to be a self that is vulnerable to the issues of separation that arise at mid-life.

But this construction reveals the limitation in an account which measures women's development against a male standard and ignores the possibility of a different truth. In this light, the observation that women's embeddedness in lives of relationship, their orientation to interdependence, their subordination of achievement to care, and their conflicts over competitive success leave them personally at risk in mid-life seems more a commentary on the society than a problem in women's development.

The construction of mid-life in adolescent terms, as a similar crisis of identity and separation, ignores the reality of what has happened in the years between and tears up the history of love and of work. For generativity to begin at mid-life, as Vaillant's data on men suggest, seems from a woman's perspective too late for both sexes, given that the bearing and raising of children take place primarily in the preceding years. Similarly, the image of women arriving at mid-life childlike and dependent on others is belied by the activity of their care in nurturing and sustaining family relationships. Thus the problem appears to be one of construction, an issue of judgment rather than truth.

In view of the evidence that women perceive and construe social reality differently from men and that these differences center around experiences of attachment and separation, life transitions that invariably engage these experiences can be expected to involve women in a distinctive way. And because women's sense of integrity appears to be entwined with an ethic of care, so that to see themselves as women is to see themselves in a relationship of connection, the major transitions in women's lives would seem to involve changes in the understanding and activities of care. Certainly the shift from childhood to adulthood witnesses a major redefinition of care. When the distinction between helping and pleasing frees the activity of taking care from the wish for approval by others, the ethic of responsibility can become a self-chosen anchor of personal integrity and strength.

In the same vein, however, the events of mid-life—the meno-
pause and changes in family and work—can alter a woman's activities of care in ways that affect her sense of herself. If mid-life brings
an end to relationships, to the sense of connection on which she relies, as well as to the activities of care through which she judges her
worth, then the mourning that accompanies all life transitions can
give way to the melancholia of self-deprecation and despair. The
meaning of mid-life events for a woman thus reflects the interaction
between the structures of her thought and the realities of her life.

When a distinction between neurotic and real conflict is made
and the reluctance to choose is differentiated from the reality of having no choice, then it becomes possible to see more clearly how wom-
en's experience provides a key to understanding central truths of
adult life. Rather than viewing her anatomy as destined to leave her
with a scar of inferiority (Freud, 1931), one can see instead how it
gives rise to experiences which illuminate a reality common to both
of the sexes: the fact that in life you never see it all, that things unseen undergo change through time, that there is more than one path
to gratification, and that the boundaries between self and other are
less clear than they sometimes seem.

Thus women not only reach mid-life with a psychological history different from men's and face at that time a different social reality having different possibilities for love and for work, but they also
make a different sense of experience, based on their knowledge of
human relationships. Since the reality of connection is experienced
by women as given rather than as freely contracted, they arrive at an
understanding of life that reflects the limits of autonomy and control. As a result, women's development delineates the path not only
to a less violent life but also to a maturity realized through interdependence and taking care.

In his studies of children's moral judgment, Piaget (1932/1965)
describes a three-stage progression through which constraint turns
into cooperation and cooperation into generosity. In doing so, he
points out how long it takes before children in the same class at
school, playing with each other every day, come to agree in their
understanding of the rules of their games. This agreement, however,
signals the completion of a major reorientation of action and thought
through which the morality of constraint turns into the morality of

cooperation. But he also notes how children's recognition of differences between others and themselves leads to a relativizing of equality in the direction of equity, signifying a fusion of justice and love.

There seems at present to be only partial agreement between men and women about the adulthood they commonly share. In the absence of mutual understanding, relationships between the sexes continue in varying degrees of constraint, manifesting the "paradox of egocentrism" which Piaget describes, a mystical respect for rules combined with everyone playing more or less as he pleases and paying no attention to his neighbor (p. 61). For a life-cycle understanding to address the development in adulthood of relationships characterized by cooperation, generosity, and care, that understanding must include the lives of women as well as of men.

Among the most pressing items on the agenda for research on adult development is the need to delineate *in women's own terms* the experience of their adult life. My own work in that direction indicates that the inclusion of women's experience brings to developmental understanding a new perspective on relationships that changes the basic constructs of interpretation. The concept of identity expands to include the experience of interconnection. The moral domain is similarly enlarged by the inclusion of responsibility and care in relationships. And the underlying epistemology correspondingly shifts from the Greek ideal of knowledge as a correspondence between mind and form to the Biblical conception of knowing as a process of human relationship.

Given the evidence of different perspectives in the representation of adulthood by women and men, there is a need for research that elucidates the effects of these differences in marriage, family, and work relationships. My research suggests that men and women may speak different languages that they assume are the same, using similar words to encode disparate experiences of self and social relationships. Because these languages share an overlapping moral vocabulary, they contain a propensity for systematic mistranslation, creating misunderstandings which impede communication and limit the potential for cooperation and care in relationships. At the same time, however, these languages articulate with one another in critical ways. Just as the language of responsibilities provides a weblike imagery of relationships to replace a hierarchical ordering that dissolves with the coming of equality, so the language of rights underlines the importance of including in the network of care not only the other but also the self.

As we have listened for centuries to the voices of men and the theories of development that their experience informs, so we have come more recently to notice not only the silence of women but the difficulty in hearing what they say when they speak. Yet in the different voice of women lies the truth of an ethic of care, the tie between relationship and responsibility, and the origins of aggression in the failure of connection. The failure to see the different reality of women's lives and to hear the differences in their voices stems in part from the assumption that there is a single mode of social experience and interpretation. By positing instead two different modes, we arrive at a more complex rendition of human experience which sees the truth of separation and attachment in the lives of women and men and recognizes how these truths are carried by different modes of language and thought.

To understand how the tension between responsibilities and rights sustains the dialectic of human development is to see the integrity of two disparate modes of experience that are in the end connected. While an ethic of justice proceeds from the premise of equality—that everyone should be treated the same—an ethic of care rests on the premise of nonviolence—that no one should be hurt. In the representation of maturity, both perspectives converge in the realization that just as inequality adversely affects both parties in an unequal relationship, so too violence is destructive for everyone involved. This dialogue between fairness and care not only provides a better understanding of relations between the sexes but also gives rise to a more comprehensive portrayal of adult work and family relationships.

As Freud and Piaget call our attention to the differences in children's feelings and thought, enabling us to respond to children with greater care and respect, so a recognition of the differences in women's experience and understanding expands our vision of maturity and points to the contextual nature of developmental truths. Through this expansion in perspective, we can begin to envision how a marriage between adult development as it is currently portrayed and women's development as it begins to be seen could lead to a changed understanding of human development and a more generative view of human life.

REFERENCES

Erikson, Erik H. *Childhood and Society*. New York: W.W. Norton, 1950.

Gilligan, Carol, and Murphy, John Michael. "Development from Adolescence to Adulthood: The Philosopher and the 'Dilemma of the Fact.' " In D. Kuhn, ed. *Intellectual Development Beyond Childhood*. New Directions for Child Development, no. 5. San Francisco: Jossey-Bass, 1979.

Joyce, James. *A Portrait of the Artist as a Young Man* (1916). New York: The Viking Press, 1956.

Levinson, Daniel J. *The Seasons of a Man's Life*. New York: Alfred A. Knopf, 1978.

McCarthy, Mary. *Memories of a Catholic Girlhood*. New York: Harcourt Brace Jovanovich, 1946.

McClelland, David C. *Power: The Inner Experience*. New York: Irvington, 1975.

Miller, Jean Baker. *Toward a New Psychology of Women*. Boston: Beacon Press, 1976.

Murphy, J.M., and Gilligan, C. "Moral Development in Late Adolescence and Adulthood: A Critique and Reconstruction of Kohlberg's Theory." *Human Development* 23 (1980): 77–104.

Perry, William. *Forms of Intellectual and Ethical Development in the College Years*. New York: Holt, Rinehart and Winston, 1968.

Piaget, Jean. *The Moral Judgment of the Child* (1932). New York: The Free Press, 1965.

Rubin, Lillian. *Worlds of Pain*. New York: Basic Books, 1976.

Stack, Carol B. *All Our Kin*. New York: Harper and Row, 1974.

Vaillant, George E. *Adaptation to Life*. Boston: Little, Brown, 1977.

The Evolving Self

Robert Kegan

[The self evolves in five stage-like phases. See the chart at the end of this article. This section of Kegan's explanation has been edited to omit the childhood stages, (1) Impulsive and (2) Imperial, and begins with stage three which is most significant for women.]

With the emergence from an embeddedness in one's needs, gradually a new evolutionary truce is struck. "I" no longer *am* my needs (no longer the imperial I); rather, I *have* them. In having them I can now coordinate, or integrate, one need system with another, and in so doing, I bring into being that need-mediating reality which we refer to when we speak of mutuality. The theory presented in this book is at once a theory of interpersonal and intrapsychic reconstruction. The context of meaning-evolution is taken as prior to the interpersonal *and* the intrapsychic; it gives rise to each. The interpersonal consequence of moving the structure of needs from subject to object is that the person, in being able to coordinate needs, can become mutual, empathic, and oriented to reciprocal obligation. But during the transition the old balance can experience this change as an unwelcome intrusion upon the more independent world of personal control and agency. The intrapsychic consequence of moving the structure of needs from subject to object is that the person is able to coordinate points of view within herself, leading to the experience of subjectivity, the sense of inner states, and the ability to talk about feelings experienced now *as* feelings rather than social negotiations. But once again, *during* the transition, this change can be felt as a perplexing complexification of one's inner experience, the most common expression of which is adolescent moodiness.

88

THE INTERPERSONAL BALANCE (STAGE 3)

In the interpersonal balance the feelings the self gives rise to are, a priori, shared; somebody else is in there from the beginning. The self becomes conversational. To say that the self is located in the interpersonal matrix is to say that it embodies a plurality of voices. Its strength lies in its capacity to be conversational, freeing itself of the prior balance's frenzy-making constant charge to find out what the voice will say on the other end. But its limit lies in its inability to consult itself about that shared reality. It cannot because it *is* that shared reality.

My stage 3 ambivalences or personal conflicts are not really conflicts between what I want and what someone else wants. When looked into they regularly turn out to be conflicts between what I want to do as a part of this shared reality and what I want to do as part of that shared reality. To ask someone in this evolutionary balance to resolve such a conflict by bringing both shared realities before herself is to name precisely the limits of this way of making meaning. "Bringing before oneself" *means* not being subject to it, being able to take it as an object, just what this balance cannot do.

When I live in this balance as an adult I am the prime candidate for the assertiveness trainer, who may tell me that I need to learn how to stand up for myself, be more "selfish," less pliable, and so on, as if these were mere skills to be added on to whoever else I am. The popular literature will talk about me as lacking self-esteem, or as a pushover because I want other people to like me. But this does not quite address me in my predicament, or in my "hoping." It is more that there *is* no self independent of the context of "other people liking." It is not as if this self, which is supposedly not highly esteemed, is the same as one that can stand up for itself independent of the interpersonal context; it is rather a wholly different self, differently constructed. The difference is not just an affective matter—how much I like myself, how much self-confidence I have. The difference goes to that fundamental ground which is itself the source of affect and thought, the evolution of meaning. With no coordinating of its shared psychological space, "pieced out" in a variety of mutualities, this balance lacks the self-coherence from space to space that is taken as the hallmark of "identity." From such perspectives this more public coherence is what is meant by ego itself, but in my view it would be wrong to say that an ego is lacking at stage 3, just as it would be wrong to say that at stage 3 there is a weaker ego. What there is is a qualitatively—not a quantitatively—different ego, a different way of making the self cohere.

This balance is "interpersonal" but it is not "intimate," because what might appear to be intimacy here is the self's *source* rather than its aim. There is no self to share with another; instead the other is required to bring the self into being. Fusion is not intimacy. If one can feel manipulated by the imperial balance, one can feel devoured by the interpersonal one.

A person in stage 3 is not good with anger, and may, in fact, not even *be* angry in any number of situations which might be expected to make a person angry. Anger owned and expressed is a risk to the interpersonal fabric, which for this balance is the holy cloth. My getting angry amounts to a declaration of a sense of self separate from the relational context—that I still exist, that I am a person too, that I have my own feelings—which I would continue to own apart from this relationship. It is, as well, a declaration that you are a separate person, that you can survive my being angry, that it is not an ultimate matter for you. If my meaning-making will not permit me to know myself this way, it will surely not permit me to guarantee this kind of distinctness to you either. There are a myriad of reasons why people might find it hard to express anger when they feel it, but it appears that persons in this balance undergo experiences, such as being taken advantage of or victimized, which do not make them angry at all, because they cannot know themselves separate from the interpersonal context; instead they are more likely to feel sad, wounded, or incomplete.

Thus, if the interpersonal balance is able to bring inside to itself the other half of a conversation the imperial balance had always to be listening for in the external world, the interpersonal balance suffers the vicissitudes of its own externalities. It cannot bring onto itself the obligations, expectations, satisfactions, purposes, or influences of interpersonalism; they cannot be reviewed, reflected upon, mediated—and so they rule.

Diane, too, discussed Kohlberg's famous dilemmas. She was told the story of Heinz, who needed a drug to save his dying wife, but faced a druggist who had invented the drug and wanted a huge sum of money for it which Heinz had no way of paying.

He had created this thing to try to help people and then shut it off for his own monetary gains. I think that's wrong. His aim couldn't have been to help people, but to glorify and enrich himself. And that sets up the whole subject of selfishness, which selfishness to that degree I think is wrong.

Get back to Heinz—what if he doesn't feel close or affectionate to his wife, does he have the obligation—first of all, do you think he has any obligation in any case to steal the drug? You said it was the right thing to do.

No, I don't think it is an obligation, I think it comes under does he care enough about his wife, for his wife, to put himself in jeopardy.

But if he doesn't, would he be right not to, if he decided that he doesn't care enough about his wife to put himself in jeopardy, do you think what he is doing is the right thing to do?

I think he should go to his wife and let her know how he feels and help her; they have spent a number of years together, parts of themselves and their lives together, and he should help her to see if there is any way that she can get the drug, but if he feels that he can't—if he puts getting himself in trouble over his wife—

I am trying to get oriented. I understand when you say you think it was more important to try to save the woman's life than observe the druggist's rights.

Yah, I don't think he or any person on the street is under any obligation to steal.

So when you say the value of life would make it right to do it, you are saying the husband has an obligation to do it?

No.

Would it be just as right to do it if he no longer loved her, or he was no longer intimately concerned about her welfare?

I think it would be right, I think doing something like that would show that he did care, I don't think he would do it if he didn't care. But I still think it would be right if he didn't, if he felt that he wanted to do this, he would probably feel in that sense, that he owed her something, but I think if he felt he wanted to do this for her, as another human being, it would be all right.

Why do you think it wouldn't be an obligation? Or a duty? Do you think the wife would have a right to expect him to do it for her?

No. Not at all.

Why not?

Because I don't know that you can expect to put other people in that jeopardizing situation for your own good if they don't care to. Anyone doing this for this woman obviously cares a great deal for the woman and I don't think that she could expect that from someone who didn't care about her.

Because someone who didn't wouldn't do it? Or it would be wrong to expect it?

If she has invested nothing in this other person, I don't see how she can expect a return.

So suppose it was not for a person, but it was Heinz's pet dog? Would it be right for him to steal to save the dog's life?

Save the dog's life—I think I would look at that as being somewhat an extreme and an irrational measure for a dog. Then that is putting human life over animal life, and separating the two. But I could go back to the same argument of he has invested in the dog, and I guess I do have some tendency of feeling that animals aren't independent in their own right and I don't think that the dog really has invested himself in a person. I can see how he could, just somehow, I don't see what it is, but something in me is not letting me justify that.

You think it would be wrong if he did it, would you say that was wrong? Or wouldn't you want to talk about it as being right or wrong?

I think you could talk about it being right or wrong, but I just feel at this point I am not able to make that decision.

Whatever it is about a human's life that you are willing to base a justification on it, the person's investment in that life, wouldn't hold for a dog.

Yah, there is something of a sense in here, that dogs hold a shorter life than humans and you can get over those things. There is an interaction between humans that I think becomes much stronger than that of an animal and a person, and that difference, taking that, I guess I would say it was wrong.

Diane spontaneously frames the dilemma either in terms of the relative affective "investments" persons might have in profit-making "things" versus other human beings, or in terms of "selfishness" (what stage 2 looks like from the perspective of stage 3) versus caring for others. The rightness of Heinz's theft is lodged entirely within the expectations, requirements, satisfactions, and influences of mutual, interpersonal relationships. Life is valuable by virtue of people's investment in it, or its investments in others (rather than by virtue of its benefits to me, as was the case in the earlier balance). But stealing is sanctioned with no spontaneous construction of a social or legal system generalized beyond the interpersonal, to some extent regulative of the interpersonal, and requiring some kind of "answer" in the face of a sanctioned theft. The subordination of the druggist's rights are justified finally in terms of the inferior claims of selfishness in comparison to altruism. ("He has created this thing to help people and then shut it off for his own monetary gains. I think that's wrong. His aim couldn't have been to help people, but to glorify himself and enrich himself. And that sets up the whole subject of selfishness, which selfishness to that degree I think is wrong.") Thus this much of the interview suggests the kind of self-and-other balance in which the universe is subject to the interpersonal, the self is constructive of the interpersonal, and the important question for the "other" is framed in terms of its recognition of, and availability for, the rigors of mutuality. Does this give us some sense of how great were the proportions of Diane's loss when her relationship ended? Does it suggest something of what must be further lost if she is to be able to live more successfully outside the hospital?

Each new balance sees you (the object) more fully as you; guarantees, in a qualitatively new way, your distinct integrity. Put another way, each new balance corrects a too-subjective view of you; in this sense each new balance represents a qualitative reduction of what another psychology might call "projected ambivalence." In the imperial balance (stage 2), you are an instrument by which I satisfy my needs and work my will. You are the other half of what, from the next balance, I recognize as my own projected ambivalence. In the move to the new evolutionary grammar of stage 3, I claim both sides of this ambivalence and become internally "interpersonal." But stage 3 brings on a new "projected ambivalence." You are the other by whom I complete myself, the other whom I need to create the context out of which I define and know myself and the world. At stage 4, I recognize this as well, and again claim both sides as my own, bringing them onto the self. What does this mean for my inner life?

THE INSTITUTIONAL BALANCE (STAGE 4)

In separating itself from the context of interpersonalism, meaning-evolution authors a self which maintains a coherence across a shared psychological space and so achieves an identity. This authority—sense of self, self-dependence, self-ownership—is its hallmark. In moving from "I am my relationships" to "I have relationships," there is now somebody who is doing this having, the new I, who, in coordinating or reflecting upon mutuality, brings into being a kind of psychic institution (*in* + *statuere*: to set up; *statutum*: law, regulation; as in "statute" and "state").

As stage 3, in appropriating a wider other, was able to bring onto itself the other half of a conversation stage 2 had always to be listening for in the external world, stage 4's wider appropriation brings inside those conflicts between shared spaces which were formerly externalized. This makes stage 4's emotional life a matter of holding both sides of a feeling simultaneously, where stage 3 tends to experience its ambivalences one side at a time. But what is more central, perhaps, to the interior change between the interpersonal and the institutional, is the way the latter is regulative of its feelings. Having moved the shared context over from subject to object, the feelings which arise out of interpersonalism do not reflect the structure of my equilibrative knowing and being, but are, in fact, reflected upon by that structure. The feelings which depend on mutuality for their origin and their renewal remain important but are relativized by that context which is ultimate, the psychic institution and the time-bound constructions of role, norm, self-concept, auto-regulation, which maintain that institution. The sociomoral implications of this ego balance are the construction of the legal, societal, normative system. But what I am suggesting is that these social constructions are reflective of that deeper structure which constructs the self itself as a system, and makes ultimate (as does every balance) the maintenance of its integrity.

Talk of "transcending the interpersonal" often makes people uneasy who want to point out—and rightly, I think—that other people should remain what is important to us throughout our lives. But others are not lost by an emergence from embeddedness in the interpersonal. (On the contrary, in a sense they are found.) The question always is *how* "other people" are known. The institutional balance does not leave one bereft of interpersonal relationships, but it does appropriate them to the new context of their place in the maintenance of a personal self-system.

A strength of this is the person's new capacity for independence, to own herself, rather than having all the pieces of herself owned by various shared contexts; the sympathies which arise out of one's shared space are no longer determinative of the "self," but taken as preliminary, mediated by the self-system. But in this very strength lies a limit. The "self" is identified with the organization it is trying to run smoothly; it *is* this organization. The "self" at ego stage 4 is an administrator in the narrow sense of the word, a person whose meanings are derived out of the organization, rather than deriving the organization out of her meaning/principles/purposes/reality. Stage 4 has no "self," no "source," no "truth" before which it can bring the operational constraints of the organization, because its "self," its "source," its "truth" is invested within these operational constraints. In this sense, ego stage 4 is inevitably ideological (as Erikson, 1968, recognized must be the case for identity formation), a truth for a faction, a class, a group. And it probably requires the recognition of a group (or persons as representatives of groups) to come into being; either the tacit ideological support of American institutional life, which is most supportive to the institutional evolution of white males, or the more explicit ideologies in support of a disenfranchised social class, gender, or race.

Emotional life in the institutional balance seems to be more internally controlled. The immediacy of interpersonalist feeling is replaced by the mediacy of regulating the interpersonal. Regulation, rather than mutuality itself, is now ultimate. For stage 3 it is those events risking the integrity of the shared context that mobilize the "self's" defensive operations; for stage 4 it is those events that threaten chaos for the interior polity. The question is not, as it was earlier, "Do you still like me?" but, "Does my government still stand?" A variety of feelings, particularly erotic or affiliative feelings and doubts around performance and duty discharge, come to be viewed as potential dissidents which must be subjected to the psychic civil polity. Stage 4's delicate balance is that in self-government it has rescued the "self" from its captivity by the shared realities, but in having no "self" before which it can bring the demands of that government, it risks the excesses of control that may obtain to any government not subject to a wider context in which to root and justify its laws.

Rebecca is in her mid-thirties. The very self-sufficiency Diane desperately needed when she entered the hospital has long been familiar to Rebecca. It has become now too familiar; it has worn out its welcome. But because "it" is how Rebecca is herself composed, she is herself worn out. We will return to her in more detail later, but in her words, presented here, I think one can hear: (1) a fleeting glance back to the interpersonalist balance, long ago transcended; (2) the personal authority and integrity of the institutional self; and (3) the courage and fatigue of experiencing its limits:

> I know I have very defined boundaries and I protect them very carefully. I won't give up the slightest control. In any relationship I decide who gets in, how far, and when.

> What am I afraid of? I used to think I was afraid people would find out who I really was, and then not like me. But I don't think that's it anymore. What I feel now is—"That's me. That's mine. It's what makes me." And I'm powerful. It's my negative side, maybe, but it's also my positive stuff—and there's a lot of that. What it is is me, it's my self—and if I let people in maybe they'll take, maybe they'll use it—and I'll be gone.

> Respect above all is the most important thing to me. You don't have to like me. You don't have to care about me, even, but you do have to respect me.

> This "self," if I had to represent it I think of two things: either a steel rod that runs through everything, a kind of solid fiber, or sort of like a ball at the center that is all together. What you just really can't be is weak.

> I wasn't always this way. I used to have two sets of clothes— one for my husband and one for my mother who visited often. Two sets of clothes, but none for me. Now *I* dress in *my* clothes. Some of them are like what my mother would like me to wear but that's a totally different thing.

> How exhausting it's becoming holding all this together. And until recently I didn't even realize I was doing it.

THE INTERINDIVIDUAL BALANCE (STAGE 5)

The rebalancing that characterizes ego stage 5 separates the self from the institution and creates, thus, the "individual," that self who can reflect upon, or take as object, the regulations and purposes of a psychic administration which formerly was the subject of one's attentions. "Moving over" the institutional from subject to object frees the self from that displacement of value whereby the maintenance of the institution has become the end in itself; there is now a self who runs the organization, where before there was a self who *was* the organization; there is now a source before which the institutional can be brought, by which it is directed, where before the institution was the source.

Every ego equilibrium amounts to a kind of "theory" of the prior stage; this is another way of speaking about subject moving to object, or structure becoming content. Stage 2 is a "theory" of impulse; the impulses are organized or ordered by the needs, wishes, or interests. Stage 3 is a "theory" of needs; they are ordered by that which is taken as prior to them, the interpersonal relationships. Stage 4 is a kind of theory of interpersonal relationships; they are rooted in and reckoned by institutions. Stage 5 is a theory of the institutional; the institutional is ordered by that new self which is taken as prior to the institutional. Kohlberg's moral stage 5 requires a "prior-to-society perspective," by which he refers to that dislodging by which the self is no longer subject to the societal; this is accomplished at the transitional disequilibration between his stages 4 and 5. To be at stage 5 in Kohlberg's framework, a person must have, in addition to this prior-to-society perspective, a kind of theory that roots the legal institution in principles which give rise to it, to which conflicts in the law might be appealed, and by which the rights that the legal institution protects might be hierarchized. What this amounts to, more than disequilibrial transition out of the stage 4 balance, is the re-equilibration by which the legal institution has been recovered or recollected as object in a new balance. No longer is "the just" derived from the legal, but the legal from a broader conception of the just. And no longer is the past balance disowned (as in, " 'Should' is no longer in my vocabulary"). The hallmark of every rebalancing is that the past, which may during

transition be repudiated, is not finally rejected but reappro-
priated.

But that which is a kind of theory of the legal institution may
be an expression, in the moral domain, of the deep structure which
is a theory of the self as institutional. And that which constructs this
theory—the new subjectivity—is the next ego balance.

What happens to one's construction of community at ego stage
5? The capacity to coordinate the institutional permits one now to
join others not as fellow-instrumentalists (ego stage 2) nor as partners in fusion (ego stage 3), nor as loyalists (ego stage 4), but as individuals—people who are known ultimately in relation to their
actual or potential recognition of themselves and others as value-
originating, system-generating, history-making individuals. The
community is for the first time a "universal" one in that all persons,
by virtue of their being persons, are eligible for membership. The
group which this self knows as "its own" is not a pseudo-species,
but the species. One's self is no longer limited to the mediation and
control of the interpersonal (the self as an institution) but expands
to mediate one's own and others' "institutions." If the construction
of the self as an institution brought the interpersonal "into" the self,
the new construction brings the self back into the interpersonal. The
great difference between this and stage 3 is that there now is a "self"
to be brought to, rather than derived from, others; where ego stage
3 is interpersonal (a fused commingling), ego stage 5 is interindividual (a commingling which guarantees distinct identities).

This new locating of the self, not in the structure of my psychic
institution but in the *coordinating* of the institutional, brings about
a revolution in Freud's favorite domains, "love" and "work." If one
no longer *is* one's institution, neither is one any longer the duties,
performances, work roles, career which institutionality gives rise to.
One *has* a career; one no longer *is* a career. The self is no longer so
vulnerable to the kind of ultimate humiliation which the threat of
performance-failure holds out, for the performance is no longer ultimate. The functioning of the organization is no longer an end in
itself, and one is interested in the way it serves the aims of the new
self whose community stretches beyond that particular organization.
The self seems available to "hear" negative reports about its activities; before, it *was* those activities and therefore literally "irritable"
in the face of those reports. (Every balance's irritability is simulta-

neously testimony to its capacity to grow and its propensity to preserve itself.) Every new balance represents a capacity to listen to what before one could only hear irritably, and the capacity to hear irritably what before one could hear not at all.

But the increased capacity of the stage 5 balance to hear, and to seek out, information which might cause the self to alter its behavior, or share in a negative judgment of that behavior, is but a part of that wider transformation which makes stage 5 capable, as was no previous balance, of intimacy. At ego stage 4, one's feelings seem often to be regarded as a kind of recurring administrative problem which the successful ego-administrator resolves without damage to the smooth functioning of the organization. When the self is located not in the institutional but in the coordinating of the institutional, one's own and others, the interior life gets "freed up" (or "broken open") within oneself, and with others; this new dynamism, flow, or play results from the capacity of the new self to move back and forth between psychic systems within itself. Emotional conflict seems to become both recognizable and tolerable to the "self." At ego stage 3, emotional conflict cannot yet be recognized by the self; one can feel torn between the demands from one interpersonal space and those from another, but the conflict is taken as "out there"; it is the ground and I am the figure upon it. At ego stage 4, this conflict comes inside. The dawn of the "self-as-a-self" (the institutional self) creates the self as the ground for conflict and the competing poles are figures upon it. Emotional conflict is recognized but not tolerable; that is, it is ultimately costly to the self. The self at ego stage 4 was brought into being for the very purpose of resolving such conflict, and its inability to do so jeopardizes its balance. Ego stage 5 which recognizes a plurality of institutional selves within the (interindividual) self is thereby open to emotional conflict as an interior conversation.

Ego stage 5's capacity for intimacy, then, springs from its capacity to be intimate with itself, to break open the institutionality of the former balance. Locating itself now in the coordination of psychic institutions, the self surrenders its counter-dependent independence for an interdependence. Having a self, which is the hallmark of stage 5's advance over stage 4, it now has a self to share. This sharing of the self at the level of intimacy permits the emotions and impulses to live in the intersection of systems, to be "re-solved" between one self-system and another. Rather than the attempt to be both close and auto-regulative, "individuality" permits one to "give oneself up" to another; to find oneself in what Erikson has called "a counter-pointing of identities," which at once shares experiencing and guarantees each partner's distinctness, which permits persons— again Erikson's words—"to regulate with one another the cycles of work, procreation, and recreation" (Erikson, 1968). Every re-equilibration is a qualitative victory over isolation.

The stories of Terry (omitted here), Diane, and Rebecca are not complete.

But perhaps a last picture of them now will help me to suggest an overarching image for this history of evolutionary truces.

Although I said that Terry, Diane, and Rebecca all seem to be involved with boundary issues, it should be clear that some distinctions within this generalization can be made. Chief among these is that Terry and Rebecca (the youngest and oldest of the three) seem to express their concerns in terms of preserving a boundary which feels like it is giving way. Diane, on the other hand, expresses her concerns in terms of a fearful inability to preserve the lack of a boundary. Terry and Rebecca seem to be guarding a precious sense of differentiation or separateness, whereas Diane seems to be guarding an equally precious sense of inclusion or connection.

These two orientations I take to be expressive of what I consider the two greatest yearnings in human experience. We see the expression of these longings everywhere, in ourselves and in those we know, in small children and in mature adults, in cultures East and West, modern and traditional. Of the multitude of hopes and yearnings we experience, these two seem to subsume the others. One of these might be called the yearning to be included, to be a part of, close to, joined with, to be held, admitted, accompanied. The other might be called the yearning to be independent or autonomous, to experience one's distinctness, the self-chosenness of one's directions, one's individual integrity. David Bakan called this "the duality of human experience," the yearnings for "communion" and "agency" (1966). Certainly in my experience as a therapist—a context in which old-fashioned words such as "yearn" and "plea" and "long for" and "mourn" have great meaning—it seems to me that I am often listening to one or the other of these yearnings; or to the fear of losing a most precious sense of being included or feeling independent; or to their fearful flip sides—the fear of being completely unseparate, of being swallowed up and taken over; and the fear of being totally separate, of being utterly alone, abandoned, and remote beyond recall. Those who are religiously oriented will note that the same old-fashioned language finds its way into prayer, and that much liturgy and scripture is an expression of one or the other of these two longings. I think of Schleiermacher's "ultimate dependence," on the one hand (1958), and Luther's "Here I Stand," on the other; of the fervent communalism of Hasidism, on the one hand (1960), and the lonely Job, talking to (even cursing) the Lord, on the other.

But what is most striking about these two great human yearnings is that they seem to be in conflict, and it is, in fact, their *relation*—this tension—that is of more interest to me at the moment than either yearning by itself. I believe it is a lifelong tension. Our experience of this fundamental ambivalence may be our experience of the unitary, restless, creative motion of life itself.

Biologists talk about evolution and its periods of adaptation— of life organization—as involving a balance between differentiation and integration. These are cold and abstract words. I suggest they are a biological way of speaking of the phenomena we experience as the yearnings for autonomy and inclusion.

Every developmental stage, I said, is an evolutionary truce. It sets terms on the fundamental issue as to how differentiated the organism is from its life-surround and how embedded. It would be as true to say that every evolutionary truce—each stage or balance I have sketched out in this chapter—is a temporary solution to the lifelong tension between the yearnings for inclusion and distinctness. Each balance resolves the tension in a different way. The life history I have traced involves a continual moving back and forth between resolving the tension slightly in the favor of autonomy, at one stage, in the favor of inclusion, at the next. We move from the overincluded, fantasy-embedded impulsive balance to the sealed-up self-sufficiency of the imperial balance; from the overdifferentiated imperial balance to overincluded interpersonalism; from interpersonalism to the autonomous, self-regulating institutional balance; from the institutional to a new form of openness in the interindividual. Development is thus better depicted by a spiral or a helix, as in Figure 1, than by a line.[1]

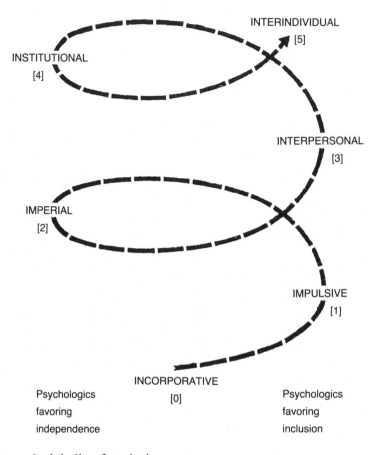

Figure 1. A helix of evolutionary truces

While any "picture" of development has its limitations, the helix has a number of advantages. It makes clear that we move back and forth in our struggle with this lifelong tension; that our balances are slightly *im*balanced. In fact, it is because each of these temporary balances is slightly imbalanced that each *is* temporary; each self is vulnerable to being tipped over. The model suggests a way of better understanding the nature of our vulnerability to growth at each level.

The model also recognizes the equal dignity of each yearning, and in this respect offers a corrective to *all* present developmental frameworks which univocally define growth in terms of differentiation, separation, increasing autonomy, and lose sight of the fact that adaptation is equally about integration, attachment, inclusion. The net effect of this myopia, as feminist psychologists are now pointing out (Gilligan, 1978; Low, 1978), has been that differentiation (the stereotypically male overemphasis in this most human ambivalence) is favored with the language of growth and development, while integration (the stereotypically female overemphasis) gets spoken of in terms of dependency and immaturity. A model in pursuit of the psychological meaning and experience of *evolution*—intrinsically about differentiation *and* integration—is less easily bent to this prejudice.

NOTE

1. The general notion of depicting development as a helix I owe to conversation with William Perry. George Vaillant, I have since discovered, has a similar conception which grows out of his reconstruction of Erikson's model.

Forms and functions of embeddedness cultures

Evolutionary balance and psychological embeddedness	Culture of embeddedness	Function 1: Confirmation (holding on)	Function 2: Contradiction (letting go)	Function 3: Continuity (staying put for reintegration)	Some common natural transitional "subject-objects" (bridges)[a]
(0) INCORPORATIVE Embedded in: reflexes, sensing, and moving.	Mothering one(s) or primary caretaker(s). *Mothering culture.*	Literal holding: close physical presence, comfort and protecting. Eye contact. Recognizing the infant. Dependence upon and merger with oneself.	Recognizes and promotes toddler's emergence from embeddedness. Does not meet child's every need, stops nursing, reduces carrying, acknowledges displays of independence and willful refusal.	Permits self to become part of bigger culture, i.e., the family. High risk: prolonged separation from infant during transition period (6 mos.–2 yrs.).	Medium of 0–1 transition: *blankie, teddy,* etc. A soft, comforting, nurturant representative of undifferentiated subjectivity, at once evoking that state and "objectifying" it.
(1) IMPULSIVE Embedded in: impulse and perception.	Typically, the family triangle. *Parenting culture.*	Acknowledges and cultures exercises of fantasy, intense attachments, and rivalries.	Recognizes and promotes child's emergence from egocentric embeddedness in fantasy and impulse. Holds child responsible for his or her feelings, excludes from marriage, from parents' bed, from home during school day, recognizes child's self-sufficiency and asserts own "other sufficiency."	Couple permits itself to become part of bigger culture, including school and peer relations. High risk: dissolution of marriage or family unit during transition period (roughly 5–7 yrs.).	Medium of 1–2 transition: *imaginary friend.* A repository for impulses which before *were* me, and which eventually will be part of me, but here a little of each. E.g., only I can see it, but it is not me.

104

(2) IMPERIAL Embedded in: enduring disposition, needs, interests, wishes.	*Role recognizing culture.* School and family as institutions of authority and role differentiation. Peer gang which requires role-taking.	Acknowledges and cultures displays of self-sufficiency, competence, and role differentiation.	Recognizes and promotes preadolescent's (or adolescent's) emergence from embeddedness in self-sufficiency. Denies the validity of only taking one's own interests into account, demands mutuality, that the person hold up his/her end of relationship. Expects trustworthiness.	Family and school permit themselves to become secondary to relationships of shared internal experiences. High risk: family relocation during transition period (roughly early adolescence, 12–16).	Medium of 2–3 transition: *chum.* Another who is identical to me and real but whose needs and self-system are exactly like needs which before *were me,* eventually a part of me, but now something between.
(3) INTERPERSONAL Embedded in: mutuality, interpersonal concordance.	Mutually reciprocal one-to-one relationships. *Culture of mutuality.*	Acknowledges and cultures capacity for collaborative self-sacrifice in mutually attuned interpersonal relationships. Orients to internal state, shared subjective experience, "feelings," mood.	Recognizes and promotes late adolescent's or adult's emergence from embeddedness in interpersonalism. Person or context that will not be fused with but still seeks, and is interested in, association. Demands the person assume responsibility for own initiatives and preferences. Asserts the other's independence.	Interpersonal partners permit relationship to be relativized or placed in bigger context of ideology and psychological self-definition. High risk: interpersonal partners leave at very time one is emerging from embeddedness. (No easily supplied age norms.)	Medium of 3–4 transition: *going away to college, a temporary job, the military.* Opportunities for provisional identity which both leave the interpersonalist context behind and preserve it, intact, for return; a time-limited participation in institutional life (e.g. 4 years of college, a service hitch).

105

Evolutionary balance and psychological embeddedness	Culture of embeddedness	Function 1: Confirmation (holding on)	Function 2: Contradiction (letting go)	Function 3: Continuity (staying put for reintegration)	Some common natural transitional "subject-objects" (bridges)[a]
(4) INSTITUTIONAL Embedded in: personal autonomy, self-system identity.	Culture of identity or self-authorship (in love or work). Typically: group involvement in career, admission to public arena.	Acknowledges and cultures capacity for independence; self-definition; assumption of authority; exercise of personal enhancement, ambition or achievement; "career" rather than "job," "life partner" rather than "helpmate," etc.	Recognizes and promotes adult's emergence from embeddedness in independent self-definition. Will not accept mediated, noninitimate, form-subordinated relationship.	Ideological forms permit themselves to be relativized on behalf of the play between forms. High risk: ideological supports vanish (e.g., job loss) at very time one is separating from this embeddedness. (No easily supplied age norms.)	Medium of 4–5 transition: *ideological self-surrender (religious or political); love affairs protected by unavailability of the partner.* At once a surrender of the identification with the form while preserving the form.
(5) INTERINDIVIDUAL Embedded in: interpenetration of systems.	Culture of intimacy (in domain of love and work). Typically: genuinely adult love relationship.	Acknowledges and cultures capacity for interdependence, for self-surrender and intimacy, for interdependent self-definition.			

a. In the construction of this column I am indebted to the thinking of Mauricia Alvarez.

Toward a New Psychology of Women

Jean Baker Miller

TIES TO OTHERS

Male society, by depriving women of the right to its major "bounty"—that is, development according to the male model—overlooks the fact that women's development *is* proceeding, but on another basis. One central feature is that women stay with, build on, and develop in a context of attachment and affiliation with others. Indeed, women's sense of self becomes very much organized around being able to make and then to maintain affiliations and relationships. Eventually, for many women the threat of disruption of an affiliation is perceived not as just a loss of a relationship but as something closer to a total loss of self.

Such psychic structuring can lay the groundwork for many problems. Depression, for example, which is related to one's sense of the loss of affiliation with another(s), is much more common in women, although it certainly occurs in men.

What has not been recognized is that this psychic starting point contains the possibilities for an entirely different (and more advanced) approach to living and functioning—very different, that is, from the approach fostered by the dominant culture. In it, affiliation is valued as highly as, or more highly than, self-enhancement. Moreover, it allows for the emergence of the truth: that for everyone—men as well as women—individual development proceeds *only* by means of affiliation. At the present time, men are not as prepared to *know* this. This proposition requires further explanation. Let us start with some common observations and examples and then return to unravel this complex, but basic, issue.

107

Paula, a married woman with children, was similar in some ways to Edith, who was described in Chapter Six. Paula, too, had been raised to make a relationship with a man "who would make her happy," and she had organized her life around serving his needs. Most of her sense of identity and almost all of her sense of value rested on doing so. She believed that Bill "made her valuable," even though, in fact, few could surpass her ability to run a big household and respond to everyone's needs. As time went on, she felt some diminution in her central importance to Bill. As this feeling increased, she doubled her efforts to respond to and serve him and his interests, seeking to bind him to her more deeply. The actual things she did were not in themselves important to her. (In fact, she accomplished what she set out to do with great ease and efficiency.) They counted only as they produced an inner sense that Bill would be attached to her intensely and permanently, and that this, in turn, would make her worthwhile. Thus, her successful life activity did not bring satisfaction in itself; it brought satisfaction only insofar as it brought Bill's interest and concern.

When Paula's efforts did not produce the result she was after, she became depressed, although she did not know why. She was filled with feelings that she was "no good," that she "didn't matter," that "nothing mattered." She felt Bill did not care enough, but she could not document convincing evidence for this feeling. He was fulfilling his role as a husband and father according to the usual standards; in fact, he was "a better husband than most," said Paula. This factor, of course, made her feel even more "crazy." She *knew* Bill cared, but she could not *feel* that he did somehow. She became persuaded then that there must be something terribly wrong with *her*. At the same time, none of the worthwhile things she did, provided her with any satisfaction at all.

It is important to note here that Paula was not "dependent," at least in the meaning usually implied by that term. In fact, she "took care" of Bill and their children in many ways. It is rather that Paula's whole existence "depended on" Bill's word that she existed or that her existence mattered.

Paula, like many depressed patients, was a very active, effective person. But underlying her activity was an inner goal: that the significant other person—in this case Bill—must affirm and confirm her. Without his affirmation, she became immobilized, she felt like no one at all. What did it matter how she thought of herself? Such words had no meaning.

Even women who are very accomplished "in the real world" carry with them a similar sort of underlying structure. One woman, Barbara, holds a high academic appointment. In discussion she is a rigorous and independent thinker. Yet she struggles with an inner feeling that all of her accomplishment is not worthwhile unless there is another person there to make it so. For her, that other person must be a man.

Beatrice, a very successful business woman who could "sell" and persuade shrewd bargainers who intimidated many men, used to ask, "But what does it all mean if there isn't a man who cares about me?" Indeed, when there was, she found her activities alive and stimulating. When there was not, she became depressed. All of her successes became meaningless, devoid of interest. She was still the same person doing the same things but she could not "feel them" in the same way. She felt empty and worthless.

Kate, a woman who was actively working for women's development, was sophisticated in her understanding of women's situation. At certain times she would become acutely aware of her need for others and condemn herself for it. "See, I'm not so advanced at all. I'm as bad as I always was. Just like a woman."

While Barbara and Kate did not become depressed, they felt the same underlying factor operating. Depression is used here only as an illustration of one end result of this factor. There are many other negative consequences.

How Affiliation Works

All of the women cited offer hints of the role that affiliations with other people play for women. We see the kinds of problems that can result when all affiliations, as we have so far known them, grow out of the basic domination-subordination model.

According to psychological theory, the women discussed above might be described as "dependent" (needing others "too much") or immature in several ways (not developed past a certain early stage of separation and individuation or not having attained autonomy). I would suggest instead that while these women do face a problem, one that troubles them greatly, the problem arises from the dominant role that affiliations have been made to play in women's lives. Women are, in fact, being "punished" for making affiliations central in their lives.

We all begin life deeply attached to the people around us. Men, or boys, are encouraged to move out of this state of existence—in which they and their fate are intimately intertwined in the lives and fate of other people. Women are encouraged to remain in this state but, as they grow, to transfer their attachment to a male figure.

Boys are rewarded for developing other aspects of themselves. These other factors—power or skills—gradually begin to displace some of the importance of affiliations and eventually to supersede them. There is no question that women develop and change too. In an inner way, however, the development does not displace the value accorded attachments to others. The suggestion here is that the parameters of the female's development are not the same as the male's and that the same terms do not apply. Women can be highly developed and still give great weight to affiliations.

Here again, women are geared all their lives to be the "carriers" of the basic necessity for human communion. Men can go a long distance away from fully recognizing this need because women are so groomed to "fill it in" for them. But there is another side: women are also more thoroughly prepared to move toward more advanced, more affiliative ways of living—and less wedded to the dangerous ways of the present. For example, aggression will get you somewhere in this society if you are a man; it may get you quite far indeed if you are one of the few lucky people. But if you continue to be directly aggressive, let us say in pursuit of what seem to be your rights or needs as a man, you will at some time find that it will get you into trouble too. (Other inequalities such as class and race play an important part in this picture.) However, you will probably find this out somewhat later, *after* you have already built up a belief in the efficacy of aggression; you already believe it is important to your sense of self. By then it is hard to give up the push toward aggression and the belief in its necessity. Moreover, it is still rewarded in some measure: you can find places to get some small satisfaction and applause for it, even if it is only from friends in the local bar, by identifying with the Sunday football players, or by pushing women around. To give it up altogether can seem like the final degradation and loss—loss especially of manhood, sexual identification. In fact, if events do not go your way you may be inclined to increase the aggression in the hope that you can force situations. This attempt can and often does enlarge aggression into violence, either individual or group. It is even the underlying basis of national policy, extending to the threat of war and war itself.

Instead, one can, and ultimately must, place one's faith in others, in the context of being a social being, related to other human beings, in their hands as well as one's own. Women learn very young that they must rest primarily on this faith. They cannot depend on their own individual development, achievement, or power. If they try, they are doomed to failure; they find this out early.

Men's only hope lies in affiliation, too, *but* for them it can *seem* an impediment, a loss, a danger, or at least second best. By contrast, affiliations, relationships, make women feel deeply satisfied, fulfilled, "successful," free to go on to other things.

It is not that men are not concerned about relationships, or that men do not have deep yearnings for affiliation. Indeed, this is exactly what people in the field of psychodynamics are constantly finding—evidence of these needs in men as well as in women, deep *under the surface* of social appearance. This has been said in many different ways. One common formulation states, for example, that men search all their lives for their mothers. I do not think that it is *a* mother *per se* that they seek. I do think men are longing for an affiliative mode of living—one that would not have to mean going back to mother if one could find a way to go on to greater human communion. Men have deprived themselves of this mode, left it with women. Most important, they have made themselves unable to really *believe* in it. It is true that the time with their mothers was the time when they could really believe in and rely on affiliation. As soon as they start to grow in the male mold, they are supposed to give up this belief and even this desire. Men are led to cast out this faith, even to condemn it in themselves, and build their lives on something else. *And they are rewarded for doing so.*

Practically everyone now bemoans Western man's sense of alienation, lack of community, and inability to find ways of organizing society for human ends. We have reached the end of the road that is built on the set of traits held out for male identity—advance at any cost, pay any price, drive out all competitors, and kill them if necessary. The opportunity for the full exercise of such manly virtues was always available only to the very few, but they were held out as goals and guidelines for all men. As men strove to define themselves by these ideas, they built their psychic organizations around this striving.

It may be that we had to arrive at a certain stage of "mastery" over the physical environment or a certain level of technology, to see not only the limits but the absolute danger of this kind of social organization. On the other hand, it may be that we need never have come this long route in the first place; perhaps it has been a vast, unnecessary detour. It now seems clear we have arrived at a point from which we must return to a basis of faith in affiliation—and not only faith but recognition that it is a requirement for the existence of human beings. The basis for what seem the absolutely essential next steps in Western history if we are to survive is already available.

A most basic social advance can emerge through women's outlook, through women putting forward women's concerns. Women have already begun to do so. Here, again, it is not a question of innate biological characteristics. It is a question of the kind of psychological structuring that is encompassed differentially by each sex at this time in our development as a society of human beings—and a question of who can offer the motivation and direction for moving on from here.

The central point here is that women's great desire for affiliation is both a fundamental strength, essential for social advance and at the same time the inevitable source of many of women's current problems. That is, while women have reached for and already found a psychic basis for a more advanced social existence, they are not able to act fully and directly on this valuable basis in a way that would allow it to flourish. Accordingly, they have not been able to cherish or even recognize this valuable strength. On the contrary, when women act on the basis of this underlying psychological motive, they are usually led into subservience. That is, the only forms of affiliation that have been available to women are subservient affiliations. In many instances, the search for affiliation can lead women to a situation that creates serious emotional problems. Many of these are then labeled neuroses and other such names.

But what is most important is to see that even so-called neuroses can, and most often do, contain within them the starting points, the searching for a more advanced form of existence. The problem has been that women have been seeking affiliations that are impossible to attain under the present arrangements, but in order to conduct the search women have been willing to sacrifice whole parts of themselves. And so women have concluded, as we so readily do, that we must be wrong or, in modern parlance, "sick."

The Search for Attachment—"Neuroses"

We have raised two related topics: one is social and political, the other more psychological. One is the question of how women can evolve forms of affiliation which will advance women's development and help women to build on this strength to effect real change in the real world? Secondly, until we accomplish this task—and along the way—can we understand more about the psychological events of our lives? Can we better understand why we suffer? At the very least, we may be able to stop undermining ourselves by condemning our strengths.

In the attempt to understand the situation further we can return to some of the women mentioned at the beginning of this chapter. They all expressed a common theme: the lack of ability to really value and credit their own thoughts, feelings, and actions. It is as if they have lost a full sense of satisfaction in the use of themselves and all of their own resources—or rather, never had the full right to do so in the first place. As Beatrice put it, there is the sense "that there has to be that other person there." Alone, her being and her doing do not have their full meaning; she becomes dry, empty, devoid of good feeling. It is not that Beatrice needs someone else to reflect herself back to her. (She knew she was, in fact, an excellent and accurate judge herself.) Her need seems even more basic than that. Unless there is another person present, the entire event—the thought, the feeling, the accomplishment, or whatever it may be—lacks pleasure and significance. It is not simply that she feels like half a person, lacking total satisfaction and wanting another person, but still able to take some satisfaction from her own half. It is like being no person at all—at least no person that matters. As soon as she can believe she is using herself *with* someone else and *for* someone else, her own self moves into action and seems satisfying and worthwhile.

The women referred to in this chapter are not so-called "symbiotic" or other immature types of personalities. (Such terms, incidentally, may well require re-examination in relation to women.) In fact, they are very highly developed and able people who could not possibly be categorized in such a way. Nor, on a more superficial level, do phrases like "seeking approval" or "being afraid of disapproval," really cover the situation, although these factors play a part.

Their shared belief that one needs another person in a very particular way manifests itself in different ways for different people. In one form it leads readily into depression. The experiences of the women described here may thus provide some further clues to depression, may help us understand some aspects of it. While Paula and Beatrice did suffer depression, for other women there are different manifestations.

Everyone in the various psychological fields would probably readily admit that we do not fully understand depression (or fully understand anything else for that matter). Depression, in general, seems to relate to feeling blocked, unable to do or get what one wants. The question is: what is it that one really wants? Here we find difficult and complicated depressions that do not seem to "make sense." On the surface it may even seem that a person has what she wants. It often turns out, however, that, instead, she has what she has been led to believe she should want. (For many young middle-class women it was the house in the suburbs, a nice husband, and children.) How then to discover what one is really after? And why does one feel so useless and hopeless?

Beatrice's experience may offer some understanding on this point. She eventually said that she sought to bind the important other person to her absolutely, and she wanted a guarantee of that bond. She was anything but a passive, dependent, or helpless woman; but all of her activity was directed to this goal, which she believed she needed to attain. While she did not really need *that* kind of relationship, she was not convinced of it internally. (Often her activity in search of this goal took on a very forceful and manipulative character. Although the goal was usually pursued covertly and obscured from herself, it was felt very distinctly by those around her.)

Beatrice had developed the inner belief that everything she does feels right *only* if she does it for that other person, not for herself. Above all, she had lost the sense that the fulfillment of her needs or desires could *ever* bring her satisfaction. It is almost as if she had lost the inner "system" that registers events and tells her whether they make *her* happy or satisfied. The "registering" of what feels like satisfaction has shifted; it now comes only through her sense that she can make the other person remain in a particular kind of relationship to her. Only then can she feel strong and good. (In more complex depressions, like Beatrice's, it may not be the other person *per se* that one desires to bind but the image of the *kind* of relationship one believes one needs. For example, women whose children have grown up may not want to retain the individual children but they feel they must have the mother-child kind of relationship. In fact, one may not really need such a relationship; but the belief is strong, and a person who has spent a long time organizing her psyche on that basis will not easily relinquish the idea. Further, she has long since lost the belief that she can really have any other kind of relationship.)

Another facet of Beatrice's problem was the large amount of anger generated. To compound the problem, like many other women, she had great difficulty in allowing herself to recognize her own wrath, much less express it. Even so, she was likely to become furious if the other person did anything that seemed to threaten to alter the bond. It seems clear that being in such a position is very conducive to rage. How could she not get angry at that other person to whom she had given so much control over her life? But Beatrice would become even more depressed because of the anger. In spite of her deep unhappiness, she could not really believe that there was any other possible way to live.

Like Beatrice, people liable to depression are often very active, very forceful; but the activity must be conceived of as benefiting others. Furthermore, it is organized around a single pursuit—seeking affiliation in the only form that seems possible: "I will do anything if only you will let me stay in this kind of relationship to you."

Some other aspects of depression may help to explain these points. It has long been recognized that there are so-called paradoxical depressions, which are most often observed in men. They occur after a man who has been competent receives a promotion or other advance that presumably should make him happy and even more effective. Such depressions may reflect the fact that the individual is forced to admit to increased self-determination and to admit that he, himself, is responsible for what happens. He is not doing it for someone else or under the direction of someone else. Women do not get promotion depressions so commonly because they do not get many promotions. Nonetheless, in Beatrice, who could accomplish prodigious feats as long as she had at least one person in a position superior to her, a very similar dynamic was at work. She would absolutely never let herself have the top job, although several had been offered to her.

A similar process may be at work in a phenomenon seen in psychoanalysis. It has long been recognized that people sometimes have what are called "negative therapeutic reactions." This means that they make a major gain and then seem to get worse after it. Bonime has suggested that many of these reactions are in fact depressions and that they occur when a person has made a major step toward taking on responsibility and direction in her/his own life.[1] The person has seen that she/he can move out of a position of inability and can exert effective action in her/his own behalf, but then becomes frightened of the implications of that new vision; for example, it would mean the person really doesn't need the old dependent relationships. She/he then pulls back and refuses to follow through on the new course. Such retreats occur in men as well as women, but for women this situation is an old story, very similar to what goes on in life.

The significance for women of these two examples may be this: "If I can bring myself to admit that I can take on the determination and direction of my own life rather than give it over to others, can I exist with safety? With satisfaction? And who will ever love me, or even tolerate me, if I do that?" Only after these questions are confronted, at least to some degree, can one begin to ask the even more basic question: what do I really want? And this question, too, will not always be answered easily. Most women have been led too far from thinking in those terms. It often takes strenuous exploration, but usually it turns out that there are deeply felt needs that are not being met at all. Only then can one begin to evaluate these desires and to see the possibility of acting to bring about their attainment; *and* only then does one realize that there can be satisfaction in such a course. Moreover, it then becomes apparent that one does not need or want the kind of binding one believed was so essential.[2] Since the process described in this paragraph is so often thwarted, it seems obvious why women are set up for depression.

Many complications come in to compound the situation for women, as they did for Beatrice. If one believes that safety and satisfaction lie in relationships structured in particular kinds of bonds, then one keeps trying to push people and situations into these forms. Thus, Beatrice was constantly working very actively at getting a man into this kind of relationship. She had a program for action, the only one she was able to construct, but the program created her own bondage. This is why psychological troubles are the worst kind of slavery—one becomes enlisted in creating one's own enslavement— one uses so much of one's own energies to create one's own defeat.

All forms of oppression encourage people to enlist in their own enslavement. For women, especially, this enlistment inevitably takes psychological forms and often ends in being called neuroses and other such things. (Men, too, suffer psychological troubles, as we all know; and the dynamic for them is related, but it *does* take a different path.)

In this sense, psychological problems are not so much caused by the unconscious as by deprivations of full consciousness. If we had paths to more valid consciousness all along through life, if we had more accurate terms in which to conceptualize (at each age level) what was happening, if we had more access to the emotions produced, and if we had ways of knowing our own true options—if we had all these things, we could make better programs for action. Lacking full consciousness, we create out of what is available. For women only distorted conceptions about what is happening and what a person can and should be have been provided. (The conceptions available for men may be judged as even more distorted. The possible programs for action and the subsequent dynamic are, however, different.)

Even the very words, the terms in which we conceptualize, reflect the prevailing consciousness—not necessarily the truth about what is happening. This is true in the culture at large and in psychological theory too. We need a terminology that is not based on inappropriate carryovers from men's situation. Even a word like *autonomy*, which many of us have used and liked, may need revamping for women. It carries the implication—and for women therefore the threat—that one should be able to pay the price of giving up affiliations in order to become a separate and self-directed individual. In reality, when women have struggled through to develop themselves as strong, independent individuals they did, and do, threaten many relationships, relationships in which the other person will not tolerate a self-directed woman. But, when men are autonomous, there is no reason to think that their relationships will be threatened. On the contrary, there is reason to believe that self-development will win them relationships. Others—usually women—will rally to them and support them in their efforts, and other men will respect and admire them. Since women have to face very different consequences, the word *autonomy* seems possibly dangerous; it is a word derived from men's development, not women's.

There is a further sense in which the automatic transfer of a concept like autonomy as a goal for women can cause problems. Women are quite validly seeking something more complete than autonomy as it is defined for men, a fuller not a lesser ability to encompass relationships to others, simultaneous with the fullest development of oneself. Thus, many of our terms need re-examination.

Many women have now moved on to determine the nature of their affiliations, and to decide for themselves with whom they will affiliate. As soon as they attempt this step, they find the societal forms standing in opposition. In fact, they are already outside the old social forms looking for new ones. But, they do not feel like misfits, wrong again, but like seekers. To be in this unfamiliar position is not always comfortable, but it is not wholly uncomfortable either—and indeed it begins to bring its own *new* and different rewards. Here, even on the most immediate level, women now find a community of other seekers, others who are engaged in this pursuit. No one can undertake this formidable task alone. (Therapy, even if we knew how to do it in some near perfect way—which we do not— is not enough.)

It is extremely important to recognize that the pull toward affiliation that women feel in themselves is not wrong or backward; women need not add to the condemnation of themselves. On the contrary, we can recognize this pull as the basic strength it is. We can also begin to choose relationships that foster mutual growth.

Other questions are equally hard. How do we conceive of a society organized so that it permits both the development and the mutuality of all people? And how do we get there? How do women move from a powerless and devalued position to fully valued effectiveness?

How do we get the power to do this, even if we do not want or need power to control or submerge others? It would be difficult enough if we started from zero, but we do not. We start from a position in which others have power and do not hesitate to use it. Even if they do not consciously use it against women, all they have to do is remain in the position of dominance, keep doing what they are doing, and nothing will change. The women's qualities that I believe are ultimately, and at all times, valuable and essential are not the ones that make for power in the world as it is now. How then can we use these strengths to enhance our effectiveness rather than let them divert us from action?

One part of the answer seems clear already. Women will not advance except by joining together in cooperative action. What has not been as clear is that no other group, so far, has had the benefit of women's leadership, the advantage of women's deep and special strengths. Most of these strengths have been hidden in this culture, and hidden from women themselves. I have been emphasizing one of these strengths—*the* very strength that is most important for concerted group action. Unlike other groups, women do not *need* to set affiliation and strength in opposition one against the other. We can readily integrate the two, search for more and better ways to use affiliation to enhance strength—and strength to enhance affiliation.

For women to derive strength from relationships, then, clearly requires a transformation and restructuring of the nature of relationships. The first essential new ingredients in this process are self-determination and the power to make the self-determination a reality. But even before getting to this major issue, there are questions facing many women: "If I want self-determination, what is it I really want to determine? What do I want? Who am I anyhow?" The difficulty of answering these questions has sometimes served to discourage women. The discouragement occurs even in women who are convinced that there is something deeply wrong with the old way. Given the history that women's lives have been so totally focused on others, it is easy to see that such questions bear a special cogency and come from a particularly hidden place in women.

It is important here to note that this discussion of the importance of affiliations for women is by no means exhaustive. Nor is it a full discussion of any of the related, complicated problems, such as depression. Rather, it is an attempt to unravel a topic that requires much new examination. I hope that it will give rise to further discussion.

RECLAIMING CONFLICT

Conflict has been a taboo area for women and for key reasons. Women were supposed to be the quintessential accommodators, mediators, the adapters, and soothers. Yet conflict is a necessity if women are to build for the future.

All of us, but women especially, are taught to see conflict as something frightening and evil. These connotations have been assigned by the dominant group and have obscured the necessity for conflict. Even more crucially, they obscure the fundamental nature of reality—the fact that, in its most basic sense, conflict is inevitable, the source of all growth, and an absolute necessity if one is to be alive.

As women learn to make use of conflict, they will accomplish two major tasks: first, they will escape the trap of the "rigged" conflict—one conducted solely in terms set by others, terms that guarantee that women will lose. Simultaneously, they will illuminate the understanding that conflict is an inevitable fact of life and is not bad by any means.

I have stated that the dominant group's attempt to ignore and deny the existence of certain crucial unsolved conflicts and problems has led it to use women as convenient depositories of these aspects of life. (I am referring here to the societal level, although this is certainly true on the most intimate personal level as well.) In doing so, a dominant group tends to say that "things are what they are" and that "what they are, is right." What psychoanalysts found, instead, is that things are *not* what they are said to be. They are expressions of conflict and attempts at resolution. Whatever "is" originated in conflict and continues to operate in conflict. The important questions are: what really causes conflict, and have we accurately formulated the terms of the conflict?

The major initial psychoanalytic discovery was that symptoms are not what they seem—they are not fixed and static. For example, a hysterical paralysis is not *like* a physical paralysis. It is not a paralysis in any sense of the term. It is, or it expresses, an attempt to move when movement, for important reasons, is simultaneously blocked. This "paralysis" is a *process* of conflict, not a "thing" or even a static state of being. It is in motion and therefore capable of change.

The fact of the existence of conflict is the point of emphasis here. Not only are symptoms the embodiment of conflict; all of life is too. Put simply, the big secret that psychoanalysis found—and it is basic to all of its other secrets—is the secret of conflict itself.

As women seek self-definition and self-determination, they will, perforce, illuminate, on a broad new scale, the existence of conflict as a basic process of existence. As long as women were used in a massive attempt to suppress certain fundamental human conflicts, the basic process of conflict itself remained obscure. As women move out of that position, conflict can become known and therefore available for more appropriate attention—with much greater hope of eventually understanding our minds. That is, women are not *creating* conflict; they are exposing the fact that conflict exists. Here again, we must start with an attempt to redefine some of the terms to which we have become accustomed.

In addition to these general and somewhat abstract levels, there are concrete conflicts that women face today economically, socially, and politically. This is blazingly clear. Precisely because women face such grinding everyday conflicts as soon as they try to move ahead, they are better able to open up the more difficult abstract levels. Members of the dominant group can more easily avoid knowledge of the existence of conflict. Women's present ability to recognize the *necessity* for conflict if they are to pursue their self-defined self-interest can therefore be a first, great, primary source of strength—a strength that women can take into their own hands and use. The second great source of strength can be the possibility—again, one that the dominant group cannot so easily grasp—that the *conduct* of conflict does not have to be the way it has been. That is, the methods of conducting conflict do not have to be those we have always known. There can be others.

Suppressed Conflict

In earlier chapters it was suggested that as soon as a group attains dominance it tends inevitably to produce a situation of conflict and that it also, simultaneously, seeks to suppress conflict. Moreover, subordinates who accept the dominants' conception of them as passive and malleable do not *openly* engage in conflict. Conflict occurs between dominants and subordinates, but it is forced underground. Such covert conflict is distorted and saturated with destructive force. Knowing only the pain and futility of hidden conflict, one believes that *that* is what conflict *is*.

It is not practically useful, however, to urge subordinates to conduct open conflict on the personal level as if they were not dependent and powerless. Women as a group, therefore, have been able to conduct almost nothing but indirect conflict until they could begin to act from a base of strength "in the real world." It is practically impossible to initiate open conflict when you are totally dependent on the other person or group for the basic material and psychological means of existence. Moreover, because women's lives have been tied to biology and childrearing, there have been additional major obstacles in the path of gaining economic and social power and authority. Obviously, such role definitions need not keep women from full participation in the world; but to change this situation requires major reorganization of our institutions and the paths to power in them. It is easy to devise work schedules and arrangements that will allow both women and men to share in childrearing and fully participate in the life of our time, if both desire to do so. But to bring these about for any large number of people will require more changes in social and economic arrangements than other oppressed groups have had to accomplish. It requires us to ask, not how can women fit into, and advance in, the institutions as organized for men, but how should these institutions be reorganized so as to include women. For example, the question is still asked of women: "How do you propose to answer the need for child care?" That is an obvious attempt to structure conflict in the old terms. The questions are rather: "If we *as a human community want* children, how does the total society propose to provide for them? How can it provide for them in such a way that women do not have to suffer or forfeit other forms of participation and power? How does society propose to organize so that men can benefit from equal participation in child care?" Obviously none of these major changes will come about without opposition. But it is most important to define the overall goals and to debate on that basis rather than be diverted into fighting on false terms.

The fact that such necessary changes seem still so far off and so radically different can serve as another possible source of discouragement. Also, women find it difficult to believe they have the *right* to ask for so much. They are *not* irrational or immoderate demands. It is important to ask instead why the provision for such clear and obvious women's needs can still *seem* like so much to ask. It is necessary therefore to reconsider some of the more basic dimensions of conflict.

The Crucible of Conflict

Conflict begins at the moment of birth. The infant, and then the child, immediately and continually initiates conflict around its desires. The older participant in this interaction approaches the infant bringing along her/his state of psychological organization, filled with a history of conceptions about what she/he wants to do, and she/he should do, what the result should be, and so on. As these two people, with two very different states of psychological organization and desires, interact, the outcome will be the creation of a new state in each person. The result will also be somewhat different from what either of them "intended." (Of course, the infant doesn't consciously "intend," but she/he has real and important purposes that she/he is pursuing.) As a result of the interaction, both parties will change, but each in different ways and at a different rate. Out of a myriad of such interactions—*conflicts* repeated over and over and in slightly different ways—each person develops a new conception of what she/he is. This continually new conception in turn forms a subsequent new desire; new action will flow from the new desire. This is conflict as the term is used here. Both parties approach the interaction with different intents and goals, and each will be forced to change her/his intent and goals as a result of the interaction—that is, as a result of the conflict.

Ideally, the new intent and goals will be larger and richer each time, rather than more restricted and cramped. That is, each party should perceive more, and want *more* as a result of each engagement and have more resources with which to act. All too often, the opposite is true, and conflicts result in *lowered* goals and diminution of resources.

Productive conflict can include a feeling of change, expansion, joy. It may at times have to involve anguish and pain, too; but even these are different from the feelings involved in destructive or blocked conflict. Destructive conflict calls forth the conviction that one cannot possibly "win" or, more accurately, that nothing can really change or enlarge. It often involves a feeling that one must move away from one's deeply felt motives, that one is losing the connection with one's most importantly held desires and needs.

Children and young people gradually come to "know" that it is dangerous to initiate conflict. Adults have been well schooled in suppressing conflict but not in conducting constructive conflict. Adults don't seem to know how to enter into it with integrity and respect and with some degree of confidence and hope. It is hardly surprising then that many conflicts turn out badly, leaving adults with anguish and fear of conflict, which children are quick to sense.

This basic difficulty with conflict, which underlies the problems encountered in handling any specific conflict, bears a strong resemblance to the way conflict is viewed and conducted by any dominant group in an unequal situation. It is important then to look at how conflict has been viewed and conducted on the larger scene— and why it has been so hard to put it on a productive base.

Old Views and Forms of Conflicts

If we ask how can we move toward putting conflict on a productive basis, it is important to recognize that this ability is not one that anyone has learned well in our society, nor in many others. We have only relatively recently emerged from a state in which conflict was barely tolerated at all. There was absolute rule and severe penalties for those who did not comply. Today conflicts between various groups in male society are still carried out on an extremely frightening and dangerous basis.

Within this context, conflict itself can necessarily appear highly destructive. It is more likely, however, that it becomes dangerous when its necessity has been suppressed. It then tends to explode in an extreme form—on the societal and on the individual level. This tendency of conflict, when suppressed, to turn toward violence, acts as a massive deterrent to subordinates. Conflict is made to look as if it *always* appears in the image of extremity, whereas, in fact, it is actually the lack of recognition of the need for conflict and provision of appropriate forms for it that lead to danger. This ultimate destructive form is frightening, but it is also *not* conflict. It is almost the reverse; it is the end result of the attempt to avoid and suppress conflict.

In addition to this massive psychological deterrent, there is the bedrock fact that in any situation in the real world the dominants have most of the real power. This, too, obviously is a powerful deterrent. But even with these two strong general deterrents against conflict, it is still important to ask why, in particular, do not women move ahead as rapidly and as well as they can. An important factor is the unwillingness to initiate conflict.

Initiating Conflict

For a woman, even to *feel* conflict with men has meant that something is wrong with her "psychologically" since one is supposed to "get along" if one is "all right." The initial sensing of conflict then becomes an almost immediate proof that she is wrong and moreover "abnormal." Some of women's best impulses and sources of energy are thus nipped in the bud. The overwhelming pressure is for women to believe they must be wrong: they are to blame, there must be something very wrong with *them*.

Instead, we would assert that when women *feel* in conflict, there is a good reason to believe they should *be* in conflict. This, at least, can help at the start. Women's energies and hopes will not be drained before they even begin to accumulate. In the past, women lived under a framework of conceptions and prescriptions that was destructive of them. They were attempting to fit themselves into a model of behavior that did not fit anyone; then they blamed themselves if they could not squeeze into it, or if they even felt conflicted in the process. (Men too have sensed, in their own way, that they are attempting to be "fit in an unfit fitness," as Kenneth Burke said, but the specific misfitting is very different for each sex.)

Moving from these generalizations to some of the specifics of women today, we can return briefly to Jane, Doris, and Nora, the women whose seeking for self-knowledge and self-directed action we reviewed in earlier chapters. Each of them faced a particular personal obstacle in her path, and in order to take the next step, each had to initiate conflict. For Doris it was with her husband; for Nora it was with the women in her women's group; and for Jane, it was her co-workers.

Each woman demonstrated yet a further dimension to the initiation of conflict, for each also had to initiate conflict with the old image of herself, the image she believed she needed. This was equally as hard as handling conflict with others. Doris and Nora had an image of themselves as the consistently "strong woman" that was not valid or necessary. Jane saw herself as the weak, clinging woman. In each case, the images constituted blocks to fuller development; they stood in the way of gaining greater true strength.

Waging Good Conflict

We have suggested that moving to the new, developing further, brings conflict all along the way. There will inevitably be conflict with one's own old level of consciousness—in the broadest sense. In the midst of such a process, we have an absolute need for other people. Nora, for example, could not have understood her old images by herself. She needed other people with whom to share and to take risks, people to trust (or with whom to begin building a basis of trust, since trust does not come all at once).

Further, as one attempts to develop in opposition to the prevailing framework of the dominant culture, it is difficult to be certain that one is perceiving things clearly. It is not easy to believe one is right and, more basically, that one *has* rights. For all this, a community of like-minded people is essential.

In the past, probably the greatest threat facing women at the hint of conflict was the threat of condemnation and isolation—most of all isolation. (For anyone, this is probably the ultimate weapon but, as we have seen so often, the situation was structured so that for women it appeared *most imminent.*) Women have already constructed supportive environments to help overcome this threat. Certainly, all of us need as much help as we can get. It is difficult to see one's way all alone, to have a true vision about which aspects of conflict are appropriate or inappropriate, to know when we have the right to ask or assert and when we are making exaggerated or distorted demands.

It is not an easy or straightforward path. Meanings change along the way and are influenced by the course of the conflict itself. Who can clearly and directly know her own needs at all times? More often they emerge unclearly. Especially, if they are important, they may be highly charged with emotion and difficult to discern. To undertake such conflict in the first place requires courage. The hope for success lies in respectful engagement with other people. Until now women were encouraged to stop before they started; they did not have to be told they had little chance of winning, and even less hope of respectful engagement. All this can now be different. Women have begun to create the environment in which they can engage in respectful interaction and in real conflict.

NOTES

1. Walter Bonime, "The Psychodynamics of Neurotic Depression," in Silvano Arieti, ed., *American Handbook of Psychiatry*, vol. 3 (New York: Basic Books, 1966).

2. Jean B. Miller and Stephen M. Sonnenberg, "Depression following Psychotic Episodes: A Response to the Challenge of Change?" *Journal of the American Academy of Psychoanalysis* 1 (1973), 253–70.

The Construction of Femininity

Luise Eichenbaum and Susie Orbach

Psychological development starts at birth and occurs within the context of the relationship the infant has with the caregiver. Women's psychological development is thus shaped in the mother-daughter relationship, the critical relationship in the formation of women's psychology.

Mothers and daughters share a gender identity, a social role, and social expectations. They are both second-class citizens within a patriarchal culture and the family. In mothering a baby girl a woman is bringing her daughter up to be like her, to be a girl and then a woman. In mothering her son she is bringing him up to be other, to be a boy and then a man. Because of the social consequences of gender, mothers inevitably relate differently to their daughters and their sons. Much of the difference is intentional and prescribed by the requirements of sex-role stereotyping—for example, encouraging an adolescent son's sexual adventures and restricting an adolescent daughter's. Some of the difference is subtle and mothers may not be aware of it—girls are encouraged to be neat, messiness is tolerated in boys; or girls are encouraged to be "pretty" and boys to be "bright." And some of the difference comes from a mother's unconscious feelings about being a woman and raising a daughter or raising a son.

In looking at the significance of the shared gender of mothers and daughters, the most obvious and most important point is that all mothers were and are daughters themselves. A second obvious and important point is that all daughters are brought up by their mothers to become mothers. The third point is that all mothers learned from their mothers about their place in the world. In each woman's experience is the memory, buried or active, of the struggles she had with her mother in the process of becoming a woman, of learning to curb her activities and to direct her interests in particular ways. Mothers and daughters thus have a tremendous amount of common experience, although this is often obscured by the fact that they are always in different phases of their social role vis-à-vis each other. A fifty-year-old mother and a twenty-five-year-old mother each experiences similar emotional pushes and pulls in relation to their children. Yet the mothering requirements for each of them are very different. Adult women with girl children play two roles simultaneously in the mother-daughter relationship: they are their mother's daughters and their daughter's mothers.

The interplay between a woman's conscious and unconscious feelings about being both a daughter and a mother are an essential part of what she brings to maternal nurturance. The psychology that the infant girl will embody in the process of becoming a person will be imbued with the mother's sense of self. Growing up female and being a woman means that one's sense of self reflects what each woman has had to learn in her development. Aspects of the mother's psychology that are inextricably bound up with being socialized to the feminine role are absorbed and then shared by the daughter in her own psychology.

In our practice we often hear women describe how startling it is to hear themselves speaking to their daughters just as their mothers spoke to them. As one woman put it, "I couldn't believe it came out of my mouth. The same tone of voice, practically the very same words. It was as if my mother's voice came from my lips." It is often after a woman has a child that she becomes more aware of the ways in which she is like her mother. The mother's influence becomes apparent as aspects of her personality resonate for the daughter in herself as mother. Traversing the generations from grandmother to mother to daughter is a particular psychology which has its roots and its flesh in the experience of being female in a patriarchal culture. The social requirements of deference, submission, and passivity generate many complicated feelings. Often women do not feel complete, substantial, or good within themselves. They feel afraid of their emotional needs, their insecurities and dependencies; they are fearful and guilty about their sexuality and their strivings for independence, nurturance, and power. The social requirements of patriarchy surround a girl from the moment of her birth. This means that she has a particular psychology which she transmits to her daughter.

Men's and women's psychologies reflect patriarchal attitudes in different ways. A boy will be raised to expect to be looked after and attended to, a girl to provide the looking after and attending.

For a woman, the process of pregnancy, giving birth, and becoming a mother can be a very satisfying experience. Having a baby may fulfill an important personal desire and enrich a woman's sense of self. Since motherhood is traditionally the apex of woman's social role, approved by family and society, giving birth enables a woman to feel a certain contentment. In turn she is able to transmit these positive feelings to her daughter. Mother reads the communications of her daughter and is responsive. The infant in turn expresses her pleasure, and this communication adds to mother's feelings of self-worth and potency. Positive interactions between mother and daughter establish a pattern of relating and a feeling of closeness between them. As a relationship forms, the mother experiences great pleasure in seeing her daughter's daily developments. Mother's time and care and tiring long hours of work through the day and night have moments of overpowering reward as she sees her daughter grow, and she continues to express her feelings of competence, strength, and ability to care and protect within the relationship. In this nurturing relationship the mother gives her daughter the essential emotional food that helps the infant establish her very sense of existence as well as her security and well-being. The daughter's psychological development is built on the feelings of acceptance and love in this first and most important relationship.

Beyond these positive feelings that mother has toward herself, however, lie mother's other experiences of self. The effect of having to curtail one's wants and desires over many years is that many women are not aware of the fact that they feel needy, and they have complicated feelings about their repressed needs. Over the years in our practice we have seen many women reveal the part of them that is needy and uncared for, undeserving, inadequate, and inarticulate. A woman often feels that nobody sees this part of her or gives her what she needs, and that even she herself cannot locate what she wants—"everybody sees me as so strong, they don't know that I have my moments, too, when I want to give up and weep and feel unsure and anxious." These negative and complicated feelings, conscious or unconscious, also have a profound effect on the daughter's psychology. The mother's negative self-image is as important a factor in the mother-daughter interaction, and hence in the daughter's psychology, as her positive experiences of self through motherhood and in other areas.

We can identify the following major aspects of the mother-daughter interaction which make for a particular shaping of a daughter's psychology. The first of these is that the mother will *identify* with her daughter because of their shared gender, for when a woman gives birth to a daughter she is in a sense reproducing herself. When she looks at her daughter she sees herself. Laura, a thirty-three-year-old mother of a daughter aged three and (an infant) son, talked about this point in her therapy. "When Ruth was an infant I can remember looking down at my body at I lay in a certain position in my bed and thinking it was Ruth's body. The shape of my knee or my arm looked to me like Ruth's body. And when she had her first cold I felt ill. It was very strange. These things have not happened with Barry. Somehow it just isn't the same. I've never had the feeling I *was* him or he *was* me."

Vivian, a forty-year-old woman, expressed it this way: "When my daughter was born, each time I looked at her I thought she *was* me; I couldn't tell at all that she was different from me. You know that feeling when you look at yourself in a mirror? Well, it felt something like that. When my son was born that never even crossed my mind. He was different, he was something else [motioning "out there" and "away" with her hand]. It was completely clear that he was a different person."

When a mother looks at an infant son she sees someone who is quite other, who is going to have a very different life, and for whom she can imagine a whole world of differing possibilities. But she knows that her daughter will follow her own footsteps. Mother must introduce her daughter to the ways of behaving and feeling that go along with being a girl. Mother must prepare her for a life spent, like hers, in taking care of others. Mother, whether she is consciously aware of it or not, must also prepare her daughter to take her place in society as a second-class citizen.

When a woman bears a son, the difference in sex and gender helps her to be more aware of her own boundaries. A woman does not have this aid with a daughter. The boundaries are blurred. When she looks at her daughter she sees mirror images of her own experience of being mothered, her own childhood and growing up; her whole life as a woman.

The second major aspect of the mother-daughter relationship is that a mother not only identifies with her daughter but also *projects* onto her some of the feelings she has about herself. Having super-imposed these deeply buried feelings which are inaccessible and un-conscious she experiences them as if expressed in her daughter. In this projection she is seeing her daughter not as another person but as an extension of herself. Thus when she holds her infant daughter in her arms she reads the child's communications in a particular way. She sees a vulnerable, undefended, expressive, eager little girl. This in turn reawakens—still at an unconscious level—the part of her that feels needy and wants to be nurtured, responded to, en-couraged.

Such feelings are almost inevitable because of the importance in women's social role, and thus in their psychology, of deferring to and caring for others. Women today pay a high psychological price for the ability to nurture. In developing emotional antennae for the desires of others, women place their own needs second. The expe-rience of receiving nurturance is not symmetrical for women and men. There is an unequal emotional exchange between men and women, and the emotional caretaking is not reciprocal. Because of this social-psychological construct a woman hides and represses many of her own emotional needs as she develops an adult stance in the world. She appears to be a person with little need. These needs do not disappear, however, and in experiencing and responding to the needs of her infant daughter the mother unconsciously first iden-tifies and then projects her *own* needy parts, what we call her little-girl onto her daughter.

In responding to her daughter the mother is full of contradic-tory feelings, some conscious and some not. She wants to meet her daughter's needs: sometimes she is able to and at other times she is not. The reasons are complex. On the one hand she hopes for a fuller and less restricted life for her daughter, while on the other she is fearful for a daughter who does not learn the essential feminine characteristics of restraining her own needs and desires and curbing her moves toward independence. This conflict is often unconscious. Mothers generally raise and relate to their daughters much as they themselves were raised. Unbeknownst to them they are caught in a paradox. Mother has the difficult task of showing her daughter how to limit her strivings toward independence. At the same time she must wean her very early from relying, at an emotional level, upon having her dependency desires met. For mother to continue to meet them would go deeply against the grain of socialization to the feminine role. Mother knows that she has had to manage and contain her own desires for emotional nurturance; that she has had to swallow her disappointment and anger many times and that she has had to learn how to adjust her expectations for emotional care and relating.

Their own social experience prevents mothers from setting up false expectations about what awaits a daughter in womanhood. Unconsciously mother gives the message to the daughter. "Don't be emotionally dependent; don't expect the emotional care and attention you want; learn to stand on your own two feet emotionally. Don't expect too much independence; don't expect too much from a man; don't be too wild; don't expect a life much different from mine; learn to accommodate." Mother demonstrates these unconscious injunctions by relating to her daughter in this way herself. Consciously and unconsciously mother acts toward her daughter in the ways she experiences others relating to herself. Unable to respond continually and directly to her daughter's needs because her own needs have not been met in this way, she relates to the child inconsistently.

At times the mother is able to see her daughter as a separate little person and to respond to her freely. At other times, however, the mother's unconscious identification makes her annoyed with the child for displaying her needs and for not controlling them as she herself does. At these times mother is unconsciously driven to respond to her daughter with resentment and disapproval, thus transmitting the message that there is something wrong with her daughter, something wrong with her desires, something that needs to be kept at bay. Unwittingly, mother provides her daughter with her first lesson in emotional deprivation.

At the same time that mother pushes her daughter's neediness away she pulls her daughter to stay within the boundaries that she herself inhabits. There is a push-pull dynamic in the mother-daughter relationship. Mother wishes to see her daughter contented, but she is again caught in a paradox, for she herself does not have the experience of contentment. Mother has learned throughout her childhood to curb her desires and wants, to split her needs off, to hide that part of herself from others and not to expect to be responded to. Mother herself has a little-girl hidden inside herself.

This repressed little-girl inside mother is a third important shaper of the mother-daughter relationship. Mother comes to be frightened by her daughter's free expression of her needs, and unconsciously acts toward her infant daughter in the same way she acts internally toward the little-girl part of herself. In some ways the little daughter becomes an external representation of that part of herself which she has come to dislike and deny. The complex of emotions that results from her own deprivation through childhood and adult life is both directed inward in the struggle to negate the little-girl part of herself and projected outward onto her daughter.

A vivid example of this dynamic is the relationship between Beth and her daughter Alice. . . .

In Beth's therapy we were able to see the ways in which her daughter expressed many of Beth's own feelings and desires. Gradually Beth was able to see her identification with Alice and to see the ways she had rejected the child just as she rejected the little-girl part of herself.

This mother-daughter relationship illustrates the sensitivity that a mother can develop toward the needs and desires of a daughter, needs and desires that imitate her own. These features of mother-daughter interaction make for extreme intensity in the relationship. This intensity is often marked by a staccato quality, an inconsistency in the relating. The inconsistency stems from the way a mother copes with her feeling of identification with her daughter and her own deep feelings about herself as a woman. At those times when mother relates to daughter as a separate person she can be responsive and unambiguously caring. She can give her daughter what she needs and convey a sense of security and well-being. At other times, however, mother's sense of herself as a separate person dissolves and she experiences her daughter and herself as having the same feelings, thoughts, and desires.[1] When this occurs it is hard for a mother to be appropriately responsive; she may be withdrawn at one moment and overinvolved the next. She is acting on her unconscious feelings of identification and relating to her daughter in the same inconsistent way that she relates to the little-girl part of herself. Such toing and froing between a mother's sense of herself as separate and her merger with her daughter creates the staccato quality in the relationship.

The shape of this relationship, first established in infancy, is maintained throughout the daughter's life. As she slowly becomes her own person and needs her mother in different ways, the intense push-pull nature of the relationship persists. The daughter is absorbing essential lessons about what it means to be female, with her mother as both model and guide, and beyond that their relationship is absorbed by the daughter as a blueprint for other love relationships. The picture of mother that the daughter takes into herself is complex. Mother is the person who gives her what she needs—feeds her, bathes her, cuddles her, plays with her, talks to her, responds to her. She opens up wider and wider horizons. At the same time mother is the person who can say no, who can disappoint or withhold, who can be short-tempered and can misunderstand. Mother holds tremendous power to please and to hurt.

Many of mother's actions are thus incomprehensible, because the daughter receives contradictory messages in the push-pull dynamic. She experiences her mother giving the unconscious injunctions of staying close by but not expecting too much for doing so. The little girl cannot fathom why mother is so approving and loving at times and so disappointed and disappointing at others. The little girl tries to make sense of mother's actions. The part of her that has felt nurtured and understood by mother has contributed to a psychological experience of solidity and goodness, but she has also experienced that some parts of herself are not acceptable. The little girl absorbs the idea that to get love and approval she must show a particular side of herself. She must hide her emotional cravings, her disappointments and her angers, her fighting spirit. She must hide *her self*. She comes to feel that there must be something wrong with who she really is, which in turn must mean there is something wrong with what she needs and what she wants. A feeling that she is inauthentic develops, and she is unsure in her reactions and distanced from her wants. This soon translates into feeling unworthy and hes-

itant about pursuing her impulses. Slowly she develops an acceptable self, one that appears self-sufficient and capable and will receive
more consistent acceptance. Here in this first relationship with
mother the little girl learns to fear and hide away the little-girl part
of herself. And she comes to feel like a fraud, for an external part
of her is developing that is different from who she feels she is inside.

Here we can begin to see the way in which a feminine psychology is reproduced from generation to generation. Girls' psychologies develop within the context of their social world and social
role. In our practice we hear women talk about their needs with contempt, humiliation, and shame. They feel exposed and childish,
greedy and insatiable. Mothers and daughters both attempt to curb
their little-girl inside while showing only one part of themselves to
others, a part they feel others will find acceptable because it is not
needy.

This psychological split, which occurs in the first years of life,
is not a conscious act but a protective feature of psychic structural
development. The hidden part (the little-girl) does not disappear; it
has to go underground and seek nurturance within the girl's inner
world. And since this little-girl part of the developing psyche still
yearns for nurturance, there is confusion about its rejection in the
first place. This part of the psyche tends to carry feelings of isolation
and depression, even despair. When contact with it is evoked she
may be flooded with feelings of anger, disappointment, or rejection.
Hurt by the mother's rejections, the daughter may not be able to
show this needy part to anyone again, and so lives primarily in her
inner world of relationships (internal object relations). These both
excite and disappoint her little-girl inside. The girl constructs seemingly more satisfactory relationships in her inner world. Mother continues to live on inside, alternately presenting herself as giver and
withholder. She is still very powerful and still much needed. Inside
too, the little-girl is trying to challenge the deep conviction that if
she shows herself she will continue to be rejected and disliked. In
her private world the child tries to rewrite history, but time and
again her previous painful experiences are reinforced. So the little-
girl part builds boundaries; it is as though the needy, frightened part
is surrounded by a fortress. She cannot send messages out and others
cannot penetrate her defenses. Nobody can come in and hurt her

and she cannot get out and hurt others or humiliate herself by exposing her needs. . . .

A daughter hides the little-girl part of herself because she has picked up a painful and powerful message from mother that tells her she should not have expectations of being looked after emotionally, or of having her desires met, either by mother or by anyone else. Mother encourages her daughter to look to a man to be emotionally involved with; she teaches her daughter to direct her energies toward men and to someday depend on a man. But at the same time there is another message. As she lets her daughter know she must look to men, mother simultaneously transmits a message of disappointment and frustration. She conveys that her daughter must not expect a man to really help or understand her. Mothers often let their daughters know both overtly and covertly that men are disappointments. They may convey disdain and contempt for them. Mother's messages about men are thus more than a little ambivalent. She conveys both the necessity and the limitations of a daughter's emotional ties to a man.

Lorraine was perplexed by her mother's interest in the job status of the men she went out with. Her mother seemed terribly interested in these relationships, yet Lorraine always felt uncomfortable about discussing them with her mother because she realized that her mother had very little interest in what Lorraine felt about the personalities of her men friends. Indeed, her mother never discussed men in terms of emotional exchange or feelings. On a conscious level Lorraine felt pressure from her mother to find the right man and settle down, but on another level she felt that her mother dismissed men completely, that she didn't think of them as people capable of relationships or feelings. Consciously the mother was pushing her daughter to be with a man, but unconsciously, she was transmitting a message not to expect anything from a man except a house and children. Lorraine began to understand that essentially her mother thought of men as economic providers and that was all.

Even though a daughter comes to look toward men, she still yearns for mother's support and care. From girlhood to womanhood women live with the experience of having lost these aspects of maternal nurturance. This nurturance is never replaced. Women look to men to mother them but remain bereft. These needs for nurturance do not decrease any the less for loss. This loss, which causes tremendous pain, confusion, disappoint-

*ment, rage, and guilt for the daughter, is buried and denied in the culture
at large as well as in the unconscious of the little girl.*

We have mentioned that infants who have had sufficient good
contact to embody the caregiver's positive feelings within themselves come to feel secure. They are confident that their needs will
be met and that the large world they can now see outside themselves
and mother is full of exciting possibilities and new relationships. As
the baby begins to separate from mother she or he acquires a sense
of individuality. For the developing girl, still yearning for mother's
reassurance, psychological separation and individuation can only be
partial. The experience of the initial relating with mother means that
the girl is left with feelings of deprivation, unworthiness, and rejection. As she still needs mother very badly it is hard for her to feel
unambiguously receptive to new experiences or to have confidence
that others will be receptive to her needs and desires. She tries to
move toward others to express herself but she feels nervous, at once
disloyal and abandoned. Enjoying being with an aunt may be complicated; she may seek contact with her and yet feel guilty for leaving
mother and for getting nurturance from elsewhere. This is an example of the way in which the social requirement for women to be
connected to others rather than full, autonomous people is reflected
in the development of a feminine psychology.

Too often a little girl's attempts at separation take place under
conditions of opposition from mother and consequent fear. There is
no feeling of strength and wholeness to make the world outside seem
exciting; instead it is tantalizing and frightening. In some ways it
echoes aspects of the painful inner world of the child's reality.
Mother is still a focal point; she encourages some attempts at separation—even forces them—and thwarts others. Because the little-
girl part of the girl's psyche has been split off, it continues to be
deprived of the nourishment and contact it needs for maturation.
The girl both fears and longs to remerge with mother and to be held
and cared for, but the inconsistencies in the relationship push her
toward separation, with the construction of boundaries between self
and the little-girl inside. These are in some sense false boundaries;
they do not come from an integrated ego structure which can clearly
distinguish between self and the outside world, but are internal
boundaries, separating one part of herself from another part and
keeping the little-girl inside shut away from the outside world.

At the same time, the daughter's sense of self is fused with her sense of mother, so that in her attempts to separate from mother she may not know who she herself is. Trying to be her own person, she is nevertheless confused about where she begins and mother ends. In her early development she has taken mother into her, and now, because she does not have a strong sense of her own separate self, the sense of mother inside her may outweigh her own independent identity. Unlike her brother, she cannot use gender difference to differentiate herself. Psychologically and socially she is a miniversion of mother, someone who will have a life like mother's.

And so her sense of self as unique, separate, and other is entwined with a sense of mother. There is a shared social role, a shared prescription for life, and a shared psychology.

Inevitably, then, the daughter's attempts at separation are somewhat ambiguous and dovetail with mother's ambivalence. The message from mother during the period of infantile dependency has been, "Take care of yourself, don't depend on others, don't want too much," but these injunctions, which in effect seem to push the daughter away, have been combined with the unstated, unconscious message: "Stay close, don't stray, don't go too far, it's dangerous." As a result, the process toward separation has to contend with a tug to stay close to mother and share the boundaries she inhabits.

Ideally, as daughter tries to separate from mother, mother in turn must let go just enough. She must allow her daughter to explore the limits of her developing identity from a secure base. The broadening of boundaries and setting of new ones that daughter and mother negotiate require enormous emotional and psychological shifting for the mother. In the daughter's infancy the mother may experience a tension between her sense of the baby's utter dependency and helplessness, which confirms her essentiality, and her desires for the child's separateness. The mother may be reassured by being needed and simultaneously resent and begrudge her own loss of independence. If she worked outside the home before the birth and intends to do so again, she must shift her focus from her former job to that of child rearing and then remove herself psychologically and emotionally from her absorption in her infant's world back toward the outside world and her other work.[2]

There is a delicate pushing away and pulling together between mother and baby as each attempts to separate from the other. Mother's wish to keep her daughter close reflects her own psychology and social experience. Having a child has filled up her life, and if she has been living through her child, accruing an identity through mothering, she may have great difficulty letting her daughter separate. She may need to keep her daughter close to her to maintain this sense of herself, and this psychological need may exist whether or not she has worked outside the home. A daughter's moves toward independence are bound to diminish a mother's sense of being needed. Brought up to see her central role as that of mother, she may feel empty, depressed, confused about who she is; she may lose her sense of purpose. If she has not been able to separate psychologically from her mother, she may in turn cling to her daughter. The period of her child's separation-individuation can make the mother feel that she is already "losing" her child, in a foretaste of future separations (nursery school, adolescence) that jolts and hurts. She clings in the hope that her daughter will not abandon her.

If the mother's psychological development has been similar to her daughter's, and she herself has not had a solid experience of separation and selfhood, she too has false boundaries. Her daughter's moving away involves a loss at the psychic structural level because she has attempted to complete herself in her attachment to and merger with her daughter. The distinction between the two of them is blurred, so that the daughter's development toward independence brings feelings of loss as well as pride.

As a baby daughter reaches this stage, a woman often finds herself wanting another baby. "I thought I wanted only one child," said one of our clients. "I never intended to have more. But when Jennie was two I started having dreams about another baby and thinking about it every single day. I sort of forgot about my previous thoughts on the subject of how many children I wanted. It wasn't on a rational, thinking level. I just *felt* intensely that I wanted another baby." Mother's unconscious feelings of loss as her daughter attempts separation constantly reinforce the jagged attachment between the two of them. As mother now pulls her daughter to stay close, as she indicates to her the shape of a girl's life, she instructs her in an essential feminine skill. She teaches her to look after others. The daughter, as she learns to hide her needy little-girl part, becomes extremely sensitive to neediness in others. She develops the radar to pick up the needs of others; *she learns to give what others need; and she gives to others out of the well of her own unmet needs.*

Once again we see the reproduction of a feminine psychology. Just as mother responds to and anticipates the needs of others, and just as mother identifies with the yearnings and needs of others, so the daughter comes to embody this same capacity for giving. And like mother, she too wishes for someone to respond to her needs. So the giving capacity starts very early on in her life and becomes an important part of her identity and self-image.

As the mother transmits to her daughter the importance of caring for others, she brings to the relationship her *own* unmet emotional needs. Inside each mother lives a hungry, needy, deprived, and angry little-girl. She turns to her daughter for nurturance, looking to the child to make up the loss of her own maternal nurturance and satisfy her continued yearnings.

The psychological attachment and lack of separation between mothers and daughters and daughters and mothers continues through generations of women. The daughter becomes involved in a cycle that is part of each woman's experience: attempting to care for mother. As the daughter learns her role as nurturer, *her first child is her mother.*

Women do not usually bring these same needs to their sons. Built into a mother's experience with a son from the beginning of his life is the knowledge that he will become his own person in the world. She accepts the fact that he will become a man and move out into the world to create and commit himself to a family of his own. But although she expects her daughter to have a family too, she expects this to be an extension of her own family rather than a separate entity. Whether or not a woman still lives with her husband after her children are grown, her daughter tends to remain available and responsible for her care and companionship. In fact, we often see daughters-in-law taking on this responsibility as well. Although an adult daughter may resent this responsibility, at the same time she is consciously and unconsciously aware of her mother's needs. The social position of women, which often forces them to hide their loneliness or pain even from themselves, is a strong adhesive in the mother-daughter relationship.

Just as she transmits messages to her daughter about her role as a woman, a mother also transmits what her sexuality may be. The mother's feelings about her own body and her sexuality are a critical influence on the way a daughter will come to feel about herself. Nancy Friday writes: "When we were learning to walk, mother helped us to practice and her confidence in our success encouraged us to keep trying. When it came to sex her emotions became communicated to us too, this time what we learned from her was anxiety and failure."[3]

Our complex cultural attitudes toward women's bodies—that they are sexual, ugly, mysterious, extraordinary, dark, bloody, and bad smelling—find a place in each woman's sense of self. The female body is both degraded and deified; it is felt to be so powerful that men will destroy themselves or die for it. Female sexuality is held responsible for male sexuality and male aggression (an extreme example is the myth that it is a woman's fault if a man rapes her). Women, then, often come to their relationship with their daughters with, at the very least, apprehension about the female body and the power of female sexuality.

In the generational transmission of feminine sexuality it is mothers who begin the process of shaping a daughter's sexuality. But mother's sexuality has developed within particular constraints, so that many mothers feel uncomfortable within their own bodies and hide their sexual desires and needs. In our therapeutic work we rarely hear a woman say that sexuality was openly accepted, that the parents' sexuality was visible, that mother or father informed the girl of the changes her body would go through in a positive and exciting way, telling her that when her body became a woman's body it would be a proud, joyful transition. We hear instead remembrances of shame, embarrassment, fear; of women not liking their breasts because they are too big or too small, not liking their pubic hair, big hips, or rounded bottoms. Women also recall adolescent warnings and restrictions (boys are encouraged to be experienced). Female sexuality seems to be dangerous; it is unknown, unspoken. You must have it to become a grown-up woman and yet you must hide it. Thus many adolescent girls and young women learn to be frightened of their own sexuality and to dislike their own bodies.

At the same time many daughters perceive their mothers as nonsexual and know that they do not want to be like mother in that respect. From quite an early age they may be aware of wanting to be quite a different sort of woman. A girl may want to be "sexy," like a movie star or the woman at the beauty shop. She may feel ashamed of the way her mother dresses or embarrassed by her behavior. Whether mother conveys her sexuality through dress or physicality or hides it, it will make an impression on her daughter. The daughter compares herself to her mother as she tries to find her own independent sexuality.

As the girl's sexuality explodes during adolescence, it drives her to seek freedom and independence from her family. Her new sexual body means that she comes face to face with both her reproductive and her erotic capacities. This is a painful time for many young women, because they are already uncomfortable with their sexuality and know that women's social heritage does not allow them to act on these new desires for freedom.

The thread of sexuality is entwined in the issues of separation and merger, although its meaning is not always confluent. Sexual connection with another is in part a demonstration of a woman's attempt to separate from mother. Her physical attachment to another symbolizes her relatedness outside the family, but this new relatedness highlights the complexities of separation and attachment. In many parts of society cultural law still dictates that the only way a woman can leave her family is by starting another family. Even if she lives apart from her parents, she leaves their home only to go into her husband's. In patriarchy the daughter is passed from father to husband, as ritualized in the wedding ceremony, when the bride is "given away" by the father. But often mother is crying nearby, filled with a sense of loss due to her daughter's new attachment. The paradox lies in the fruition of mother's ambiguous message. On the one hand, mother has instructed her daughter to go toward a man; on the other, when the daughter does so it brings mother tremendous pain, for she experiences the loss of her daughter. (Mother's own memory of leaving her mother may also be unconsciously reevoked.) The marriage highlights the cultural prohibition against separation—psychological or social—for a woman. She must leave home and yet she cannot. Women are at psychic crossroads.

A daughter's personality takes shape in her relationship with her mother, a relationship weighted heavy with longing, identification, disappointment, betrayal, anger, and guilt. As mothers transmit the knowledge of how to survive within the structure that they and all women inhabit, they bind their daughters with the chains of femininity. Thus mothers and daughters share complex and powerful emotions of love, neediness, insecurity, low self-esteem, and identification. Many women never feel free of their mothers. They are not separate people, but experience mother as living inside, judging, binding, tempting, and disappointing. At the same time mothers and daughters often feel the pain of not being able to share honesty, to show themselves to each other in direct ways.

As Adrienne Rich writes, "Mother stands for the victim in ourselves, the unfree woman, the martyr. Our personalities seem dangerously to blur and overlap with our mothers." The consequence of this painful identification is that we deny that our mother has anything to do with us: "We develop matraphobia and try to split ourselves off from her, to purge ourselves of her bondage, in a desperate attempt to know where mother ends and daughter begins, we perform radical surgery."[4]

Although the nuances and particulars of each woman's experience vary, although what each woman brings to mothering is different, and although the specifics of each mother-daughter relationship are unique, these two crucial determinants—a mother's feelings about herself and her identification with her daughter—are reproduced in all mother-daughter relationships. They are the key features in the development of a woman's psychology.

As a girl develops, her father's presence in her life continues to be very different from mother's. In a traditional family the little girl learns that father is very important to family survival, and that his daily abandonment is for the purpose of providing security, especially economic security, for the family. She learns that she must rely on him in particular ways. She also sees the complexity of mother's relationship with father. She sees how mother defers to and depends on father and she also sees that father depends on mother for many things. His daily life is an expression of his need for a woman in order to survive. His dependency needs are met in an unstated way at home, emotionally and physically.

The girl may feel excluded and pushed away from mother when father is around. She senses that she does not have the power to hold mother in the same way he does. She may feel jealous of mother's availability to another, and she may feel excluded from her parents' relationship. In her infancy she and mother were a couple; as she develops, her awareness of the world shifts and she is confronted by mother and father as a couple. She takes in how important a man, a partner, is in a woman's life. Whether the marriage is satisfactory and cooperative or not, the little girl sees the intensity of her parents' relationship, and the seeds for her own future relating to a man are fertilized. As she watches mother she learns to relate to father in specific ways. For example, most little girls learn that an important part of the relationship with father is pleasing him. They are encouraged to transfer their primary dependency from mother to father, the embodiment of all future males. This is part of learning to become a woman in a heterosexual society, and, because mother is aware of this, and how she must help her daughter to make this transfer of love and dependency needs from her to father, there is a tension expressed in the mother-daughter relationship. It shows up in the push-pull dynamic.

Both parents encourage their daughter to look to father in several ways. He is the link to the world outside the family and the daughter must use him as access to that world. Because he is more secure and sure of himself in the world, she can imagine that he will protect her. However, she cannot fully identify with father because of his sexual identity. Father encourages his daughter to charm him and a male audience, to attract and hold his attention in specifically defined feminine ways, as she will later need to do. She learns that she must not attempt to make decisions which challenge his authority; she must not show too much independence and power.

Very few little girls have much contact with their fathers in the very early period of psychological development. Father plays a tremendously important role very soon, but he builds on the ego development that has occurred between mother and daughter. Father is a person with whom the daughter can identify when she is in the process of separation-individuation, and as she tries to differentiate herself from her mother, she may try to emulate him, incorporating characteristics she admires.[5] If he is outgoing, humorous, or a good storyteller, for example, the daughter may develop these aspects in her own personality.

The father's relationship with his daughter is complex. He stands outside the physical experiences of pregnancy, birth, and lactation. He may feel excluded from the mother-child relationship or inadequate to participate in it. He may appreciate the sensuality and tenderness it brings into his life, and he may very much want to participate fully, but he may be consciously or unconsciously unsure about his place. Because of his lack of preparedness he may feel inadequate in relating to the baby, and his own insecurities may be reinforced by the mother's anxiety about his capabilities at mothering. In her worry about his inexperience mother may unintentionally undercut his confidence. His feelings about having a daughter or having a son will inevitably influence his relationship to a new baby. And with a daughter, especially, he may feel in the dark about who she is, what to do with her, how to relate. With a boy child he can rely on his own experience of boyhood and maleness to aid him in building a relationship.

Father may feel excluded from the early mother-infant couple and become jealous. His relationship with his partner has changed with the entry of the third person, and his partner is no longer available to him in the same way. If the child is a girl, his feeling of being the "outsider" in the triangle may be increased. The closeness between mother and infant may also evoke happy or unsatisfactory experiences from his own infancy, when he was very close to a woman.

In our practice many women report having no real contact with their fathers. As adults they still wonder where father fits in their lives.[6] We often find that a daughter's relationship with father was not straightforward, that she experienced barriers and interceptions. The mother strongly affects the father-daughter relationship. A father's loving relationship with his daughter may cause friction, because mother may experience jealousy at his attention to daughter as well as anger because of what she feels is lacking in her life. Mother may feel that father shows gentle, caring affection to a daughter in ways he does not with her, and since her needy little-girl inside yearns for just this kind of attention, seeing it between her partner and their daughter can be painful. Mothers may unwittingly intercept this loving contact between a father and a daughter.

In addition, because father often spends very little time each day with a daughter, his availability to his daughter in those moments may stir up mother's resentment. She sees the child thrilled at father's attention and feels that all she gives is taken for granted or even negated. (She may also have a burden of unconscious jealousy: father's time at home used to be hers alone.)

These dynamics in the mother-father-daughter triangle are likely to be part of the girl's psychological development and they help explain why a daughter's relationship to her father is often undeveloped. Because she is so attuned to her mother, the daughter picks up mother's feelings, including any ambivalent feelings about daughter's relationship to father. The daughter may have to hide the contact she does have with him. As one woman put it, "Each time I phoned my parents I essentially talked to my mother. If my mother answered, then I never even had a word with my father. I would just tell my mother to send him my love. When my father answered the phone we talked for ten seconds, very superficially, and then my mother would come on the phone. When I became aware of this I tried to talk longer to my father and then my mother actually started picking up the extension."

Another dynamic we have consistently seen in our practice is that of a daughter's alliance with mother about father's inadequacies. Women often express contempt and disdain for their fathers because they are involved in mother's anger. Indeed, the daughter often carries her mother's rage. Women report feeling their fathers to be weak because they did not "stand up" to mother, especially in relation to them. "He wasn't strong enough to stop my mother's interceptions." "He didn't fight for a relationship with me." Once again daughter and mother share an experience. Both feel disappointed with father, both feel disdain, and thus they tighten their unspoken bond.

Father's position in the emotional triangle of the family is a critical piece in the puzzle of why it is so difficult for women to separate psychologically. The father-daughter relationship no more provides for unambiguous relating than the mother-daughter one does. Father is outside daughter's primary ambivalent relationship with mother but cannot offer an unambivalent one himself. Adolescence, then, the time of struggle toward independence, creates a psychic hiatus. Mother continues to relate in the push-pull while father is confronted with a daughter who is now a sexual being. This may well make him uncomfortable and as a result distant and inconsistent in his relating. Women who had good contact with their fathers and felt it changed dramatically during adolescence are likely to feel that there is something dangerous and wrong with their sexuality and that they are being punished because of it. The adolescent girl living in an emotional storm has no constant buoy.

The father-daughter relationship illustrates one of the tragedies of patriarchy. A man's position in the family and the significance of gender in his early psychological development means that he is often both ill prepared to give nurturance and afraid of women.[7] Men do not provide the emotional stability girls and women need either in their early struggles for psychological separation or in adult heterosexual relationships.

Father, then, stands at once outside the mother-daughter relationship and as the representative of the patriarchal order. Symbolically he represents for his daughter many things that are outside the world of women, the world of her mother, the world she is supposed to enter.

A daughter's psychology, then, is created in this nexus of family relations in a particular way. Like her mother before her, the woman's internal sense of self will be somewhat shaky and her psychological boundaries malleable.[8] She will have learned to hide her needy and would-be independent and initiating parts and will find herself searching in various ways for the missing connection in her life that will allow her the unambiguous nurturance she needs to continue her developmental task of separation. She will look to her husband and children to fill in the missing pieces, because the psychological merger with her mother thwarts her from achieving a solid sense of self and separateness. As a result she is well suited for her social role of handmaiden to others' activities. Her inner sense of unworthiness and unentitledness have been reinforced over and over again in the social constraints of her childhood and in the learning of her adult role. She has buried part of her self.

NOTES

1. Psychologists have observed this as part of "normal" development without considering the conditions that make this possible and the impact of mother-and-daughter psychology. For example, Winnicott, describing the mother's ability to respond to her infant's needs in the first year of life, writes: "Towards the end of the pregnancy and for a few weeks after the birth of a child the mother is preoccupied with (or better 'given over to')

the care of her baby, which at first seems like a part of herself; moreover she is very much identified with the baby and knows quite well what the baby is feeling like. For this she uses her own experience as a baby." (*Dependence Towards Independence: The Maturational Processes and the Facilitating Environment,* London, 1963.) He writes of the mother's primary maternal preoccupation as an "extraordinary condition which is almost like an illness. . . ." (*The Family and Individual Development,* London, 1965, pp. 15–16.) In the period when the mother is providing for the needs of the infant, and "finding the part of her that identifies with the infant, the mother is herself in a dependent state and vulnerable." (*The Maturational Processes and the Facilitating Environment,* London, 1963.)

2. Andrea Egan, who is doing a study on the experience of mothering, has informed us that many of the women she interviewed found that after the initial period of merger in infancy, as the baby turned more toward the world at six months of age, so mother had to readjust and redirect some of her interests outside her baby.

3. Nancy Friday, *My Mother, My Self,* New York, 1977.

4. Adrienne Rich, *Of Woman Born,* New York, 1976, p. 236.

5. From Freud's development of the concept of the Oedipus complex onward throughout psychoanalytic theory we see the analyst's attempt to incorporate the father as the central figure in psychological development. Freud himself recognized the critical nature of the early years of life for the girl's psychology and called this preoedipal—that is, he had to keep father in the picture and name everything else in relation to the father's entry into the world of the child. Even Melanie Klein could not abandon the father and so saw the oedipal conflict as happening in the first year of life.

6. Signe Hammer, *Passionate Attachments: Fathers and Daughters in America Today,* New York, 1982.

7. Men's psychology is obviously not the subject of this book, but for an explication of men's fear of women see Robert J. Stoller, *Sex and Gender,* New York, 1968, London, 1969; Dorothy Dinnerstein, *The Mermaid and the Minotaur: Sexual Arrangements and Human Malaise,* New York, 1976; and Luise Eichenbaum and Susie Orbach, *What Do Women Want? Exploding the Myth of Dependency,* New York, 1983.

8. Nancy Chodorow, *The Reproduction of Mothering: Psychoanalysis and the Sociology of Gender,* Berkeley, Calif. 1978; Jean Baker Miller, *Toward a New Psychology of Women,* Boston, Mass., 1976; and Carol Gilligan, *A Different Voice,* Cambridge, Mass., 1982. All have a more positive view of the developmental repercussions of women's malleable boundaries. They point to the certainty of affiliation in relating and the ways in which a feminine view of the world provides for safety and containment.

A Feminist Critique of Jung

Naomi R. Goldenberg

Feminist scholarship in religious studies has explored the reasons why many women feel estranged from traditional religious institutions. Rejecting conventional views of what their subordinate place in the world should be, women can hardly be content with theological formulations which both reflect and justify that place.[1]

Portions of Jungian theory may prove helpful in the search for new formulations. Jung hypothesized that there is a religious process in every human being which dreams, symbols, and myths manifest. He saw such religions as Christianity, Judaism, and Buddhism as elaborate communal ways of organizing a basic religious progression. He thought a person quite lucky if she or he could be a devout follower of an inherited religion, for then the road would be easy, well planned, and secure. In *The Collected Works* Jung often states that his first effort in therapy is to try to connect patients to their native religions, since many of his patients did not suffer from a sense of the impossibility of coping but, rather, from a sense of the meaningless, barren quality of life. Contact with "religion" could help in their cure. If the connection with the native religion could not work, the patient had to become expert in listening and being guided by her or his own religious authority and adept in seeing a basic process within.

However, Jungian psychology particularly warrants a feminist critique because it has largely become a form of patriarchal religion itself. The first step in such a feminist critique is to question the veneration of Jung himself. He is regarded as a "prophet" by the vast majority of Jungians, whose self-assigned role is to teach and explicate the Jungian opus.[2] Most "original" Jungian works simply extend Jung's assumptions without questioning any premises. Erich Neumann, for example, assumed the archetypes as already proven and then arranged them in succession.[3] Marie Louise von Franz looked at the archetypal truth of various fairy tales.[4] Even a work such as Ann Belford Ulanov's study of *The Feminine in Jungian Thought and Christian Theology* does not in any way disagree with Jung in the classification of the concept of the feminine.[5] Given such attitudes, Jungians tend to overlook the several contradictory statements Jung may make within a single work, to veil his complexities and failures in an effort to make everything simple, cohesive, and inoffensive.[6] They will not admit that his statements were often misinformed, ignorant, or just plain prejudiced. (To paraphrase one unpublished seminar, for example, Jung virtually equated the Negro with the gorilla.)[7]

More important, feminist scholars must confront the sexism of Jung's theories which has also been glossed over by his followers. In fact, it is often argued that, in comparison with Freud, Jung valued the feminine and therefore valued women more. To look at a characteristic statement of Jung's on women, however, is to gain a very different impression:

> Woman is compensated by a masculine element and therefore her unconscious has, so to speak, a masculine imprint. This results in a considerable difference between men and women, and accordingly, I have called the projection-making factor in women the animus, which means mind or spirit. The animus corresponds to the paternal Logos just as the anima corresponds to the maternal Eros. But I do not wish to give these two intuitive concepts too specific a definition. I use Eros and Logos merely as conceptual aids to describe the fact that woman's consciousness is characterized more by the connective quality of Eros than by the discrimination and cognition associated with Logos. In men, Eros, the function of relationship, is usually less developed than Logos. In women, on the other hand, Eros is an expression of their true nature, while their Logos is often only a regrettable accident.[8]

Despite his caveats that his "intuitive concepts" should not be taken too literally, Jung is certain that women are characterized by Eros, an ability to make connections, while men are oriented toward Logos, the function of analytic thought. It is true that Jung genuinely values woman for her remarkable and all too often overlooked Eros, but it is equally true that he confines her to this sphere. Once she moves into a Logos arena, she is not only at a great disadvantage but is behaving unnaturally as well. Jung is not content to stay on a symbolic or harmlessly vague level with his ideas of "feminine" and "masculine." Like all the thinkers that Mary Daly describes who subscribe to a concept of the "Eternal Feminine," he gets around to making "dogmatic assertions" about what should or should not be the role of "existing individuals."[9] Jung writes in his essay "Woman in Europe,"

> No one can get around the fact that by taking up a masculine profession, studying and working like a man, woman is doing something not wholly in accord with, if not directly injurious to, her feminine nature. She is doing something that would scarcely be possible for a man to do, unless he were a Chinese. [Note the racism.] Could he, for instance, be a nursemaid or run a kindergarten? When I speak of injury, I do not mean merely physiological injury, but above all psychic injury. It is a woman's outstanding characteristic that she can do anything for the love of a man. But those women who can achieve something important for the love of a thing are most exceptional, because this does not really agree with their nature. Love for a thing is a man's prerogative.[10]

Beyond the overt sexism in Jung's concept of the feminine, a feminist critique must examine the inequity of the anima-animus model of the psyche, which is never challenged by any of his immediate circle of followers.[11] The theory clearly favors men, even though it has been praised as a liberating concept because it supports that marvelous unseen creature—the "androgyne."[12] The anima-animus theory postulates a contrasexual personality in each sex. In men this personality would be female—in women, male. The word "personality," however, is too light; in Jungian thought, "anima" and "animus" conjure up associations to the unconscious and the soul. In fact, "anima" and "animus," like "Eros" and "Logos," are never clearly defined and are often used with different connotations, a slippery quality common to most Jungian concepts that serves to insulate them from much questioning. The only certain element is that an anima is man's picture of his female other side, while an animus is woman's picture of her other. Jung writes,

> Since the anima is an archetype that is found in men, it is reasonable to suppose that an equivalent archetype must be present in women; for just as the man is compensated by a feminine element, so woman is compensated by a masculine one. I do not, however, wish this argument to give the impression that these compensatory relationships were arrived at by deduction. On the contrary, long and varied experience was needed in order to grasp the nature of anima and animus empirically. Whatever we have to say about these archetypes, therefore, is either directly verifiable or at least rendered probable by the facts. At the same time, I am fully aware that we are discussing pioneer work which by its very nature can only be provisional. [13]

The hesitation, the assertion of probability, and the mention of "pioneer work" at the end of the paragraph reveal Jung's uncertainty. But the key statement is the first sentence: *"Since the anima is an archetype that is found in men, it is reasonable to suppose that an equivalent archetype must be present in women."* The presence of the animus in women certainly seems to have been deduced from Jung's contention about an anima in men. He hypothesized the former to balance the latter. According to Jungian stereotypes of masculine and feminine, however, this gives women and men qualitatively different kinds of unconscious (or soul)—an enormous assertion based on little "evidence." It is not surprising then, that Jung never developed the idea of the animus to the same extent as the anima; in my view he was forcing a mirror image where there was none. The anima-animus model is clearly more beneficial to men than to women. Barbara Charlesworth Gelpi correctly states that Jung "is primarily concerned with the integration, or, within the tradition of the myth [of androgyny], reintegration, of the feminine into the masculine psyche." [14] Jung's theory simply exemplifies the sort of androgyne Gelpi labels "the masculine personality fulfilled and completed by the feminine. . . ." [15] For women, Jung's particular model militates against change in the social sphere. While men can keep control of all Logos activities and appropriate just whatever Eros they need as a kind of psychological hobby, women are by no means encouraged to develop Logos, since they are thought of as handicapped by nature in all Logos arenas. Thus the anima-animus theory does not lead to the integration of the sexes but, rather, to more separatism.

Admittedly, it is good to urge men who have been afraid of experiencing Eros or anima because they think it is inappropriate to their sex to develop their contrasexual element. But the Jungian model functions with and sustains decidedly masculine and feminine stereotypes. I would argue that it makes far more sense to postulate a similar psychic force for both sexes. Freud did this regularly when he spoke of the "repudiation of femininity" as the task of successful psychoanalysis for men *and* women.[16] The current theology of women's religions argues positively for contact with female energy as the end toward which both sexes should strive.[17] It is less important, in my view, whether the basic human drive is labeled "male" or "female"; what matters is that the *same* primary impetus in human libido exists for men and women alike. In future work this model might be developed more profitably than the petty anima-animus division of the psyche.

To Jungians the anima, the animus, and their verbal handmaidens Eros and Logos are "archetypes," by definition, what is unchanging and unchangeable. This concept of archetype allows Jungians like Erich Neumann and Esther Harding to write studies on the "archetypal" nature of the feminine psyche which are based on their subjective selection of mythological material to document preordained conclusions.[18] Feminist scholars must examine the very idea of archetype in Jungian thought if sexism is ever to be confronted at its base.[19] Indeed, if feminists do not change the assumptions of archetype or redefine the concept, there are only two options: either (1) to accept the patriarchal ideas of the feminine as ultimate and unchanging and work within those or (2) to indulge in a rival search to find female archetypes, ones which can support feminist conclusions.

I have several reservations about this second alternative, which some feminists have chosen. Elizabeth Gould Davis's *The First Sex*, for example, is an essentially imaginative work—which claims to be "science."[20] It proclaims matriarchy as an *empirical* absolute, the very same kind of proclamation that men have made to justify the subjugation of women. I do see the great use in recovering lost, buried images of women; but if we establish these images as archetypes that define the proper experience of women, we are in danger of setting bounds to that experience. I see this as a new version of the Eternal Feminine enterprise which could become just as restrictive as the old Eternal Feminine ever was.

Instead of a new search for absolutes, feminists could abandon the idea of absolutes altogether. We could, further, renounce the Jungian idea of separating archetype from its expression in images, that is, the absolute, transcendent ideals of which our changing experiences, which usually appear visually in the mind and are expressed actively in the world, are only inferior copies.[21] This separation leads to a distinction between the ideal form out there in archetype land and the expressed content in here, in the activities, dreams, and meditations of individuals.[22] It is this separation of absolute from experience which lies at the base of all patriarchal religion: women are the way they are because they are conforming to something out there which can never change. It is such a concept which allowed much of Jungian thought to become racist, sexist, and closed to experience.

Rather than rival absolutes or superior-inferior paradigms, we could begin to equate image with archetype. This would put much greater value on what is happening in the individual psyche. Images are, after all, our psychic pictures of action, our imaginal depictions of the behavioral patterns we are continually enacting and continually modifying. All imaginal activities, all images, could then be understood as archetypes to the degree that they move things and partake of what we might want to call "numinosity." *Archetypes therefore would refer to the imaginal or religious process itself rather than to past documents of that process.* With this sort of notion, we can stay open to all the data of experience and cease looking for authority words to label that experience archetypal, mythological, or religious.

I am suggesting nothing less than breaking down the hierarchy of mind—to which all other hierarchies and authority structures are linked—whether political, economic, or religious. Since feminists have suffered more than most others from these hierarchies. I propose this as the task of the feminist scholar concerned with the psychology of religion. Like the patients Jung described who saw too much hypocrisy and too little relevance in native religion, feminists are both cursed and blessed—cursed because they cannot refer to any established text or doctrine to make the way easier and blessed because their religious innovations have a chance of being more creative.[23]

NOTES

1. See esp. Sheila D. Collins, *A Different Heaven and Earth* (Valley Forge, Pa.: Judson Press, 1974); Judith Plaskow and Joan Arnold Romero, eds., *Women and Religion* (Missoula, Mont.: Scholars' Press, 1974); and Rosemary Radford Ruether, ed., *Religion and Sexism* (New York: Simon & Schuster, 1974).

2. See, e.g., Frieda Fordham, *An Introduction to Jung's Psychology* (London: Penguin Books, 1954); and Jolande Jacobi, *The Psychology of C. G. Jung* (New Haven, Conn.: Yale University Press, 1971). Thus in bookstores one will see rows of books summarizing Jungian thought.

3. Erich Neumann, *The Origins and History of Consciousness*, trans. R. F. C. Hull (Princeton, N.J.: Princeton University Press, 1954).

4. Marie Louise von-Franz, *Creation Myths* (New York and Zurich: Spring Publications, 1972); *Interpretation of Fairy Tales* (New York and Zurich: Spring Publications, 1970); *The Problem of the Puer Aeternus* (New York and Zurich: Spring Publications, 1970); and *The Feminine in Fairy Tales* (New York and Zurich: Spring Publications, 1972).

5. Ann Belford Ulanov, *The Feminine in Jungian Psychology and Christian Theology* (Evanston, Ill.: Northwestern University Press, 1972). Ulanov begins to raise questions in the appendix to "A Note on Eros and Logos," pp. 335–41. One can only wish she had carried such questions further.

6. Philip Rieff has pointed out some of the worst features of Jung's style in *The Triumph of the Therapeutic* (New York: Harper Torchbooks, 1968), pp. 44–45.

7. All of the seminars consist of notes transcribed by some of Jung's students. These notes cannot yet be directly quoted in print; one can only report on their contents. I discovered this reference to Negroes while editing a seminar for possible publication in Zurich.

8. C. G. Jung, *The Collected Works*, ed. G. Adler et al., trans. R. F. Hull, 2d ed. (Princeton, N.J.: Princeton University Press, 1968), 9, pt. 2:4.

9. Mary Daly, *The Church and the Second Sex, with a New Feminist*

Post-Christian Introduction by the Author (New York: Harper Colophon Books, 1975), pp. 148–49.

10. Jung (2d ed., 1964), 10:117–18.

11. Jung's immediate circle of followers, in fact, were and are prone to emphasize it to an even greater degree than Jung himself. Dr. Jolande Jacobi, one of the most successful female members of the second generation of Jungians, insisted that, "just as the male by his very nature is uncertain in the realm of Eros, so the woman will always be unsure in the realm of Logos . . ." (pp. 117–18). The fact that her very successful career as author and lecturer in the realm of "Logos" seemed to contradict this statement never bothered her at all.

12. I believe that, if there is a modern-day unicorn, it has to be the androgyne. It is said to be out there somewhere, running around but nearly impossible to catch. Cynthia Secor has envisioned the androgyne as a unicorn also ("Androgyny: An Early Reappraisal," *Women's Studies* 2, no. 2 [1974]: 163). Catharine Stimpson has seen it as another species of chimera ("The Androgyne and the Homosexual," *Women's Studies* 2, no. 2 [1974]: 242–43).

13. Jung, 9, pt. 2:14.

14. Barbara Charlesworth Gelpi, "The Politics of Androgyny," *Women's Studies* 2, no. 2 (1974): 158.

15. Ibid., p. 151.

16. Sigmund Freud, *The Standard Edition of the Complete Psychological Works*, trans. James Strachey (London: Hogarth Press, 1964), 23:252.

17. From a class given in the Wicca by Star Hawk, High Priestess of the Compost coven in San Francisco, December 1975.

18. Erich Neumann, *The Great Mother: An Analysis of the Archetype*, trans. Ralph Mannheim (Princeton, N.J.: Princeton University Press, 1972); and "The Psychological Stages of Feminine Development," trans. Rebecca Jacobson, *Spring* (1959); and Esther Harding, *Women's Mysteries* (New York: Bantam Books, 1971).

19. See my article entitled "Archetypal Theory after Jung," *Spring* (1975), pp. 199–219.

20. Elizabeth Gould Davis, *The First Sex* (Baltimore: Penguin Books, 1973).

21. James Hillman pointed this out in relation to instinct in his "Essay on Pan," in *Pan and the Nightmare*, by James Hillman and Wilhelm Roscher (Zurich: Spring Publications, 1972), pp. xxiii–xxvi.

22. Toward the end of his life, Jung toyed with the idea of a psychoid continuum on which our action in the world, our images of that action, and the ideal spiritual "archetype" were linked. Although he continued to insist

on the transcendence of archetypes, he was beginning to join them to the material world of experience in images. See Jung, "On the Nature of the Psyche," in *Collected Works* (2d ed., 1970), 8:159–237.

23. See esp. Jung (1970), vol. 11; and "The Meaning of Psychology for Modern Man," in *Collected Works* (2d ed., 1964), 10:134–56.

A Feminist Perspective on
Jung's Concept of the Archetype

Demaris Wehr

In recent years, feminist discussion of the usefulness of C.G. Jung's theories, notably the theory of archetype, has been wide-ranging, with some of the most intense debate taking place in the field of religion. Conferences and journals have been the usual forum for this debate. Feminist authors like Carol Christ and Naomi Goldenberg have criticized Jung's psychological model from a feminist perspective, and Jungians have responded by either updating the theory or defending Jung against what they perceive to be misinterpretations of his theory.[1] This essay is my contribution to the debate.

Using a methodology informed by feminism and drawn from the sociology of knowledge, specifically the work of Peter Berger, I will examine the religious and social dimensions of Jung's concept of the archetype. This broad sociological emphasis allows us to uncover the central problem (and the potential value) of this concept. The central problem is this: Jung ontologizes what is more accurately and more usefully seen as socially constructed reality. Even though Jung and Jungians at times describe the archetype as simply a propensity or a predisposition to act or image in a certain way, the category of archetype is often used as a category of Being itself. Thus Jungian theory can function as quasi-religious or scientific legitimation of the status quo in society, reinforcing social roles, constricting growth, and limiting options for women. Seen for what

159

they actually describe, however, in other words, deontologized, Jung's archetypes can be useful.

A PARADIGM FOR UNDERSTANDING: SOCIOLOGY OF KNOWLEDGE

The sociology of knowledge is a subfield of sociology that emphasizes the role of institutions (religious, psychological, scientific and others) in molding human behavior and emotions. It also stresses the enormous human need for the ordering principles that institutions provide and the seemingly exorbitant price paid by individuals who defy established boundaries. Although human beings have created these institutions, the institutions have acquired an objective character, hiding the fact that they were created by humans in the first place. People collude with these structures because of the suffering they would incur if they did not, and also, more importantly, because the very structures of consciousness itself come to be isomorphic with the social structures. By a similar process, one which Jung seems to have overlooked, the archetypal images of the collective unconscious and social structures, institutions, and roles also become congruent with one another.

In *The Social Construction of Reality*, written with Thomas Luckmann, and *The Sacred Canopy*,[2] Peter Berger has elaborated his sociology of knowledge as it applies to the individual in society. In *The Sacred Canopy*, a sociological study of religion, Berger concentrates on the interaction between a human being and society and on the role of religion in ensuring that society's mandates gain the necessary, sacred legitimation that will ensure their enforcement. Berger emphasizes that a society is nothing but a human product, and yet this product attains an objective status which allows it to "continuously act back upon its producer."[3] While it is obvious that society is a human product, it is perhaps not so obvious that each human being is also a product of society, and not merely in a simple and benign sense, for society becomes not only an objective reality but a coercive force in the lives of individuals. Although human beings are entirely responsible for creating institutions, they come to perceive institutions as something that can act over and against them. Their role in the creation of these institutions becomes entirely lost to them, and their relationship to institutions is thus characterized by alienation and even self-deception. This socialization process occurs in three phases—externalization, objectivation, and internalization.

Externalization, the first phase, takes place almost on the level of instinct. It is an "anthropological necessity." Human beings, by definition, must pour themselves and their activities into the world and, by so doing, create the world. This necessity springs from the unfinished character of human beings and the "relatively unspecialized character of our instinctual structure."[4]

Objectivation, the second phase, refers to the process by which the human outpouring of activity in the world attains an objective character so that human products come to confront human beings over and against themselves. These products then seem to have what Berger calls a "facticity" outside of the factor of human agency. "The humanly produced world becomes something 'out there.' It consists of objects, both material and non-material, that are capable of resisting the desires of their producer."[5]

The third phase, internalization, is the process whereby human beings come to be determined by society. Internalization refers to the "reabsorption into consciousness of the objectivated world" so that the structures of the world and the structures of consciousness are isomorphic. In other words, society produces people with structures of thought that coincide with the social institutions people created in the first place.

JUNG, JUNGIANS, AND DEFINITIONS OF THE ARCHETYPE

Jung's understanding of the archetype evolved during his lifetime and his conceptualization of it became clearer. His use of the term remained persistently ambiguous, however, because he failed to distinguish between "archetype" and "archetypal image." His lack of precision in using these two terms led to frequent attempts at clarification by his disciples and students. In the beginning, a certain fuzziness, as Jung formulated his concept, was perhaps natural. Also, Jung seemed to be motivated by a strong desire to be accepted by the scientific community. This may account for his use of medical language, equating archetypes with instincts. The instincts, he said, "form very close analogies to the archetypes, so close, in fact, that there is good reason for supposing that the archetypes are the unconscious images of the instincts themselves, in other words, that they are patterns of instinctual behavior."[6] While the biological model may have been useful in legitimizing Jung's theories, the analogy with instincts has not added clarity to the concept of the archetype, which continued to be associated with images.

When associating the archetype with motifs from literature, myth, and folklore, Jung arrives at a much clearer definition:

> The concept of the archetype . . . is derived from the repeated observation that, for instance, the myths and fairytales of world literature contain definite motifs which crop up everywhere. We meet these same motifs in the fantasies, dreams, deliria, and delusions of individuals living today. These typical images and associations are what I call archetypal ideas. . . . They impress, influence, and fascinate us. They have their origin in the archetype, which in itself is an irrepresentable, unconscious, pre-existent form that seems to be part of the inherited structure of the psyche and can therefore manifest itself spontaneously anywhere, at any time.[7]

This definition makes a distinction between archetype and archetypal image (idea), a distinction so crucial to Jung's thinking that it is unfortunate that he was not careful to speak of "archetypal images" every time he meant them, rather than lapse into the linguistically simpler "archetypes." Even if this distinction had been maintained, however, the concept of the archetype is still problematical in ways having to do with Jung's particular use of "numinosity"—a quality attributed to the experience of the archetype.

ON NUMINOSITY: JUNG AND OTTO

Jung borrowed the concept of numinosity from Rudolf Otto's *The Idea of the Holy* (1923). There are some interesting implications of this borrowing. Otto's premise is that the rationalist conception of God lacks something essential, leading to a "wrong and one-sided interpretation of religion."[8] Otto thought that orthodox Christianity had failed to recognize the value in the non-rational and hence had kept that element out of its interpretation of God. His aim was to restore to the understanding of God the element of the non-rational. Thus Otto brings us to the category of the "holy" or "sacred." He calls the "holy" a category of interpretation and locates it squarely within the sphere of religion.

Jung applies the notion of numinosity to the experience of archetypal images residing in the collective unconscious, but his use of the term remains very close to Otto's. In carrying over a concept that pertains to the experience of the Divine and applying it to human (psychological, mythological, imaginal, fanciful, and social) interaction, is Jung divinizing the human psyche, or at least part of it, the unconscious? His use of the word "numinous" to apply to an experience of the archetype is congruent with Otto's description of an experience of the "holy," a category of interpretation and valuation peculiar to the sphere of religion.

Jung is careful in some of his statements to separate the psychological and theological dimension of inquiry, claiming that theologians are the only ones who can legitimately speculate about Reality or the Beyond. He states that as a psychologist he can only speak of human psychological experience and claims only to have demonstrated that a God archetype exists in the human psyche. In his theoretical explanation of the concept of God, however, he comes close to collapsing the distinction between the psychological and theological realms. Jung gives religious legitimation to irrational behavior such as "an inexplicable mood, a nervous disorder, or an uncontrollable vice" by equating "autonomous psychic contents" with what has previously been labeled in our culture as divine, or even daemonic.[9]

In the following passage Jung goes even further in conflating psychology and theology:

It is only through the psyche that we can establish that God acts upon us, but we are unable to distinguish whether these actions emanate from God or the unconscious. We cannot tell whether God and the unconscious are two different entities. Both are border-line concepts for transcendental contents.[10]

The admission by Jung of a possible fusion, or at least a possible confusion, of God and the unconscious is crucial for our understanding of how the collective unconscious can serve to legitimate socially constructed roles for women.

On the negative side: the quarrel I have with Jung is with his willingness to consider archetypal phenomena as manifestations of the Divine and with his assertion that we lose something valuable psychologically if we do not see them as such. While a plunge into Jung's theology is outside the scope of this essay, it is enough here to note that Jung's theory confers religious and ontological status on behaviors, moods, and even uncontrollable vices, which can be explained on other grounds, grounds that do not involve us in categories of the sacred as we try to understand ourselves and others, to change our behavior, and to become free from stultifying roles and compulsions.

On the positive side: although the theological underpinnings of Jung's psychology are fundamentally flawed in this way, and although he mixes the levels of psychology, ontology and theology to a confusing degree, his *method* of differentiating oneself from unconscious contents has much to recommend it. It gives us a greater awareness of the unconscious pulls operating on us—greater self-awareness in other words—and a measure of freedom from those irrationalities.

ANIMUS AND ANIMA

Our understanding of archetypes can illuminate the way women's and men's psyches both reflect and conflict with images of women and men given to us by a patriarchal society. In particular, the experience of "being possessed by an archetype" (acting out of an unconscious identification with an archetypal image, so that a man acts like the anima and a woman acts like the animus—both of which are inferior "feminine" and "masculine" ways of acting) when viewed in cultural context, exposes the human tendency to internalize imprisoning and oppressive images. Understood ontologically, as Jung's archetypes often are, the concept has the capacity to imprison us further. Because of his gift for grasping fantasy and dream images, Jung offers a more imaginal description than Freud does of the inner world of women and men bound by a patriarchal culture. Women caught in seemingly isolated individual struggles are acting out the culture-wide struggle of all women to realize their full humanity (one that includes, for example, a strong intellect) in a society which devalues them and offers no complete vision of their possibilities of empowerment.

The anima and the animus are two especially powerful archetypes. Both Emma and Carl Jung used the terms anima and animus to indicate the unconscious contra-sexual element (the anima being the feminine component of the male psyche and the animus the masculine component of the female psyche) in the male and female personalities. These are lopsided concepts given that the cultural positions of men and women differ, with men generally having, and women generally lacking, power and respect. This inequality is not discussed by the Jungs, although Emma Jung comes close to recognizing it. Jung summarizes the distinction between anima and animus as follows:

> If I were to attempt to put in a nutshell the difference between man and woman in this respect, i.e., what it is that characterizes the animus as opposed to the anima, I could only say this: as the anima produces *moods*, so the animus produces *opinions*.[11]

Emma Jung's version of the animus was clearer and less pejorative than C.G. Jung's. She describes the animus in terms more likely to resonate with women's inner experience. For example, with respect to the way in which the animus functions within the female psyche, Emma Jung says:

> The most characteristic manifestation of the animus is not in a configured image (Gestalt) but rather in words (logos also means word). It comes to us as a voice commenting on every situation in which we find ourselves. . . . As far as I have observed, this voice expresses itself chiefly in two ways. First, we hear from it a critical, usually negative comment on every movement, an exact examination of all motives and intentions, which naturally always causes feelings of inferiority, and tends to nip in the bud all initiative and every wish for self-expression. From time to time, this same voice may also dispense exaggerated praise, and the result of these extremes of judgment is that one oscillates to

and fro between the consciousness of complete futility and a blown-up sense of one's own value and importance.[12]

Had Emma Jung gone one step further in her analysis, she would have realized that the animus can emerge as harsh self-criticism in a male voice and that this internal, critical voice is an accurate reflection of the culture's derogatory view of women's motives, intentions, and self-expressions. Since, from a Jungian standpoint, the psyche operates by compensation, the animus' exaggerated praise is the opposite of devaluation. The woman's inner evaluation of herself swings back and forth between these two extremes. But this phenomenon, too, reflects the polarized images of women that our society offers. As many scholars have noted, images of women presented by modern media, as well as in fairy tales, myths and religious stories, tend to be extreme rather than balanced, fragmented rather than holistic.[13]

A positive contribution of Jung's concept of the anima is that it offers us a unique view of the inner world of the male who struggles to accept a side of himself which is devalued by society. It is interesting that no devaluation of the man by his anima like that of the woman by her animus is presented. Rather, the Jungian anima appears to work primarily by seduction (again, a replication of the way in which society has encouraged women to behave).

Carol Christ has astutely observed that "the strength of [Jung's] theory lies in its insight into the psyches and psychic tasks of educated (and culture-creating) white males in Western culture."[14] Christ feels that Jung's eros/logos model does seem to account for white males' under-developed eros function and highly developed intellect, and suggests that the model be kept as a "useful tool for analyzing white males and the culture they have created."[15] I agree with Christ here, and I also think that the archetypal model of the psyche has some value for understanding women as well as men if the model is seen in relationship to society and its values, in other words, if it is contextualized and hence deontologized.

Jung and the Jungians omit from their descriptions of the animus and anima three crucial elements: the ubiquitous nature of patriarchy, the equally ubiquitous and persistent problem of misogyny, and the dialectic relationship between the individual and society.[16] If these three phenomena are explained and incorporated in the Jungian system, we discover a useful description of our culture as it is *experienced inwardly*, and as it is reflected by the psyche in dreams, fantasies, and moods.

Jung not only ontologizes a socially constructed reality, but his emphasis on religion, religious experience and the numinosity of the archetypes also gives divine sanction to psychological experiences that are culturally induced experiences and motifs. These psychological experiences, or images, need to have the divine sanction removed from them.

Naomi Goldenberg has suggested that the Jungian concept of the archetype as an absolute must be discarded or revised.[17] Nonetheless, she thinks that there is much of worth in the general Jungian schema, particularly Jung's understanding of the symbolic reality of religion and of the religious value of inner experience. Goldenberg is helpful in directing our criticism to the concept of the archetype, the central Jungian concept. Without it the Jungian system loses its very foundation.

Feminist readers have asked: Why retain the Jungian model at all? Why bother about its "uniqueness" if the theory is corrupt? Part of the answer is that Jung's psychology does give us a workable view of the unconscious. Jung's understanding of the unconscious is positive and creative in many respects. That this concept has been used, like many others, to reinforce existing stereotypes about women does not warrant throwing out an idea which gives the study of soul some of its soulful dimension. Our understanding of what the unconscious is can be rescued from the notion that it is a stagnant, static eternal entity. Furthermore, the volumes of work Jung did on the collective unconscious do illustrate the ways in which it mirrors the culture. Assimilation and integration of archetypal images can be understood as an experience of wrestling with the demons of a sexist culture. Gender-linked archetypes can be seen as inner representatives of socially sanctioned, seductive but oppressive roles and behavior patterns.

THE ANIMA AND THE FEMININE:
TWO ARCHETYPAL IMAGES ILLUSTRATED

The socially constructed nature of the archetype as it affects women is best illustrated by comparing the concepts of the anima and the feminine. The anima is a component of male psychology, and the feminine a component of female psychology. Although both terms seem to refer in some way to women, "anima" is not synonymous with "the feminine." The anima is the soul-image of men's imaginations which they often project onto real women. Men must disentangle themselves from the anima in order to be able to relate to real women and to allow real women the space to be themselves. The feminine, on the other hand, is a way of perceiving and being in the world as lived out by women. The latter is a social role definition, although it becomes archetypal in Jungian thought. This essential distinction between the anima and the feminine is not always made by Jungians.[18]

Men's experience of the quality of their own souls, according to Jung, is primarily a "feminine" experience—that is, it has an emotional quality which reminds them of what they think women are like. Jung intends to make it clear that the anima is a part of male psychology. This "soul-imago" is composed of three elements. The first is the experience of real, adult women whom the particular man has known; this experience is registered as an "imprint" on his psyche. The second is the man's own femininity, usually repressed; the more repressed his own femininity, the more traditionally feminine his soul-image will be and the more likely it is that the women he is attracted to will carry that projection. ("Carrying the projection," in Jungian terminology, means being the one on whom the image is projected.) The third is an *a priori* category, an archetype, an inherited collective image of women.[19]

Though Jung placed the anima in the male psyche, he frequently mixed a discussion of the anima with a discussion of the psychology of women. In discussing "man's own femininity" he lapsed into talking about actual women. No wonder later readers have had such a hard time deciphering the meaning of the anima. Jung himself alludes to the difficulty of the concept: "I do not expect every reader to grasp right away what is meant by animus and anima."[20]

With respect to the third component of the anima, the *a priori*, or inherited, collective images of women, Jung does not slip into a discussion of real women, but keeps to the issue at hand. While Jung does not equate women with male projections onto them, he does take an androcentric perspective. Female psychology, while mentioned frequently in his writings, always has a clearly derivative character.

Another Jungian, Marie Louise von Franz, in *The Feminine in Fairytales*, provides an example of the way Jungians have confronted and rationalized inconsistencies in Jung's theory such as the ones noted above. Unlike Jung, von Franz seems at least to recognize the mixing of levels as she describes the feminine in fairytales.[21] Von Franz's description has the advantage of clarity on one level—she is undoubtedly correct about the effect of male projections on female behavior and attitudes—but she shows the same androcentric bias found in Jung's writings. Neither does it account for the social element in this interplay. There do not seem to be any accounts of the man's character being shaped and formed by women's animus projections, other than the descriptions of the man who has been plunged into an anima mood because of conversing with a woman's animus.

Like Emma Jung in *Animus and Anima*, von Franz failed to realize that men's projections shape female character and behavior to the great extent they do because women are relatively powerless in society. As Jean Baker Miller shows in *Toward a New Psychology of Women*, dominants have very different psychological characteristics from subordinates, and subordinates absorb much of the dominants' viewpoint because it is the norm. "Tragic confusion arises because subordinates absorb a large part of the untruths created by the dominants."[22]

Much about "women's nature" has crept into what is reputedly a discussion of a component of male psychology, the anima. This mixing means not only that readers must make a continual effort to clarify Jung's ideas, but also that the usefulness of the anima as a concept is seriously undermined. Disparaging comments about women can be found throughout Jung's writing and feminists who examine Jung's theory of the anima in its present state will reject all Jungian statements about female psychology.

If we consider Jung's concept of the anima in light of Otto's description of the numinous, we see that the effect of the numinous is remarkably similar to the feeling of being gripped by an archetypal image. The element of fear, whether it takes the form of dread, awe, horror, or fascination, is important in both. The experience of the anima in men seems to contain all of these elements, and parallels men's attitudes toward women in our culture and toward the feminine element in themselves. In our society men are often alienated from their own emotions and from relationships generally.[23] In this condition, they do indeed project onto women both exalted and debased images of the kind Jung describes and then are captivated by these projections.

The archetypes of the feminine were first elaborated by Toni Wolff, a member of Jung's inner circle. Drawing on Jung's own description of feminine archetypes, Wolff names and describes them: the Mother, the Hetaira, the Amazon, and the Medium. For Wolff, these four archetypal images represent the major ways in which women experience the world. Ann Ulanov explains this tetralogy in *The Feminine in Jungian Psychology and Christian Theology:*

> These fundamental archetypal forms of the feminine are described in the myths and legends of all cultures throughout history, as for example in the recurrent tales of the princess, the maiden, the wise woman, the witch, etc. In our everyday speech, when we describe women we know or know about, we often resort to typing them, unconsciously using archetypal imagery. Common examples are the references to a woman as "a witch," "a man-eater," and so forth. The archetypal forms of the feminine describe certain basic ways of channeling one's feminine instincts and one's orientation to cultural factors. They also indicate the type of woman one is or the type of anima personality a man is likely to develop.[24]

Notice that in this passage certain social categories are unquestionably accepted as categories of Being. The feminine, a social role definition and a way of relating to the world, has acquired ontological status. Moreover, archetypes of the feminine, with their aura of the numinous, have entered the dimension of religious experience. They have become part of the meaningful order, or nomos, that is "imposed upon the discrete experiences and meanings of individuals." "It may now be understandable if the proposition is made that the socially constructed world is, above all, an ordering of experience."[25] Role definitions and behaviors as well as neurotic character types have become legitimated by their relationship to the sacred.

According to Berger's framework, it is impossible for human beings to live without a nomos, or an ordering principle in their lives. Society is just such a giver of order, and it follows that socially defined roles which order and legitimate our lives in the social realm also partake of the character of the nomos. Berger's dialectic shows that an individual becomes that which she or he is addressed as being by others. On the other side of the dialectic of identity formation and society lies "anomy," a word Berger took from Durkheim's "anomie" but spells in the Anglo-American manner. "Anomy" means "loss of order." At its most extreme, anomy leads to disintegration, fragmentation, and chaos; on an individual level this can mean mental illness, suicide, or extreme anguish. These are the consequences, Berger believes, of trying to live outside of the social order (nomos).

A possible way of confronting the experience of nothingness is to attempt to live outside nomic structures which legitimate damaging or limiting social roles and identity concepts. The experience of nothingness must surely be the consequence of stepping outside the parameters of the ongoing conversation. In spite of the risk of anomy, feminists must dare to step outside of the nomizing conversation. On the other hand, all of the works cited, as well as Jung's, understand the inherent human need for order. Feminists, being human, do not escape this need.

What, then, is a possible solution? Goldenberg suggests the breaking down of mental hierarchies; Daly proposes the radical bond-breaking bonding between women; Miller stresses the need for the courage to embrace conflict with men, with other women, and with outworn self-images whose fraudulent hold on our psyches nonetheless exerts a formidable grip. All of these are signposts. None of these is a total solution. We do not and cannot know the full direction in which we are moving, as we continue to see through and reject nomic solutions with sexist implications.

NOTES

1. See Goldenberg, "Feminist Critique of Jung," *Signs* 2/2 (1976): 443–49." Also see Goldenberg, "Archetypal Theory after Jung"; Carol Christ, "Some Comments on Jung, Jungians and the Study of Women," *Anima* 3, No. 2 (Spring Equinox, 1977), 68–69; Goldenberg, "Feminism and Jungian Theory," *Anima* 3, No. 2 (Spring Equinox, 1977), 14–18. Responses to Christ and Goldenberg can be found in *Anima* 4, No. 1 (Fall Equinox, 1977).

2. Peter L. Berger and Thomas Luckmann, *The Social Construction of Reality: A Treatise in the Sociology of Knowledge* (Garden City, N.Y.: Doubleday, 1967); Berger, *The Sacred Canopy: Elements of a Sociological Theory of Religion* (Garden City, N.Y.: Doubleday, 1976).

3. Berger, *Sacred Canopy*, 3.

4. Berger, *Sacred Canopy*, 5.

5. Berger, *Sacred Canopy*, 8–9.

6. Jung, *CW* IX, Part I, par. 91.

7. Jung, *Memories*, 392–393.

8. Rudolf Otto, *The Idea of the Holy* (N.Y.: Oxford Univ. Press, 1958), 1.

9. Jung, *CW* VII, pars. 400, 403.

10. Jung, *Memories*, 395.

11. C.G. Jung, *CW* VII, par. 331.

12. Emma Jung, *Animus and Anima: Two Essays* (Zurich: Spring 1974), 20.

13. See, for example, Sarah Pomeroy, *Goddesses, Whores, Wives, and Slaves* (N.Y.: Schocken, 1975) and Sheila M. Rothman, *Woman's Proper Place* (N.Y.: Basic, 1978).

14. Christ, "Some Comments," 68.

15. *Ibid.*

16. Jung and Jungians are not totally unaware of these three social facts. For them, however, social reality is always derived from the psychic (i.e., archetypal) level and is always of secondary importance.

17. Goldenberg, "Feminist Critique."

18. Some of the authors who do make the distinction are Christ, "Some Comments," Whitmont, *Symbolic Quest*, and Ann Ulanov, *The Feminine in Jungian Psychology and in Christian Theology* (Evanston, Ill.: Northwestern Univ. Press, 1971).

19. Jung, *CW* VII, pars. 296–301.

20. Jung, *CW* VII, par. 340.

21. Marie Louise von Franz, *The Feminine in Fairytales* (Zurich: Spring 1972), 1–2.

22. Jean Baker Miller, *Toward a New Psychology of Women* (Boston: Beacon, 1976), 11.

23. They do not rate relatedness high on a scale of values. See Carol Gilligan, "In a Different Voice," *Harvard Education Review* 47, No. 4, 481–516.

24. Ulanov, *The Feminine*, 195.

25. Berger, *Sacred Canopy*, 19.

Section III

Characteristics of Religious Development

   This book aims to listen as carefully to women's experience as it does to men's; therefore, this section includes classical and contemporary models of religious development written by both women and men.

   Each selection characterizes religious development in ways compatible with the feminist conclusions about human development presented in Section II. Each author sees the goal of religious development as deep love: an inclusive love for God, others, and oneself. Feminist psychologists promote the same goal for human development: the capacity for authentic love, for genuine intimacy.

   The criterion for human maturity, according to feminist psychologists, is an integration of both attachment and independence, of both autonomy and relationship. Do the religious authors agree that both of these elements are part of the standard of religious maturity? They explicitly agree that the norm of religious maturity is relationship. The ability to sustain a wide range of loving relationships typifies the religiously mature person. I believe they agree also with the need for autonomy or self-direction, yet only the contemporary sources use this language. Agreement in the classical sources is implicit, yet clear, I believe, when one examines their description of religious maturity as the fruit of a strenuous human process. Each selection here speaks of maturity as the result of developmental phases which require love even in darkness, loneliness, or misunderstanding. This lack of consolation which throws one back upon one's deepest inner resources is, I believe, the atmosphere which can promote what contemporary language calls autonomy, or what classical language calls perseverance or fidelity to one's inner calling. It

175

can also promote depression if one has not been helped to have deep inner resources (i.e., a sense of identity as loved for oneself).

Nevertheless, this recognition of the importance of personal autonomy has seldom been taught to Christian women. Rather, as the essays in Section II reveal, women have been educated to find the meaning of themselves primarily in terms of relationships. Yet they have not had sufficient encouragement in the direction of autonomy or independence, nor have they been helped to see the dangers inherent in a self that finds its meaning only in relationships. Religious models of development so emphasize the value of loving relationships, they are used too often to reinforce motifs of women's "self-sacrifice." This simply reinforces conformity to male-approved roles unless the praise for self-sacrifice is coupled with insistence on developing a self that is also appropriately independent.

These selections from longer works have been edited to feature their two criteria for maturity. They explicitly maintain the primacy of relationship, yet they also teach, often only implicitly, the necessity of free choice, of self-directed action. This latter theme is most evident in their discussion of discernment, of fidelity in darkness, of perseverance when one feels no consolation. For it is this struggle to sustain authentic love that enables a person to experience both ultimate dependence on God and empowerment by God. What is important for women is this conviction that God's Spirit affirms their self-direction as well as their surrender. What is essential for mature religious living is the conviction that *only* an independent self can give authentic self-surrender.

The Dialogue (Truth and Love)

Catherine of Siena

5

The willing desire to suffer every pain and hardship even to the point of death for the salvation of souls is very pleasing to me. The more you bear, the more you show your love for me. In loving me you come to know more of my truth, and the more you know, the more intolerable pain and sorrow you will feel when I am offended.

You asked for suffering, and you asked me to punish you for the sins of others. What you were not aware of was that you were, in effect, asking for love and light and knowledge of the truth. For I have already told you that suffering and sorrow increase in proportion to love: When love grows, so does sorrow. So I say to you: Ask and it shall be given to you;[10] I will not say no to anyone who asks in truth. Consider that the soul's love in divine charity is so joined with perfect patience that the one cannot leave without the other. The soul, therefore, who chooses to love me must also choose to suffer for me anything at all that I give her. Patience is not proved except in suffering, and patience is one with charity, as has been said. Endure courageously, then. Otherwise you will not show yourselves to be—nor will you be—faithful spouses and children of my Truth, nor will you show that your delight is in my honor and in the salvation of souls.

6

I would have you know that every virtue of yours and every vice is put into action by means of your neighbors. If you hate me, you harm your neighbors and yourself as well (for you are your chief neighbor), and the harm is both general and particular.

I say general because it is your duty to love your neighbors as your own self.[11] In love you ought to help them spiritually with prayer and counsel, and assist them spiritually and materially in their need—at least with your good will if you have nothing else. If you do not love me you do not love your neighbors, nor will you help those you do not love. But it is yourself you harm most, because you deprive yourself of grace. And you harm your neighbors by depriving them of the prayer and loving desires you should be offering to me on their behalf. Every help you give them ought to come from the affection you bear them for love of me.

In the same way, every evil is done by means of your neighbors, for you cannot love them[12] if you do not love me. This lack of charity for me and for your neighbors is the source of all evils, for if you are not doing good you are necessarily doing evil. And to whom is this evil shown and done? First of all to yourself and then to your neighbors—not to me, for you cannot harm me except insofar as I count whatever you do to them as done to me.[13] You do yourself the harm of sin itself, depriving yourself of grace, and there is nothing worse you can do. You harm your neighbors by not giving them the pleasure of the love and charity you owe them, the love with which you ought to be helping them by offering me your prayer and holy desire on their behalf. Such is the general help that you ought to give to every reasoning creature.

9

If a soul were to do penance without discernment,[25] that is, if her love were centered mainly on the penance she had undertaken, it would be a hindrance to her perfection. But let her center be in affectionate love, with a holy hatred of herself, with true humility and perfect patience. In hungry desire for my honor and the salvation of souls let her attend to those interior virtues which give proof that her will is dead and her sensuality is continually being slain by the affection of love for virtue. She should be discerning in her penance, with her love fixed more on virtue than on the penance. For penance ought to be undertaken as a means to growth in virtue, according to the measure of one's need as well as one's capability.

Otherwise, if penance becomes the foundation, it becomes a hindrance to perfection. Being done without the discerning light of the knowledge of oneself and of my goodness, it would fall short of my truth. It would be undiscerning, not loving what I most love and not hating what I most hate. For discernment is nothing else but the true knowledge a soul ought to have of herself and of me, and through this knowledge she finds her roots. It is joined to charity like an engrafted shoot.

Charity, it is true, has many offshoots, like a tree with many branches. But what gives life to both the tree and its branches is its root, so long as that root is planted in the soil of humility. For humility is the governess and wet nurse of the charity into which this branch of discernment is engrafted. Now the source of humility, as I have already told you, is the soul's true knowledge of herself and of my goodness. So only when discernment is rooted in humility is it virtuous, producing life-giving fruit and willingly yielding what is due to everyone.

In the first place, the soul gives glory and praise to my name for the graces and gifts she knows she has received from me. And to herself she gives what she sees herself deserving of. She knows that all that she is and every gift she has is from me, not from herself, and to me she attributes all. In fact, she considers herself worthy of punishment for her ingratitude in the face of so many favors, and negligent in her use of the time and graces I have given her. So she repays herself with contempt and regret for her sins. Such is the work of the virtue of discernment, rooted in self-knowledge and true humility.

Without this humility, as I have said, the soul would be without discernment. For lack of discernment is set in pride, just as discernment is set in humility. A soul without discernment would, like a thief, rob me of my honor and bestow it on herself for her own glory. And what was her own doing she would blame on me, grumbling and complaining about my mysterious ways with her and with the rest of my creatures, constantly finding cause for scandal in me and in her neighbors.

Not so those who have the virtue of discernment. These give what is due to me and to themselves. And then they give their neighbors what is due them: first of all, loving charity[26] and constant humble prayer—your mutual debt—and the debt of teaching, and the example of a holy and honorable life, and the counsel and help they need for their salvation.

If you have this virtue, then whatever your state in life may be—whether noble or superior or subject—all that you do for your neighbors will be done with discernment and loving charity. For discernment and charity are engrafted together and planted in the soil of that true humility which is born of self-knowledge.

10

Do you know how these three virtues exist?

Imagine a circle traced on the ground, and in its center a tree sprouting with a shoot grafted into its side. The tree finds its nourishment in the soil within the expanse of the circle, but uprooted from the soil it would die fruitless. So think of the soul as a tree made for love and living only by love. Indeed, without this divine love, which is true and perfect charity, death would be her fruit instead of life. The circle in which this tree's root, the soul's love, must grow is true knowledge of herself, knowledge that is joined to me, who like the circle have neither beginning nor end. You can go round and round within this circle, finding neither end nor beginning, yet never leaving the circle. This knowledge of yourself, and of me within yourself, is grounded in the soil of true humility, which is as great as the expanse of the circle (which is the knowledge of yourself united with me, as I have said). But if your knowledge of yourself were isolated from me there would be no full circle at all. Instead, there would be a beginning in self-knowledge, but apart from me it would end in confusion.

So the tree of charity is nurtured in humility and branches out in true discernment. The marrow of the tree (that is, loving charity within the soul) is patience, a sure sign that I am in her and that she is united with me.

This tree, so delightfully planted, bears many-fragranced blossoms of virtue. Its fruit is grace for the soul herself and blessing for her neighbors in proportion to the conscientiousness of those who would share my servants' fruits. To me this tree yields the fragrance of glory and praise to my name, and so it does what I created it for and comes at last to its goal, to me, everlasting Life, life that cannot be taken from you against your will.

And every fruit produced by this tree is seasoned with discernment, and this unites them all, as I have told you.[27]

26

Then God eternal, to stir up even more that soul's love for the salvation of souls, responded to her:

Before I show you what I want to show you, and what you asked to see, I want to describe the bridge for you.[1] I have told you that it stretches from heaven to earth by reason of my having joined myself with your humanity, which I formed from the earth's clay.

This bridge, my only-begotten Son, has three stairs. Two of them he built on the wood of the most holy cross, and the third even as he tasted the great bitterness of the gall and vinegar they gave him to drink. You will recognize in these three stairs three spiritual stages.

The first stair is the feet, which symbolize the affections. For just as the feet carry the body, the affections carry the soul. My Son's nailed feet are a stair by which you can climb to his side, where you will see revealed his inmost heart.[2] For when the soul has climbed up on the feet of affection and looked with her mind's eye into my Son's opened heart, she begins to feel the love of her own heart in his consummate and unspeakable love. (I say consummate because it is not for his own good that he loves you; you cannot do him any good, since he is one with me.) Then the soul, seeing how tremendously she is loved, is herself filled to overflowing with love. So, having climbed the second stair, she reaches the third. This is his mouth, where she finds peace from the terrible war she has had to wage because of her sins.

NOTES

Excerpt 5
10. Mk. 11:24.
Excerpt 6
11. Lv. 19:18: Mk. 12:33.
12. *Non è nella caritá sua.*
13. Mt. 25:40.

Excerpt 9

25. Catherine uses *discrezione* and its related forms. I have translated "discernment" in agreement with Meattini (*Il Libro*, pp. 23, 50); Cavallini (in her preface to *Il Messagio di S. Caterina da Siena*, pp. xv–xvi); K. Foster ("Saint Catherine's Teaching on Christ," *Life of the Spirit* 16 (1962): 315; *Dictionnaire de Spiritualité* 3, c. 1258–1260, 1311–1326.

26. Cf. Rm. 13:8: "Avoid getting into debt, except the debt of mutual love."

Excerpt 10

27. Cf. also ch. 31, 113, where Catherine contrasts the "tree of love" with the "tree of death" planted on the mountain of pride.

Excerpt 26

1. The basic image of the bridge may well be drawn from Gregory the Great, but Catherine builds it up with a wealth of detail apparently original to her. She may have had in mind a bridge such as that she had seen spanning the River Arno in Florence, a walled bridge complete with shops along its sides.

2. Cf. A.M. Walz, "Il segreto del cuore di Criso nella spiritualità cateriniana," *Studii domenicani* (Rome, 1939).

The Book of Her Life
("The Four Waters")

Teresa of Avila

CHAPTER 11

Tells of the reason for the failure to reach the perfect love of God in a short time. Begins to explain through a comparison four degrees of prayer. Goes on to deal here with the first degree. The doctrine is very beneficial for beginners and for those who do not have consolations in prayer.

1. Well, let us speak now of those who are beginning to be servants of love. This doesn't seem to me to mean anything else than to follow resolutely by means of this path of prayer Him who has loved us so much. To be a servant of love is a dignity so great that it delights me in a wonderful way to think about it. For servile fear soon passes away if in this first state we proceed as we ought. O Lord of my soul and my good! When a soul is determined to love You by doing what it can to leave all and occupy itself better in this divine love, why don't You desire that it enjoy soon the ascent to the possession of perfect love? I have poorly expressed myself. I should have mentioned and complained that we ourselves do not desire this. The whole fault is ours if we don't soon reach the enjoyment of a dignity so great, for the perfect attainment of this true love of God brings with it every blessing. We are so miserly and so slow in giving ourselves entirely to God that since His Majesty does not desire that we enjoy something as precious as this without paying a high price, we do not fully prepare ourselves.

183

6. I shall have to make use of some comparison, although I should like to excuse myself from this since I am a woman and write simply what they ordered me to write. But these spiritual matters for anyone who like myself has not gone through studies are so difficult to explain. I shall have to find some mode of explaining myself, and it may be less often that I hit upon a good comparison. Seeing so much stupidity will provide some recreation for your Reverence.

It seems now to me that I read or heard of this comparison—for since I have a bad memory, I don't know where or for what reason it was used; but it will be all right for my purposes. The beginner must realize that in order to give delight to the Lord he is starting to cultivate a garden on very barren soil, full of abominable weeds. His Majesty pulls up the weeds and plants good seed. Now let us keep in mind that all of this is already done by the time a soul is determined to practice prayer and has begun to make use of it. And with the help of God we must strive like good gardeners to get these plants to grow and take pains to water them so that they don't wither but come to bud and flower and give forth a most pleasant fragrance to provide refreshment for this Lord of ours. Then He will often come to take delight in this garden and find His joy among these virtues.

7. But let us see now how it must be watered so that we may understand what we have to do, the labor this will cost us, whether the labor is greater than the gain, and for how long it must last. It seems to me the garden can be watered in four ways. You may draw water from a well (which is for us a lot of work). Or you may get it by means of a water wheel and aqueducts in such a way that it is obtained by turning the crank of the water wheel. (I have drawn it this way sometimes—the method involves less work than the other, and you get more water.) Or it may flow from a river or a stream. (The garden is watered much better by this means because the ground is more fully soaked, and there is no need to water so frequently—and much less work for the gardener.) Or the water may be provided by a great deal of rain. (For the Lord waters the garden without any work on our part—and this way is incomparably better than all the others mentioned.)

8. Now, then, these four ways of drawing water in order to maintain this garden—because without water it will die—are what are important to me and have seemed applicable in explaining the

four degrees of prayer in which the Lord in His goodness has sometimes placed my soul. May it please His goodness that I manage to speak about them in a way beneficial for one of the persons who ordered me to write this, because within four months the Lord has brought him further than I got in seventeen years. This person has prepared himself better, and so without any labor of his own the flower garden is watered with all these four waters, although the last is still not given except in drops. But he is advancing in such a way that soon he will be immersed in it, with the help of the Lord. And I shall be pleased if you laugh should this way of explaining the matter appear foolish.

9. Beginners in prayer, we can say, are those who draw water from the well. This involves a lot of work on their own part, as I have said. They must tire themselves in trying to recollect their senses. Since they are accustomed to being distracted, this recollection requires much effort. They need to get accustomed to caring nothing at all about seeing or hearing, to practicing the hours of prayer, and thus to solitude and withdrawal—and to thinking on their past life. Although these beginners and the others as well must often reflect upon their past, the extent to which they must do so varies, as I shall say afterward. In the beginning such reflection is even painful, for they do not fully understand whether or not they are repentant of their sins. If they are, they are then determined to serve God earnestly. They must strive to consider the life of Christ—and the intellect grows weary in doing this.

These are the things we can do of ourselves, with the understanding that we do so by the help of God, for without this help as is already known we cannot have so much as a good thought. These things make up the beginning of fetching water from the well, and please God that it may be found. At least we are doing our part, for we are already drawing it out and doing what we can to water these flowers. God is so good that when for reasons His Majesty knows—perhaps for our greater benefit—the well is dry and we, like good gardeners, do what lies in our power, He sustains the garden without water and makes the virtues grow. Here by "water" I am referring to tears and when there are no tears to interior tenderness and feelings of devotion.

10. But what will he do here who sees that after many days there is nothing but dryness, distaste, vapidness, and very little de-

sire to come to draw water? So little is the desire to do this that if he doesn't recall that doing so serves and gives pleasure to the Lord of the garden, and if he isn't careful to preserve the merits acquired in this service (and even what he hopes to gain from the tedious work of often letting the pail down into the well and pulling it back up without any water), he will abandon everything. It will frequently happen to him that he will even be unable to lift his arms for this work and unable to get a good thought. This discursive work with the intellect is what is meant by fetching water from the well.

But, as I am saying, what will the gardener do here? He will rejoice and be consoled and consider it the greatest favor to be able to work in the garden of so great an Emperor! Since he knows that this pleases the Lord and his intention must be not to please himself but to please the Lord, he gives the Lord much praise. For the Master has confidence in the gardener because he sees that without any pay he is so very careful about what he was told to do. This gardener helps Christ carry the cross and reflects that the Lord lived with it all during His life. He doesn't desire the Lord's kingdom here below or ever abandon prayer. And so he is determined, even though this dryness may last for his whole life, not to let Christ fall with the cross. The time will come when the Lord will repay him all at once. He doesn't fear that the labor is being wasted. He is serving a good Master whose eyes are upon him. He doesn't pay any attention to bad thoughts. He considers that the devil also represented them to St. Jerome in the desert.

11. These labors take their toll. Being myself one who endured them for many years (for when I got a drop of water from this sacred well I thought God was granting me a favor), I know that they are extraordinary. It seems to me more courage is necessary for them than for many other labors of this world. But I have seen clearly that God does not leave one, even in this life, without a large reward; because it is certainly true that one of those hours in which the Lord afterward bestowed on me a taste of Himself repaid, it seems to me, all the anguish I suffered in persevering for a long time in prayer.

I am of the opinion that to some in the beginning and to others afterward the Lord often desires to give these torments and the many other temptations that occur in order to try His lovers and know whether they will be able to drink the chalice and help Him carry the cross before He lays great treasures within them. I believe

His Majesty desires to bring us along this way for our own good so that we may understand well what little we amount to. The favors that come afterward are of such great worth that He desires first that before He gives them to us we see by experience our own worthlessness so that what happened to Lucifer will not happen to us.

12. My Lord, what do You do but that which is for the greater good of the soul You understand now to be Yours and which places itself in Your power so as to follow You wherever You go, even to death on the cross, and is determined to help You bear it and not leave You alone with it?

Whoever sees in himself this determination has no reason, no reason whatsoever, to fear. Spiritual persons, you have no reason to be afflicted. Once you are placed in so high a degree as to desire to commune in solitude with God and abandon the pastimes of the world, the most has been done. Praise His Majesty for that and trust in His goodness who never fails His friends. Conceal from your eyes the thought about why He gives devotion to one after such a few days and not to me after so many years. Let us believe that all is for our own greater good. Let His Majesty lead the way along the path He desires. We belong no longer to ourselves but to Him. He grants us a great favor in wanting us to desire to dig in His garden and be in the presence of its Lord who certainly is present with us. Should He desire that for some these plants and flowers grow by the water they draw, which He gives from this well, and for others without it, what difference does that make to me? Do, Lord, what You desire. May I not offend You. Don't let the virtues be lost, if You only out of Your goodness have already given me some. I desire to suffer, Lord, since You suffered. Let Your will be done in me in every way, and may it not please Your Majesty that something as precious as Your love be given to anyone who serves you only for the sake of consolations.

13. It should be carefully noted—and I say this because I know it through experience—that the soul that begins to walk along this path of mental prayer with determination and that can succeed in paying little attention to whether this delight and tenderness is lacking or whether the Lord gives it (or to whether it has much consolation or no consolation) has travelled a great part of the way. However much it stumbles, it should not fear that it will turn back, because the building has been started on a solid foundation. This is

true because the love of God does not consist in tears or in this delight and tenderness, which for the greater part we desire and find consolation in; but it consists in serving with justice and fortitude of soul and in humility. Without such service it seems to me we would be receiving everything and giving nothing.

14. In the case of a poor little woman like myself, weak and with hardly any fortitude, it seems to me fitting that God lead me with gifts, as He now does, so that I might be able to suffer some trials He has desired me to bear. But when I see servants of God, men of prominence, learning, and high intelligence make so much fuss because God doesn't give them devotion, it annoys me to hear them. I do not mean that they shouldn't accept it if God gives it, and esteem it, because then His Majesty sees that this is appropriate. But when they don't have devotion, they shouldn't weary themselves. They should understand that since His Majesty doesn't give it, it isn't necessary; and they should be masters of themselves. They should believe that their desire for consolation is a fault. I have experienced and seen this. They should believe it denotes imperfection together with a lack of freedom of spirit and the courage to accomplish something.

15. Although I lay great stress on this because it is very important that beginners have such freedom and determination, I am not saying it so much for beginners as for others. For there are many who begin, yet they never reach the end. I believe this is due mainly to a failure to embrace the cross from the beginning; thinking they are doing nothing, they become afflicted. When the intellect ceases to work, they cannot bear it. But it is then perhaps that their will is being strengthened and fortified, although they may not be aware of this.

We should think that the Lord is not concerned about these inabilities. Even though they seem to us to be faults, they are not. His Majesty already knows our misery and our wretched nature better than we do ourselves, and He knows that these souls now desire to think of Him and love Him always. This determination is what He desires. The other affliction that we bring upon ourselves serves for nothing else than to disquiet the soul, and if it was incapable before of engaging in prayer for one hour, it will be so now for four. Very often this incapacity comes from some bodily disorder. I have a great deal of experience in this matter, and I know that what I say is true because I have considered it carefully and discussed it afterward with spiritual persons. We are so miserable that our poor little imprisoned soul shares in the miseries of the body; the changes in the weather and the rotating of the bodily humors often have the result that without their fault souls cannot do what they desire, but suffer in every way. If they seek to force themselves more during these times, the bad condition becomes worse and lasts longer. They should use discernment to observe when these bodily disorders may be the cause, and not smother the poor soul. They should understand that they are sick. The hour of prayer ought to be changed, and often this change will have to continue for some days. Let them suffer this exile as best they can. It is a great misfortune to a soul that loves God to see that it lives in this misery and cannot do what it desires because it has as wretched a guest as is this body.

16. I have said they should use discernment because sometimes the devil is the cause. And so it isn't always good to abandon prayer when there is great distraction and disturbance in the intellect just as it isn't always good to torture the soul into doing what it cannot do.

There are other exterior things like works of charity and spiritual reading, although at times it will not even be fit for these. Let it then serve the body out of love of God—because many other times the body serves the soul—and engage in some spiritual pastimes such as holy conversations, provided they are truly so, or going to the country, as the confessor might counsel. Experience is a great help in all, for it teaches what is suitable for us; and God can be served in everything. His yoke is easy, and it is very helpful not to drag the soul along, as they say, but to lead it gently for the sake of its greater advantage.

17. So I return to the advice—and even if I repeat it many times this doesn't matter—that it is very important that no one be distressed or afflicted over dryness or noisy and distracting thoughts. If a person wishes to gain freedom of spirit and not be always troubled, let him begin by not being frightened by the cross, and he will see how the Lord also helps him carry it and he will gain satisfaction and profit from everything. For, clearly, if the well is dry, we cannot put water into it. True, we must not become neglectful; when there is water we should draw it out because then the Lord desires to multiply the virtues by this means.

CHAPTER 13

14. The beginner needs counsel so as to see what helps him most. For this reason a master is very necessary providing he has experience. If he doesn't, he can be greatly mistaken and lead a soul without understanding it nor allowing it to understand itself. For since it sees that there is great merit in being subject to a master, it doesn't dare depart from what he commands it. I have come upon souls intimidated and afflicted for whom I felt great pity because the one who taught them had no experience; and there was one person who didn't know what to do with herself. Since they do not understand spiritual things, these masters afflict soul and body and obstruct progress. One of these souls spoke to me about a master who held her bound for eight years and wouldn't let her go beyond self knowledge; the Lord had already brought her to the prayer of quiet, and so she suffered much tribulation.

15. This path of self knowledge must never be abandoned, nor is there on this journey a soul so much a giant that it has no need to return often to the stage of an infant and a suckling. And this should never be forgotten. Perhaps I shall speak of it more often because it is very important. There is no stage of prayer so sublime that it isn't necessary to return often to the beginning. Along this path of prayer, self knowledge and the thought of one's sins is the bread with which all palates must be fed no matter how delicate they may be; they cannot be sustained without this bread. It must be eaten within bounds, nonetheless. Once a soul sees that it is now submissive and understands clearly that it has nothing good of itself and is aware both of being ashamed before so great a King and of repaying so little of the great amount it owes Him—what need is there to waste time here? We must go on to other things that the Lord places before us; and there is no reason to leave them aside, for His Majesty knows better than we what is fitting for us to eat.

22. I have wandered greatly from the subject I began to speak about. But everything is a subject for beginners that their journey on so lofty a road might begin on the true road. Now returning to what I was saying about Christ bound at the pillar: it is good to reflect awhile and think about the pains He suffered there, and why, and who He is, and the love with which He suffered them. But one

should not always weary oneself in seeking these reflections but just remain there in His presence with the intellect quiet. And if a person is able he should occupy himself in looking at Christ who is looking at him, and he should speak, and petition, and humble himself, and delight in the Lord's presence, and remember that he is unworthy of being there. When he can do this, even though it may be at the beginning of prayer, he will derive great benefit; and this manner of prayer has many advantages—at least my soul derived them.

I don't know if I have been successful in speaking about this. Your Reverence will be the judge. May it please the Lord that I succeed in always giving Him pleasure, amen.

CHAPTER 14

Begins to explain the second degree of prayer in which the Lord now starts to give the soul a more special kind of consolation. Explains how this experience is supernatural. This matter is worth noting.

1. It has been explained now how the garden is watered by labor and the use of one's arms, drawing the water up from the well. Let us speak now of the second manner, ordained by the Lord of the garden, for getting water; that is, by turning the crank of a water wheel and by aqueducts, the gardener obtains more water with less labor; and he can rest without having to work constantly. Well, this method applied to what they call the prayer of quiet is what I now want to discuss.

2. Here the soul begins to be recollected and comes upon something supernatural because in no way can it acquire this prayer through any efforts it may make. True, at one time it seemingly got tired turning the crank, and working with the intellect, and filling the aqueducts. But here the water is higher, and so the labor is much less than that required in pulling it up from the well. I mean that the water is closer because grace is more clearly manifest to the soul.

In this prayer the faculties are gathered within so as to enjoy that satisfaction with greater delight. But they are not lost, nor do they sleep. Only the will is occupied in such a way that, without

knowing how, it becomes captive; it merely consents to God allowing Him to imprison it as one who well knows how to be the captive
of its lover. O Jesus and my Lord! How valuable is Your love to us
here! It holds our love so bound that it doesn't allow it the freedom
during that time to love anything else but You.

3. The other two faculties help the will to be capable of enjoying so much good—although sometimes it happens that even though
the will is united, they are very unhelpful. But then it shouldn't pay
any attention to them; rather it should remain in its joy and quietude. Because if the will desires to gather in these faculties, they both
get lost. They are like doves that are dissatisfied with the food the
owner of the dovecot gives them without their having to work. They
go to look for food elsewhere, but they find it so scarce that they
return. And thus these faculties go away and then come back to see
if the will might give them what it enjoys. If the Lord desires to
throw them some food, they stop; and if not, they return to their
search. And they must think they are benefiting the will; and sometimes in desiring the memory or imagination to represent to the will
what they're enjoying, they do the will harm. Well, then, be advised
to behave toward them as I shall explain.

4. All this that takes place here brings with it the greatest consolation and with so little labor that prayer does not tire one, even
though it lasts for a long while. The intellect's work here is very slow
paced, and it obtains a lot more water than it pulled out of the well.
The tears God gives are now accompanied by joy; however, although
they are experienced, there is no striving for them.

5. This water of great blessings and favors that the Lord gives
here makes the virtues grow incomparably better than in the previous degree of prayer, for the soul is now ascending above its
misery and receiving a little knowledge of the delights of glory. This
water I believe makes the virtues grow better and also brings the
soul much closer to the true Virtue, which is God, from whence
come all the virtues. His Majesty is beginning to communicate Himself to this soul, and He wants it to experience how He is doing
so.

In arriving here it begins soon to lose its craving for earthly
things—and little wonder! It sees clearly that one moment of the enjoyment of glory cannot be experienced here below, neither are there
riches, or sovereignties, or honors, or delights that are able to pro-

vide a brief moment of that happiness, for it is a true happiness that, it is seen, satisfies us. In earthly things it would seem to me a marvel were we ever to understand just where we can find this satisfaction, for there is never lacking in these earthly things both the "yes" and the "no." During the time of this prayer, everything is "yes." The "no" comes afterward upon seeing that the delight is ended and that one cannot recover it nor does one know how. Were someone to crush himself with penances and prayer and all the rest, it would profit him little if the Lord did not desire to give this delight. God in His greatness desires that this soul understand that He is so close it no longer needs to send Him messengers but can speak with Him itself and not by shouting since He is so near that when it merely moves its lips, He understands it.

6. It seems impertinent to say this since we know that God always understands us and is with us. There is no doubt about this understanding and presence. But our Emperor and Lord desires that in this prayer we know that He understands us, and what His presence does, and that He wants to begin to work in the soul in a special way. All of this that the Lord desires is manifest in the great interior and exterior satisfaction He gives the soul and in the difference there is, as I said, between this delight and happiness and the delights of earth, for this delight seems to fill the void that through our sins we have caused in the soul. This satisfaction takes place in its very intimate depths, and the soul doesn't know where the satisfaction comes from or how, nor frequently does it know what to do or what to desire or what to ask for. It seems it has found everything at once and doesn't know what it has found.

Nor do I know how to explain this experience because for so many things learning is necessary. Here it would be helpful to explain well the difference between a general and a particular grace— for there are many who are ignorant of this difference—and how the Lord desires that the soul in this prayer almost see with its own eyes, as they say, this particular grace. Learning is also required to explain many other things, which I perhaps did not express correctly. But since what I say is going to be checked by persons who will recognize any error, I'm not worrying about it. In matters of theology as well as in those of the spirit I know that I can be mistaken; yet, since this account will end in good hands, these learned men will understand and remove what is erroneous.

CHAPTER 15

Continues on the same subject and gives some advice about how to act in this prayer of quiet. Discusses the fact that many souls reach this prayer but few pass beyond. Knowledge of the things touched on here is very necessary and beneficial.

1. Now let's return to the subject. This quietude and recollection is something that is clearly felt through the satisfaction and peace bestowed on the soul, along with great contentment and calm and a very gentle delight in the faculties. It seems to the soul, since it hasn't gone further, that there's nothing left to desire and that it should willingly say with St. Peter that it will make its dwelling there. It dares not move or stir, for it seems that good will slip through its hands—nor would it even want to breathe sometimes. The poor little thing doesn't understand that since by its own efforts it can do nothing to draw that good to itself, so much less will it be able to keep it for longer than the Lord desires.

I have already mentioned that in this first recollection and quiet the soul's faculties do not cease functioning. But the soul is so satisfied with God that as long as the recollection lasts, the quiet and calm are not lost since the will is united with God even though the two faculties are distracted; in fact, little by little the will brings the intellect and the memory back to recollection. Because even though the will may not be totally absorbed, it is so well occupied, without knowing how, that no matter what efforts the other two faculties make, they cannot take away its contentment and joy. But rather with hardly any effort the will is gradually helped so that this little spark of love of God may not go out.

2. May it please His Majesty to give me grace to explain this state well because there are many, many souls who reach it but few that pass beyond; and I don't know whose fault it is. Most surely God does not fail, for once His Majesty has granted a soul the favor of reaching this stage, I don't believe He will fail to grant it many more favors unless through its own fault.

It is very important that the soul reaching this stage realize the great dignity of its state and the great favor the Lord has bestowed on it and how with good reason it must not belong to the earth because it now seems His goodness will make it a citizen of heaven, provided it doesn't stop through its own fault; and unhappy it will be if it turns back. I think turning back would mean falling to the bottom, as I was doing, if the mercy of the Lord hadn't rescued me. For the most part, in my opinion, this turning back will come through serious faults; nor is it possible to leave so much good without the blindness caused by much evil.

3. Thus, for the love of the Lord, I beg those whom His Majesty has so highly favored in the attainment of this state that they understand it and esteem it with a humble and holy confidence so as not to return to the fleshpots of Egypt. If through weakness and wickedness and a miserable nature they should fall, as I did, let them keep ever in mind the good they have lost and be suspicious and walk with the fear—for they are right in doing so—that if they don't return to prayer, they will go from bad to worse. What I call a true fall is abhorrence of the path by which one gained so much good; and to these souls I am speaking. For I am not saying that they should never offend God or fall into sin, although it would be right for anyone who has begun to receive these favors to be very much on guard against sinning; but we are miserable creatures. What I advise strongly is not to abandon prayer, for in prayer a person will understand what he is doing and win repentance from the Lord and fortitude to lift himself up. And you must believe that if you give up prayer, you are, in my opinion, courting danger. I don't know if I understand what I'm saying because, as I said, I'm judging by myself.

4. This prayer, then, is a little spark of the Lord's true love which He begins to enkindle in the soul; and He desires that the soul grow in the understanding of what this love accompanied by delight is. For anyone who has experience, it is impossible not to understand soon that this little spark cannot be acquired. Yet, this nature of ours is so eager for delights that it tries everything; but it is quickly left cold because however much it may desire to light the fire and obtain this delight, it doesn't seem to be doing anything else than throwing water on it and killing it. If this quietude and recollection and little spark is from God's spirit and not a delight given by the devil or procured by ourselves, it will be noticed no matter how small it is. And if a person doesn't extinguish it through his own

fault, it is what will begin to enkindle the large fire that (as I shall mention in its place) throws forth flames of the greatest love of God which His Majesty gives to perfect souls.

6. What the soul must do during these times of quiet amounts to no more than proceeding gently and noiselessly. What I call noise is running about with the intellect looking for many words and reflections so as to give thanks for this gift and piling up one's sins and faults in order to see that the gift is unmerited. Everything is motion here; the intellect is representing, and the memory hurrying about. For certainly these faculties tire me out from time to time; and although I have a poor memory, I cannot subdue it. The will calmly and wisely must understand that one does not deal well with God by force and that our efforts are like the careless use of large pieces of wood which smother this little spark. One should realize this and humbly say: "Lord, what am I capable of here? What has the servant to do with the Lord—or earth with heaven?" Or other words that at this time come to mind out of love and well grounded in the knowledge that what is said is the truth. And one should pay no attention to the intellect, for it is a grinding mill. The will may desire to share what it enjoys or may work to recollect the intellect, for often it will find itself in this union and calm while the intellect wanders about aimlessly. It is better that the will leave the intellect alone than go after it, and that it remain like a wise bee in the recollection and in enjoyment of that gift. For if no bee were to enter the beehive and each were employed in going after the other, no honey could be made.

14. In the progress they observe in themselves they will know that the devil is not the cause if, even though they fall again, there remains a sign that the Lord was present in their prayer; and it is that they rise again quickly. There are other signs as well which I shall now mention. When the prayer comes from God's spirit, there is no need to go dredging up things in order to derive some humility and shame because the Lord Himself gives this prayer in a manner very different from that which we gain through our nice little reasonings. For such humility is nothing in comparison with the true humility the Lord with His light here teaches and which causes an embarrassment that undoes one. It is well known that God gives a

knowledge that makes us realize we have no good of ourselves; and the greater the favors, the greater is this knowledge. He bestows a strong desire to advance in prayer and not abandon it no matter what trial may come upon one. The soul offers itself up in all things. It feels sure, while still being humble and fearing, that it will be saved. He casts out from it all servile fear and grants a more mature trusting fear. It is aware of the beginning of a love of God that has much less self-interest. It desires periods of solitude in order to enjoy that good more.

CHAPTER 16

Treats of the third degree of prayer. Explains sublime matters and what the soul that reaches this stage can do and the effects produced by these great favors of the Lord. This prayer lifts the soul up in the praises of God and brings wonderful consolation to whoever attains it.

1. Let us come now to speak of the third water by which this garden is irrigated, that is, the water flowing from a river or spring. By this means the garden is irrigated with much less labor, although some labor is required to direct the flow of the water. The Lord so desires to help the gardener here that He Himself becomes practically the gardener and the one who does everything.

This prayer is a sleep of the faculties: the faculties neither fail entirely to function nor understand how they function. The consolation, the sweetness, and the delight are incomparably greater than that experienced in the previous prayer. The water of grace rises up to the throat of this soul since it can no longer move forward; nor does it know how; nor can it move backward. It would desire to enjoy the greatest glory. It is like a person who already has the candle in his hand and for whom little time is left before dying the death he desires: he is rejoicing in that agony with the greatest delight describable. This experience doesn't seem to me to be anything else than an almost complete death to all earthly things and an enjoyment of God.

I don't know any other terms for describing it or how to explain it. Nor does the soul then know what to do because it doesn't know whether to speak or to be silent, whether to laugh or to weep. This prayer is a glorious foolishness, a heavenly madness where the true wisdom is learned; and it is for the soul a most delightful way of enjoying.

2. In fact five or even six years ago the Lord often gave me this prayer in abundance, and I didn't understand it; nor did I know how to speak of it. Thus it was my intention, at this point, to say very little or nothing at all. I did understand clearly that it was not a complete union of all the faculties and that this type of prayer was more excellent than the previous one. But I confess that I couldn't discern or understand where the difference lay. I believe that on account of the humility your Reverence has shown in desiring to be helped by as simple-minded a person as myself, the Lord today after Communion granted me this prayer; and interrupting my thanksgiving, He put before me these comparisons, taught me the manner of explaining it, and what the soul must do here. Certainly I was startled and I understood at once. Often I had been as though bewildered and inebriated in this love, and never was I able to understand its nature. I understood clearly that it was God's work, but I couldn't understand how He was working in this stage. For the truth of the matter is that the faculties are almost totally united with God but not so absorbed as not to function. I am extremely pleased that I now understand it. Blessed be the Lord who so favored me!

CHAPTER 18

Discusses the fourth degree of prayer. Begins to offer an excellent explanation of the great dignity the Lord bestows upon the soul in this state. Gives much encouragement to those who engage in prayer that they might strive to attain so high a stage since it can be reached on earth, although not by merit but through God's goodness. This should be read attentively, for the explanation is presented in a very subtle way and there are many noteworthy things.

1. May the Lord teach me the words necessary for explaining something about the fourth water. Clearly His favor is necessary, even more so than for what was explained previously. In the previous prayer, since the soul was conscious of the world, it did not

feel that it was totally dead—for we can speak of this last prayer in such a way. But, as I said, the soul has its senses by which it feels its solitude and understands that it is in the world; and it uses exterior things to make known what it feels, even though this may be through signs.

In all the prayer and modes of prayer that were explained, the gardener does some work, even though in these latter modes the work is accompanied by so much glory and consolation for the soul that it would never want to abandon this prayer. As a result, the prayer is not experienced as work but as glory. In this fourth water the soul isn't in possession of its senses, but it rejoices without understanding what it is rejoicing in. It understands that it is enjoying a good in which are gathered together all goods, but this good is incomprehensible. All the senses are occupied in this joy in such a way that none is free to be taken up with any other exterior or interior thing.

In the previous degrees, the senses are given freedom to show some signs of the great joy they feel. Here in this fourth water the soul rejoices incomparably more; but it can show much less since no power remains in the body, nor does the soul have any power to communicate its joy. At such a time, everything would be a great obstacle and a torment and a hindrance to its repose. And I say that if this prayer is the union of all the faculties, the soul is unable to communicate its joy even though it may desire to do so—I mean while being in the prayer. And if it were able, then this wouldn't be union.

2. How this prayer they call union comes about and what it is, I don't know how to explain. These matters are expounded in mystical theology; I wouldn't know the proper vocabulary. Neither do I understand what the mind is; nor do I know how it differs from the soul or the spirit. It all seems to be the same thing to me, although the soul sometimes goes forth from itself. The way this happens is comparable to what happens when a fire is burning and flaming, and it sometimes becomes a forceful blaze. The flame then shoots very high above the fire, but the flame is not by that reason something different from the fire but the same flame that is in the fire. Your Reverence with your learning will understand this, for I don't know what else to say.

3. What I'm attempting to explain is what the soul feels when it is in this divine union. What union is we already know since it

means that two separate things become one. O my Lord, how good You are! May You be blessed forever! May all things praise You, my God, for You have so loved us that we can truthfully speak of this communication which You engage in with souls even in our exile! And even in the case of those who are good, this still shows great generosity and magnanimity. In fact, it is Your communication, my Lord; and You give it in the manner of who You are. O infinite Largess, how magnificent are Your works! It frightens one whose intellect is not occupied with things of the earth that he has no intellect by which he can understand divine truths. That you bestow such sovereign favors on souls that have offended You so much certainly brings my intellect to a halt; and when I begin to think about this, I'm unable to continue. Where can the intellect go that would not be a turning back since it doesn't know how to give you thanks for such great favors? Sometimes I find it a remedy to speak absurdities.

Signs of Transition in
The Ascent of Mount Carmel

John of the Cross

BOOK II

CHAPTER 13

The signs of recognizing in spiritual persons when they should discontinue discursive meditation and pass on to the state of contemplation.

1. To avoid obscurity in this doctrine it will be opportune to point out in this chapter when one ought to discontinue discursive meditation (a work through images, forms, and figures) so that the practice will not be abandoned sooner or later than required by the spirit. Just as it is fit to abandon it at the proper time that it may not be a hindrance in the journey to God, it is also necessary not to abandon this imaginative meditation before the due time so that there be no regression. For though the apprehensions of these faculties are not a proximate means toward union for proficients, they are a remote means for beginners. By these sensitive means beginners dispose their spirit and habituate it to spiritual things, and at the same time they void their senses of all other base, temporal, secular, and natural forms and images.

Hence we shall delineate some signs and indications by which one can judge whether or not it is the opportune time for the spiritual person to discontinue meditation.

2. The first is the realization that one cannot make discursive

meditation nor receive satisfaction from it as before. Dryness is now the outcome of fixing the senses upon subjects which formerly provided satisfaction. As long as one can, however, make discursive meditation and draw out satisfaction, one must not abandon this method. Meditation must only be discontinued when the soul is placed in that peace and quietude to be spoken of in the third sign.

3. The second sign is an awareness of a disinclination to fix the imagination or sense faculties upon other particular objects, exterior or interior. I am not affirming that the imagination will cease to come and go (even in deep recollection it usually wanders freely), but that the person is disinclined to fix it purposely upon extraneous things.

4. The third and surest sign is that a person likes to remain alone in loving awareness of God, without particular considerations, in interior peace and quiet and repose, and without the acts and exercises (at least discursive, those in which one progresses from point to point) of the intellect, memory and will; and that he prefers to remain only in the general, loving awareness and knowledge we mentioned, without any particular knowledge or understanding.

5. To leave safely the state of meditation and sense and enter that of contemplation and spirit, the spiritual person must observe within himself at least these three signs together.

6. It is insufficient to possess the first without the second. It could be that the inability to imagine and meditate derives from one's dissipation and lack of diligence. The second sign, the disinclination and absence of desire to think about extraneous things, must be present. When this inability to concentrate the imagination and sense faculties upon the things of God proceeds from dissipation and tepidity, there is then a yearning to dwell upon other things and an inclination to give up the meditation.

Neither is the realization of the first and second sign sufficient, if the third sign is not observed together with them. When one is incapable of making discursive meditation upon the things of God and disinclined to consider subjects extraneous to God, the cause could be melancholia or some other kind of humor in the heart or brain capable of producing a certain stupefaction and suspension of the sense faculties. This anomaly would be the explanation for want of thought or of desire and inclination for thought. It would foster in a person the desire to remain in that delightful ravishment.

Because of this danger, the third sign, the loving knowledge and awareness in peace, etc., is necessary.

7. Actually, at the beginning of this state the loving knowledge is almost unnoticeable. There are two reasons for this: first, ordinarily the incipient loving knowledge is extremely subtle and delicate, and almost imperceptible; second, a person who is habituated to the exercise of meditation, which is wholly sensible, hardly perceives or feels this new insensible, purely spiritual experience. This is especially so when through failure to understand it he does not permit himself any quietude, but strives after the other more sensory experience. Although the interior peace is more abundant, the individual allows no room for its experience and enjoyment.

But the more habituated he becomes to this calm, the deeper his experience of the general, loving knowledge of God will grow. This knowledge is more enjoyable than all other things, because without the soul's labor it affords peace, rest, savor, and delight.

The Dark Night

John of the Cross

BOOK I

CHAPTER 9

Signs for discerning whether a spiritual person is treading the path of this sensory night and purgation.

1. Because the origin of these aridities may not be the sensory night and purgation, but sin and imperfection, or weakness and lukewarmness, or some bad humor or bodily indisposition, I will give some signs here for discerning whether the dryness is the result of this purgation or of one of these other defects. I find there are three principal signs for knowing this.

2. The *first* is that as these souls do not get satisfaction or consolation from the things of God, they do not get any out of creatures either. Since God puts a soul in this dark night in order to dry up and purge its sensory appetite, He does not allow it to find sweetness or delight in anything.

Through this sign it can in all likelihood be inferred that this dryness and distaste is not the outcome of newly committed sins and imperfections. If this were so, some inclination or propensity to look for satisfaction in something other than the things of God would be felt in the sensory part. For when the appetite is allowed indulgence in some imperfection, the soul immediately feels an inclination toward it, little or great in proportion to the degree of its satisfaction and attachment.

Yet, because the want of satisfaction in earthly or heavenly things could be the product of some indisposition or melancholic humor, which frequently prevents one from being satisfied with anything, the second sign or condition is necessary.

3. The *second sign* for the discernment of this purgation is that the memory ordinarily turns to God solicitously and with painful care, and the soul thinks it is not serving God but turning back, because it is aware of this distaste for the things of God. Hence it is obvious that this aversion and dryness is not the fruit of laxity and tepidity, for a lukewarm person does not care much for the things of God nor is he inwardly solicitous about them.

There is, consequently, a notable difference between dryness and lukewarmness. A lukewarm person is very lax and remiss in his will and spirit, and has no solicitude about serving God; a person suffering the purgative dryness is ordinarily solicitous, concerned, and pained about not serving God. Even though the dryness may be furthered by melancholia or some other humor—as it often is—it does not thereby fail to produce its purgative effect in the appetite, for the soul will be deprived of every satisfaction and concerned only about God. If this humor is the entire cause, everything ends in disgust and does harm to one's nature, and there are none of these desires to serve God which accompany the purgative dryness. Even though, in this purgative dryness, the sensory part of the soul is very cast down, slack, and feeble in its actions, because of the little satisfaction it finds, the spirit is ready and strong.

4. The reason for this dryness is that God transfers His goods and strength from sense to spirit. Since the sensory part of the soul is incapable of the goods of spirit, it remains deprived, dry and empty, and thus, while the spirit is tasting, the flesh tastes nothing at all and becomes weak in its work. But the spirit through this nourishment grows stronger and more alert, and becomes more solicitous than before about not failing God. If in the beginning the soul does not experience this spiritual savor and delight, but dryness and distaste, it is because of the novelty involved in this exchange. Since its palate is accustomed to these other sensory tastes, the soul still sets its eyes on them. And since, also, its spiritual palate is neither purged nor accommodated for so subtle a taste, it is unable to experience the spiritual savor and good until gradually prepared by means of this dark and obscure night; the soul rather experiences dryness and distaste because of a lack of the gratification it formerly enjoyed so readily.

5. Those whom God begins to lead into these desert solitudes are like the children of Israel; when God began giving them the heavenly food which contained in itself all savors and, as is there mentioned, changed to whatever taste each one hungered after [Wis. 16:20, 21], they nonetheless felt a craving for the tastes of the fleshmeats and onions they had eaten in Egypt, for their palate was accustomed and attracted to them more than to the delicate sweetness of the angelic manna. And in the midst of that heavenly food, they wept and sighed for fleshmeat. [Nm. 11:4–6] The baseness of our appetite is such that it makes us long for our own miserable goods and feel aversion for the incommunicable heavenly good.

6. Yet, as I say, when these aridities are the outcome of the purgative way of the sensory appetite, the spirit feels the strength and energy to work, which is obtained from the substance of that interior food, even though in the beginning, for the reason just mentioned, it may not experience the savor. This food is the beginning of a contemplation that is dark and dry to the senses. Ordinarily this contemplation, which is secret and hidden from the very one who receives it, imparts to the soul, together with the dryness and emptiness it produces in the senses, an inclination to remain alone and in quietude. And the soul will be unable to dwell upon any particular thought, nor will it have the desire to do so.

If those in whom this occurs know how to remain quiet, without care or solicitude about any interior or exterior work, they will soon in that unconcern and idleness delicately experience the interior nourishment. This refection is so delicate that usually if the soul desires or tries to experience it, it cannot. For, as I say, this contemplation is active while the soul is in idleness and unconcern. It is like air that escapes when one tries to grasp it in one's hand.

7. In this sense we can interpret what the Spouse said to the bride in the Canticle: *Turn your eyes from me, because they make me fly away.* [Ct. 6:4] God conducts the soul along so different a path, and so puts it in this state, that a desire to work with the faculties would hinder rather than help His work; whereas in the beginning of the spiritual life everything is quite the contrary.

The reason is that now in this state of contemplation, when the soul has left discursive meditation and entered the state of proficients, it is God who works in it. He therefore binds the interior faculties and leaves no support in the intellect, nor satisfaction in the will, nor remembrance in the memory. At this time a person's own efforts are of no avail, but an obstacle to the interior peace and work God is producing in the spirit through that dryness of sense. Since this peace is something spiritual and delicate, its fruit is quiet, delicate, solitary, satisfying, and peaceful, and far removed from all these other gratifications of beginners, which are very palpable and sensory. For this is the peace that David says God speaks in the soul in order to make it spiritual. [Ps. 84:9] The third sign follows from this one.

8. The *third sign* for the discernment of this purgation of the senses is the powerlessness, in spite of one's efforts, to meditate and make use of the imagination, the interior sense, as was one's previous custom. At this time God does not communicate Himself through the senses as He did before, by means of the discursive analysis and synthesis of ideas, but begins to communicate Himself through pure spirit by an act of simple contemplation, in which there is no discursive succession of thought. The exterior and interior senses of the lower part of the soul cannot attain to this contemplation. As a result the imaginative power and phantasy can no longer rest in any consideration nor find support in it.

9. From the third sign it can be deduced that this dissatisfaction of the faculties is not the fruit of any bad humor. For if it were, a person would be able with a little care to return to his former exercises and find support for his faculties when that humor passed away, for it is by its nature changeable. In the purgation of the appetite this return is not possible, because upon entering it the powerlessness to meditate always continues. It is true, though, that at times in the beginning the purgation of some souls is not continuous in such a way that they are always deprived of sensory satisfaction and the ability to meditate. Perhaps, because of their weakness, they cannot be weaned all at once. Nevertheless, if they are to advance, they will ever enter further into the purgation and leave further behind their work of the senses. Those who do not walk the road of contemplation act very differently. This night of the aridity of the senses is not so continuous in them, for sometimes they experience the aridities and at other times not, and sometimes they can meditate and at other times they cannot. God places them in this night solely to exercise and humble them, and reform their appetite lest in their spiritual life they foster a harmful attraction toward sweetness. But

He does not do so in order to lead them to the life of the spirit, which is contemplation. For God does not bring to contemplation all those who purposely exercise themselves in the way of the spirit, nor even half. Why? He best knows. As a result He never completely weans their senses from the breasts of considerations and discursive meditations, except for some short periods and at certain seasons, as we said.

Rules for the Discernment of Spirits, from the Spiritual Exercises

Ignatius Loyola. Translated by Jules J. Toner, S.J.

[313]. RULES TO HELP PERSONS[3] GET IN TOUCH WITH[4] AND UNDERSTAND IN SOME MANNER THE DIVERSE MOTIONS WHICH ARE PROMPTED IN THEM, SO THAT THEY MAY RECEIVE THE GOOD ONES AND EXPEL THE EVIL ONES. THESE RULES ARE MORE APPROPRIATE TO THE FIRST WEEK.[5]

[314]. Rule 1. In the case of those persons who go from mortal sin to mortal sin, the customary tactic of the enemy is to put before them illusory gratifications, prompting them to imagine sensual delights and pleasures, the better to hold them and make them grow in their vices and sins. With such persons, the good spirit employs a contrary tactic, through their rational power of moral judgment causing pain and remorse in their consciences.

[315]. Rule 2. As for those persons who are intensely concerned with purging away their sins and ascending from good to better in the service of God our Lord, the mode of acting on them is contrary to that [described] in the first rule. For then it is connatural to the evil spirit to gnaw at them, to sadden them, to thrust obstacles in their way, disquieting them with false reasons for the sake of impeding progress. It is connatural to the good spirit to give courage and active energy, consolations, tears, inspirations and a quiet mind, giving ease of action and taking away obstacles for the sake of progress in doing good.

[316]. Rule 3. Concerning spiritual consolation. I name it [spiritual] consolation when some inner motion is prompted in the person,[6] of such a kind that he begins to be aflame with love of his Creator and Lord, and, consequently, when he cannot love any created thing on the face of the earth in itself but only in the Creator of them all. Likewise [I call it consolation] when a person pours out tears moving to love of his Lord, whether it be for sorrow over his sins, or over the passion of Christ our Lord, or over other things directly ordered to his service and praise. Finally, I call [spiritual] consolation every increase of hope, faith, and charity, and every inward gladness which calls and attracts to heavenly things and to one's personal salvation, bringing repose and peace in his Creator and Lord.

[317]. Rule 4. Concerning spiritual desolation. I call [spiritual] desolation everything the contrary of [what is described in] the third rule, for example, gloominess of soul, confusion, a movement to contemptible and earthly things, disquiet from various commotions and temptations, [all this] tending toward distrust, without hope, without love; finding oneself thoroughly indolent, tepid, sad, and as if separated from one's Creator and Lord. For just as [spiritual] consolation is contrary to [spiritual] desolation, in the same way the thoughts which spring from [spiritual] consolation are contrary to the thoughts which spring from [spiritual] desolation.

[318]. Rule 5. The time of [spiritual] desolation is no time at all to change purposes and decisions with which one was content the day before such desolation, or the decision with which one was content during the previous consolation. It is, rather, a time to remain firm and constant in these. For just as in [spiritual] consolation the good spirit generally leads and counsels us, so in [spiritual] desolation does the evil spirit. By the latter's counsels we cannot find the way to a right decision.

[319]. Rule 6. Granted that in [spiritual] desolation we ought not to change our previous purposes, it helps greatly to change ourselves intensely in ways contrary to the aforesaid desolation, for instance, by insisting more on prayer, on meditation, on much

examination, and on extending ourselves to do penance in some fitting manner.

[320]. Rule 7. Let one who is in [spiritual] desolation consider how the Lord has left him to his natural powers, so that he may prove himself while resisting the disturbances and temptations of the enemy. He is, indeed, able to do so with the divine aid, which always remains with him even though he does not clearly perceive it. For, although the Lord has withdrawn from him his bubbling ardor, surging love, and intense grace, nevertheless, he leaves enough grace to go on toward eternal salvation.

[321]. Rule 8. Let him who is in [spiritual] desolation work at holding on in patience, which goes contrary to the harassments that come on him; and, while taking unremitting action against such desolation, as said in the sixth rule, let him keep in mind that he will soon be consoled.

[322]. Rule 9. There are three principal causes which explain why we find ourselves [spiritually] desolate. The first is that we are tepid, indolent, or negligent in our spiritual exercises; and, as a result of our own failings, [spiritual] consolation departs from us. The second is that it serves to put our worth to the test, showing how much we will extend ourselves in serving and praising God without so much pay in consolations and increased graces. The third is this: spiritual desolation serves to give us a true recognition and understanding, grounding an inward experiential perception of the fact that we cannot ourselves attain to or maintain surging devotion, intense love, tears, or any other spiritual consolation, but rather that all is gift and grace from God our Lord. So, we do not build a nest on another's property, elevating our mind in a certain pride or vainglory, giving ourselves credit for devotion or other constituents of spiritual consolation.

[323]. Rule 10. Let him who is in consolation think how he will bear himself in the desolation which will follow, gathering energy anew for that time.

[324]. Rule 11. Let him who is [spiritually] consoled set about humbling and lowering himself as much as he can, reflecting on how

pusillanimous he is in the time of [spiritual] desolation without God's grace or consolation. On the other hand, let him who is in [spiritual] desolation keep in mind that, drawing strength from his Creator and Lord, he has with divine grace sufficiently great power to resist all his enemies.

[325]. Rule 12. The enemy acts like a shrewish woman, being weak and willful;[7] for it is connatural to such a woman in a quarrel with some man to back off when he boldly confronts her; and on the contrary when, losing courage, he begins to retreat, the anger vengeance, and ferocity of the woman swell beyond measure. In like manner, it is connatural to the enemy to fall back and lose courage, with his temptations fading out, when the person performing spiritual exercises presents a bold front against the temptations of the enemy, by doing what is diametrically the opposite. If, on the contrary, the person engaged in spiritual exercises begins to be fearful and to lose courage while suffering temptations, there is no beast on the face of the earth so fierce as is the enemy of human kind in prosecuting his wicked intention with such swelling malice.

[326]. Rule 13. Likewise he behaves as a seducer in seeking to carry on a clandestine affair and not be exposed. When such a frivolous fellow makes dishonourable advances to the daughter of a good father or the wife of a good husband, he wants his words and seductions to be secret. On the contrary, he is greatly displeased when the daughter discovers to her father or the wife to her husband his fraudulent talk and lewd design; for he readily gathers that he will not be able to carry out the undertaking he has initiated. In like manner, when the enemy of human kind insinuates into the faithful person his wiles and seductions, he intensely desires that they be received in secret and kept secret. It dispirits him greatly when one discloses them to a good confessor or to another spiritual person who is acquainted with his trickery and malice; for when his evident trickery is brought to light, he gets the idea that he will not be able to realize the evil plan he has set in motion.

[327]. Rule 14. So also, in order to conquer and plunder what he desires, the enemy of human kind acts like a caudillo. For, just as a military commander-in-chief pitching camp and exploring what

the forces of a stronghold are and how they are disposed, attacks the weaker side, in like manner, the enemy of human kind roves around and makes a tour of inspection of all our virtues, theological and cardinal and moral. Where he finds us weaker and more in need of reinforcement for the sake of our eternal salvation, there he attacks us and strives to take us by storm.

[Set II]

[328]. RULES FOR THE SAME PURPOSE [AS THE FIRST SET], WITH MORE ACCURATE WAYS OF DISCERNING SPIRITS. THESE RULES ARE MORE SUITED FOR USE IN THE SECOND WEEK.[8]

[329]. Rule 1. It is connatural for God and his angels, when they prompt interior motions, to give genuine gladness and spiritual joy, eliminating all sadness and confusion which the enemy brings on. It is connatural for the latter to fight against such gladness and spiritual consolation by proposing specious arguments, subtle and persistently fallacious.

[330]. Rule 2. To give a person consolation without preceding cause is for God our Lord alone to do; for it is distinctive of the Creator in relation to the created person to come in and to leave, to move the person interiorly, drawing him or her totally into love of his Divine Majesty. I say without [preceding][9] cause, that is, without any previous perception or understanding of any object such that through it consolation of this sort would come by the mediation of the person's own acts of understanding and will.

[331]. Rule 3. With a [preceding] cause, an angel, good or evil, can console a person. In doing so, the good and evil angels have contrary purposes. The purpose of the good angel is the person's progress, that he may ascend from good to better. The purpose of the evil angel is the contrary—and thereafter, to draw the person on to his damned intent and cunning trap.

[332]. Rule 4. It is characteristic of the evil spirit to take on the appearance of an angel of light, so that he can begin by going the way of a devout person and end with that person going his own way. By that I mean that he first prompts thoughts which are good and holy, harmonious with such a faithful person, and then manages, little by little, to step out of his act and lead the person to his hidden falsehoods and perverse designs.

[333]. Rule 5. We ought to pay close attention to the progression of thoughts. If the beginning, middle, and end of it are altogether good and tend entirely to what is right, that is a sign of the good angel's influence. It is, however, a clear sign that the line of thought originates from the influence of the evil spirit, the enemy of our spiritual progress and eternal salvation, if the thoughts which he prompts end up in something evil or distracting or less good than what the person had previously proposed to do, or if they weaken, disquiet, or confuse him, doing away with the peace, tranquility, and quiet experienced beforehand.

[334]. Rule 6. When the enemy of human nature has been perceived and recognized by his telltale train of thoughts terminating in the evil to which he leads, it is useful for the person who was tempted by him to look immediately at the course of good thoughts which were prompted in him, noting how they began and how, little by little, the evil spirit contrived to make him fall away from the earlier sweetness and spiritual joy until he led him to what his [the spirit's] own corrupt mind intended. The purpose is that observing such an experience and taking mental note of it will be a safeguard for the future against these customary hoaxes of the evil spirit.

[335]. Rule 7. Persons who are going from good to better the good angel touches sweetly, lightly, gently, as when a drop of water soaks into a sponge, while the evil spirit touches them sharply, with noise and disturbance, as when the drop of water falls on a rock. Those who are going from bad to worse the aforesaid spirits touch in a way contrary to the way they touch those going from good to better. The cause of this contrariety is that the disposition of the one touched is either contrary to or concordant with each of the said angels. For when it is contrary, the angels enter perceptibly, with

clamor and observable signs; when it is concordant, they come in quietly, as one comes into his own house through an open door.

[336]. Rule 8. Granted that when consolation is without [preceding] cause, it has no deception in it, since, as has been said, such consolation is from God our Lord alone; nevertheless, a spiritual person to whom God gives such consolation should, with great alertness and attention, examine his experience to discern the precise time of the actual consolation [without preceding cause] as distinct from the following time, in which the person is still glowing and still graced by the residue of [actual] consolation that is now over with. The reason for making this distinction is that frequently in this second period, either through one's own reasoning about the relations of concepts and judgments and the conclusions to be drawn from them, or through the influence of a good spirit or of an evil spirit, various purposes and opinions take shape which are not given immediately by God our Lord. Inasmuch as that is the case, these purposes and opinions are in need of prolonged and careful examination before full assent is given to them or they are put into execution.

NOTES

3. Here Ignatius' Spanish word is *ánima*. On translating it by "person" or "persons," see footnote 6 just below.

4. . . . *para en alguna manera sentir y cognoscer:* a very literal translation of Ignatius' text is "for helping in some manner to perceive and understand . . ."; his thought here moves from an initial perception (*sentir* in its primary or root meaning) of the interior motions to a better understanding (*cognoscer*) of them. Hence I translate by "get in touch with and understand." The Spanish word *sentir*, like the Latin *sentire* from which it came, has the primitive meaning of perceiving by the senses (e.g. by feeling) and then by the mind (e.g. by observing or judging); and thereafter the acquired meanings in new contexts become too numerous to list here. Ignatius used *sentir* frequently and with many meanings, some of which are peculiarly his own, especially in passages which record his mystical experiences. His shadings are treated in depth and with copious references by Iparraguirre in his *Vocabulario de Ejercicios Espirituales: Ensayo de hermeneutica Ignaciana* (Rome: Centrum Ignatianum Spiritualitatis, 1972), pp. 192–197. In the *Exercises* Ignatius uses *sentir* in its verbal form 32 times,

with the meanings and nuances varying according to the context (*Sp-ExMHSJTe*, p. 781).

Usually present in the meaning is a cognition which is basically intellectual; and often emotional or even mystical overtones are added. In various Ignatian writings *sentir* indicates cognition savored so repeatedly that it becomes a framework of reference instinctively or affectively used to guide one's thinking, deciding, and acting—for example, in *SpEx*, [352] on the directives *para el sentido verdadero que en la Iglesia debemos tener*, "toward acquiring the genuine attitude which we ought to maintain in the Church militant . . . ." (see Leturia, *Estudios Ignacianos*, II, 153; Ganss, *Studies in the Spirituality of Jesuits*, VII, no. 1 [Jan., 1975], 12). Ignatius' *Spiritual Diary*, [63] for February 21, 1544, in the words "During the Mass I was knowing, deeply feeling, or seeing, the Lord knows . . ." (*conoçia, sentia, o veia, Dominus scit . . .*), presents an instance where the basically intellectual cognition is savored amid circumstances of infused contemplation, and where all this together is used as a frame of reference in Ignatius' effort to discern God's will.

The affective and sometimes mystical overtones of *sentir* in Ignatius' works are well discussed by John Futrell in his *Making an Apostolic Community of Love* (St. Louis, 1970) pp. 111–116, and more succinctly in his brochure "Ignatian Discernment" (*Studies in the Spirituality of Jesuits*, II, no. 2 [April, 1970], 56–57). "In the process of discernment," he states on p. 57, "*sentir* comes to mean above all a kind of 'felt-knowledge,' an affective, intuitive knowledge possessed through the reaction of human feelings to exterior and interior experience."

This is undoubtedly true of many passages of Ignatius; but our present instance of Ignatius' title for his rules (*SpEx*, [313]) is not one of them. For to translate *sentir* here by "to feel" or "to have a felt-knowledge" would not make good sense. These rules for discerning spirits are certainly not calculated to help one feel anything. They presuppose feeling and other "interior motions," and are calculated to help us become aware of these and understand them, not to feel them. In the context of *SpEx*, [313], "for perceiving" or "for getting in touch with" seems to be accurate.

Futrell's two works mentioned above are highly important for the study of Ignatian discernment. However, they refer almost entirely to Ignatius' discernment of the will of God, whereas our present book is concerned with discernment of spirits. This difference of focus explains why Futrell's books do not appear more prominently in this present work.

5. The *Spiritual Exercises* are divided into four periods called "weeks," but these are not understood as periods of seven days. The distinction between the First and the Second Week is not to the point here; it

will be taken up in discussing the difference of the second set of rules from the first.

6. The Spanish is *en el ánima*. Here, as in *SpEx*, [313], and also in other occurrences in these rules where the context warrants, I translate Ignatius' *ánima* by "person" rather than "soul." Ignatius did not have a Platonic or Cartesian notion of man; he uses *ánima* merely in the figurative sense of taking the part for the whole (synechdoche). Important for understanding rightly Ignatius' use of *ánima* is the following commentary of George E. Ganss, S.J., in his translation of St. Ignatius' *Constitutions of the Society of Jesus* (St. Louis, 1970), hereafter abbreviated as (*ConsSJComm*), p. 77: ". . .*ánimas* in Ignatius' Spanish, here means the persons, the men considered as their entire selves. This was a frequent meaning of the word for 'soul' in all the languages of Christendom, as it was of the Latin *ánima* in classical times (e.g., *Aeneid*, xi, 24; Horace, *Satires*, i, 5, 41) and in Christian writers too. Ignatius also uses *ánima*, soul, in contrast to *cuerpo*, the body, e.g., in *Cons*, [312–814].

"The use of the Latin *anima* and Spanish *ánima* to mean the living man, the self, the person, is scriptural and occurs very frequently in the Latin Vulgate, especially in texts frequently quoted such as Matt. 16:26; Mark 3:48, 8:36 (Cf., e.g., Gen 2:7, 12:5, 49:6; Exod. 1:5; Acts 2:41; 1 Cor. 15:45). Hence this usage was common in all the languages of Christian Europe throughout the Middle Ages (see, e.g., Blaise, *Dictionnaire . . . des auteurs chrétiens*, s.v. 'anima', 4; also, Peter Lombard's *Sentences* II, 1, no. 8). Awareness of this usage is a key necessary for accurate interpretation of virtually all Christian writers on spirituality. Because of their heritage of Greek philosophy, medieval theologians and later spiritual writers regarded this, more frequently than modern scriptural scholars, as the figure of synecdoche by which the part (*anima*) was taken for the whole, the living man (*homo.*) Even this synecdoche, however, has a scriptural basis (Wisd. 3:1, 8:19–20). In the Spanish of the 1500's (as we gather s.v. from the *Tesoro* [A.D. 1611] of Covarrubias, who refers to Gen. 12:5 and 14:21), *ánima* and its synonym *alma* have among their meanings 'that by which we live' and are 'often used for the persons.' Ignatius' use of *ánima* rather than *hombre* or *homo* has occasionally been taken as evidence of exaggerated dualism or even of Neoplatonism in his thought. In the light of the pervading influence of the Latin Vulgate and its use of *anima* throughout the Middle Ages, this interpretation appears to be farfetched and groundless."

7. My version perhaps takes a slight liberty with the text, translating Ignatius' *muger* by "shrewish woman" (which in this context is clearly his meaning) rather than merely by "woman." The text, I think, as well as Ignatius' respect for and friendship with women, calls for such a qualification.

8. See note 5 above.

9. Careful reading of the text shows that "without cause" is simply a contraction of "without preceding cause." First, the Vulgate version and both the *Prima Versio* texts always speak of a cause that precedes. Secondly, in the autograph version of Rule II:2, where Ignatius first makes the shift, he writes, "*I say*, without cause," (emphasis mine) obviously referring back to the phrase "without preceding cause." He then adds a phrase to explain "without cause": "without any *previous* perception or understanding of any object such . . ." (italics mine).

An Inclusive-Language Translation of the Ignatian Rules for Discernment

Elisabeth Tetlow

[313.] RULES FOR THE DISCERNMENT OF SPIRITS IN THE FIRST WEEK

Rules for perceiving and understanding to some degree the different movements produced in the soul: the good, that they may be accepted, and the bad that they may be rejected. These rules are more suitable for the first week of the *Exercises*.

[314.] Rule 1. In the case of those who go from one mortal sin to another, the enemy ordinarily is accustomed to propose apparent pleasures, filling the imagination with sensual gratifications and pleasures, the more effectively to hold them fast and plunge them deeper into their vices and sins. With such persons the good spirit uses a method which is the reverse of the above, awakening the conscience to a sense of remorse through the judgment of reason.

[315.] Rule 2. In the case of those who continue earnestly striving to purify themselves from sin and who seek to advance in the service of God our Lord to greater perfection, the method pursued is the opposite of that described in the first rule. In this case it is characteristic of the evil spirit to harass with anxiety, afflict with sadness, raise obstacles based on false reasoning that disturb the soul, preventing it from progressing. It is characteristic of the good spirit, however, to give courage and strength, consolation and tears, in-

219

spirations and peace, making things easy and removing all obstacles, in order that the soul may make further progress in doing the good.

[316.] Rule 3. Spiritual Consolation. I call it consolation when the soul is aroused by an interior movement which causes it to be inflamed with love for its Creator and Lord, and as a consequence can love no created thing on the face of the earth for its own sake, but only in the Creator of all things. It is likewise consolation when one sheds tears, moved by love for God, whether it be because of sorrow for sins, or because of the sufferings of Christ our Lord, or for any other reason immediately directed to the service and praise of God. Finally I call consolation every increase of faith, hope and love, and all interior joy which calls and attracts the soul to that which is of God and to salvation by filling it with tranquillity and peace in its Creator and Lord.

[317.] Rule 4. Spiritual Desolation. I call desolation that which is entirely the opposite of what was described in the third rule, such as darkness of soul, confusion of spirit, attraction to what is base and worldly, restlessness caused by many disturbances and temptations which lead to lack of faith, hope or love. The soul finds itself completely apathetic, lukewarm, sad and as if separated from its Creator and Lord. For just as consolation is the opposite of desolation, so the thoughts coming from consolation are the opposite of those which come from desolation.

[318.] Rule 5. In time of desolation we should never make any change, but remain firm and constant in the resolution and decision which guided us before the desolation, or in the decision which we made in the preceding consolation. For just as in consolation it is the good spirit which guides and counsels us, so in desolation it is the evil one which guides and counsels. Following such counsels we can never find the way to a right decision.

[319.] Rule 6. Though in desolation we should never change former resolutions, it may be very profitable to change ourselves by insisting on more prayer, more meditation, and more examination, and by increasing our penance in some suitable way.

[320.] Rule 7. One who is in desolation should reflect that God has left the person to his or her own natural powers to resist the different agitations and temptations of the enemy as a test. One can resist with the help of God, which is always available, although one may not clearly perceive it. For though God has taken away the abundance of fervor, ardent love and intense grace, nevertheless God always leaves sufficient grace for eternal salvation.

[321.] Rule 8. One who is in desolation should strive to persevere in patience. This is contrary to the troubles bothering the person. One should also reflect that consolation will soon return, and in the meantime one should diligently use the means against desolation given in the sixth rule.

[322.] Rule 9. There are three principal reasons why we suffer from desolation. The first is because we have been lukewarm, lazy or negligent in our spiritual exercises, and so through our own fault consolation has been withdrawn from us. The second reason is because God sometimes wishes to test us, to see how much we are worth, and how much we will progress in the service and praise of the Lord when left without the generous reward of consolation and special graces. The third reason is because God wishes to give us a true knowledge and understanding of ourselves, so that we may truly perceive that it is not within our power to acquire or retain great devotion, ardent love, tears, or any other spiritual consolation, but that all this is the gratuitous gift and grace of God our Lord. God does not wish us to claim as our own what is the property of another, becoming inflated with a spirit of pride or boasting, attributing to ourselves devotion or other kinds of spiritual consolation.

[323.] Rule 10. When one enjoys consolation it is good to reflect how one will act during a time of desolation, and store up strength for that time.

[324.] Rule 11. One who enjoys consolations should be careful to remain as humble and self-abasing as possible. The person should recall how little it is possible to do in time of desolation when left without such grace or consolation. On the other hand, one who is in desolation should remember that by making use of the sufficient grace offered, one can do much to withstand the enemy, finding strength in the Creator and Lord.

[325.] Rule 12. The enemy acts in a contrary way, like a weakling before a show of strength or a tyrant when not opposed. As in human relationships one may lose courage or take flight if the other is determined and fearless; or when one loses courage and begins to run away, the anger, vindictiveness and rage of the other increase and know no bounds. In the same way, it is the custom of the enemy to become weak, lose courage and turn to flight with its seductions as soon as one leading a spiritual life faces temptations boldly, and does exactly the opposite of what the enemy suggests. However, if one begins to be afraid and to lose courage in temptations, no wild animal on earth can be more fierce than the enemy of human nature. It will carry out its evil plans with ever increasing malice.

[326.] Rule 13. The enemy may also be compared in its way of acting to a seducer, seeking to remain hidden and undetected. If such a seducer solicits with evil intent one who is virtuous, this seducer will prefer such words and solicitations kept secret. Such a one is greatly displeased if the deceitful suggestions and dishonorable intentions are revealed by the object of its misguided lust to another person. From that moment on, the seducer knows that the project will not be successful. In the same way, when the enemy of human nature tempts a righteous soul with its wiles and seductions, it earnestly desires that they be received secretly and kept secret. But if one reveals them to a good confessor or some other spiritual person with knowledge of such deceits and malicious intentions, the evil one will be quite vexed, knowing that it cannot succeed in this evil undertaking once its obvious deceptions have been revealed.

[327.] Rule 14. The conduct of the enemy may also be compared to the tactics of a military leader intent upon seizing and plundering an object desired. Such a false leader will prepare a plan, investigate the situation, and attack at the weakest point. In the same way, the enemy of human nature explores from every side all our virtues of intellect, faith and morals. Where it finds our defenses weakest and most deficient in regard to eternal salvation, it is at that point that the enemy attacks, trying to overcome us by storm.

[328.] RULES FOR THE DISCERNMENT OF SPIRITS IN THE SECOND WEEK

Further rules for understanding the different movements in the soul for a more accurate discernment of spirits. These rules are more suitable for the second week.

[329.] Rule 1. It is characteristic of God and the good spirits, when they act upon the soul, to give true happiness and spiritual joy, and to banish all the sadness and disturbances caused by the enemy. It is characteristic of the evil one to fight against such happiness and spiritual consolation by suggesting false reasonings, subtleties and continual deceptions.

[330.] Rule 2. God alone can give consolation to the soul without previous cause. It is for the Creator alone to enter into a soul, leave it, act upon it, and draw it totally toward divine love. I said without previous cause, that is, without any previous sense or knowledge of any object from which such consolation might come to the soul through the person's own acts of intellect or will.

[331.] Rule 3. If a cause precedes, consolation can come from either the good spirit or the evil one, but for quite different purposes. The good spirit consoles so that the soul may grow and progress and advance from what is good to what is better. The evil one consoles for purposes that are the contrary, and so that afterward it might draw the soul toward its own perverse intentions and toward evil.

[332.] Rule 4. It is characteristic of the evil one to assume the appearance of a good spirit. It begins by suggesting thoughts appropriate for a devout soul, and ends by suggesting its own. For example, it may suggest good and holy thoughts which are in harmony with the righteous soul. Afterward, it may endeavor little by little to draw the soul into its hidden deceits and evil plans.

[333.] Rule 5. We should carefully observe the whole course of our thoughts. If the beginning, middle and end of the course of thoughts are wholly good and directed to what is right, it is a sign that they are from the good spirit. But the end of the course of thoughts suggested to us may be something evil or distracting or less good than what the soul had formerly proposed to do, or which weakens or disquiets the soul, or causes it disturbance by destroying the peace, tranquillity and quiet it had before. These things are a clear sign that the thoughts are proceeding from the evil one, the enemy of our spiritual progress and eternal salvation.

[334.] Rule 6. When the enemy of human nature has been detected and recognized by the trail of evil which marks its course and by the evil end to which it leads us, it will be profitable for one who has been tempted immediately to review the whole course of the temptation. One should consider the series of good thoughts, how they arose, how the evil one gradually tried to make the person leave the state of spiritual joy and consolation, drawing the person toward its own evil plans. The purpose of this review is that once such an experience has been understood and carefully noted, in the future one may be better able to guard against the customary deceptions of the enemy.

[335.] Rule 7. In souls which are progressing toward greater perfection, the action of the good spirit is delicate, gentle and delightful, like a drop of water penetrating a sponge. The action of the evil one on such souls is violent, noisy and disturbing, like a drop of water falling on a stone. In souls which are going from bad to worse, the action of the spirits mentioned above is just the reverse. The reason for this is to be sought in the disposition of the soul, whether opposite or similar to the different kinds of spirits. When the disposition is contrary to a spirit, it enters with noise and commotion which are easily perceived. When the disposition is similar to a spirit, it enters silently, as when one enters one's own house when the door is open.

[336.] Rule 8. When consolation is without previous cause, as was said, there can be no deception in it, since it can come only from God our Lord. But a spiritual person who has received such a consolation should consider it very attentively and cautiously distinguish the actual time of the consolation from the period which follows it. At such a time the soul is still fervent and favored with the grace and after-effects of the consolation which has passed. In this second period the soul frequently makes various resolutions and plans which are not directly inspired by God our Lord. These may come from our own reasoning, thoughts and habits or as a result of our own judgment, or they may come from the good spirit or from the evil one. Thus they should be carefully examined before they are given full approval or put into action.

Stages of Faith

Stage 1 Intuitive-Projective faith is the fantasy-filled, imitative phase in which the child can be powerfully and permanently influenced by examples, moods, actions and stories of the visible faith of primally related adults.

The stage most typical of the child of three to seven, it is marked by a relative fluidity of thought patterns. The child is continually encountering novelties for which no stable operations of knowing have been formed. The imaginative processes underlying fantasy are unrestrained and uninhibited by logical thought. In league with forms of knowing dominated by perception, imagination in this stage is extremely productive of long-lasting images and feelings (positive and negative) that later, more stable and self-reflective valuing and thinking will have to order and sort out. This is the stage of first self-awareness. The "self-aware" child is egocentric as regards the perspectives of others. Here we find first awarenesses of death and sex and of the strong taboos by which cultures and families insulate those powerful areas.

The gift or emergent strength of this stage is the birth of imagination, the ability to unify and grasp the experience-world in powerful images and as presented in stories that register the child's intuitive understandings and feelings toward the ultimate conditions of existence.

The dangers in this stage arise from the possible "possession" of the child's imagination by unrestrained images of terror and destructiveness, or from the witting or unwitting exploitation of her or his imagination in the reinforcement of taboos and moral or doctrinal expectations.

The main factor precipitating transition to the next stage is the emergence of concrete operational thinking. Affectively, the resolution of Oedipal issues or their submersion in latency are important accompanying factors. At the heart of the transition is the child's growing concern to know how things are and to clarify for him- or herself the bases of distinctions between what is real and what only seems to be.

Stage 2 Mythic-Literal faith is the stage in which the person begins to take on for him- or herself the stories, beliefs and observances that symbolize belonging to his or her community. Beliefs are appropriated with literal interpretations, as are moral rules and attitudes. Symbols are taken as one-dimensional and literal in meaning. In this stage the rise of concrete operations leads to the curbing and ordering of the previous stage's imaginative composing of the world. The episodic quality of Intuitive-Projective faith gives way to a more linear, narrative construction of coherence and meaning. Story becomes the major way of giving unity and value to experience. This is the faith stage of the school child (though we sometimes find the structures dominant in adolescents and in adults). Marked by increased accuracy in taking the perspective of other persons, those in Stage 2 compose a world based on reciprocal fairness and an immanent justice based on reciprocity. The actors in their cosmic stories are anthropomorphic. They can be affected deeply and powerfully by symbolic and dramatic materials and can describe in endlessly detailed narrative what has occurred. They do not, however, step back from the flow of stories to formulate reflective, conceptual meanings. For this stage the meaning is both carried and "trapped" in the narrative.

The new capacity or strength in this stage is the rise of narrative and the emergence of story, drama and myth as ways of finding and giving coherence to experience.

The limitations of literalness and an excessive reliance upon reciprocity as a principle for constructing an ultimate environment can result either in an overcontrolling, stilted perfectionism or "works righteousness" or in their opposite, an abasing sense of badness embraced because of mistreatment, neglect or the apparent disfavor of significant others.

A factor initiating transition to Stage 3 is the implicit clash or contradictions in stories that leads to reflection on meanings. The transition to formal operational thought makes such reflection possible and necessary. Previous literalism breaks down; new "cognitive conceit" (Elkind) leads to disillusionment with previous teachers and teachings. Conflicts between authoritative stories (Genesis on creation versus evolutionary theory) must be faced. The emergence of mutual interpersonal perspective taking ("I see you seeing me; I see me as you see me; I see you seeing me seeing you.") creates the need for a more personal relationship with the unifying power of the ultimate environment.

In Stage 3 Synthetic-Conventional faith, a person's experience of the world now extends beyond the family. A number of spheres demand attention: family, school or work, peers, street society and media, and perhaps religion. Faith must provide a coherent orientation in the midst of that more complex and diverse range of involvements. Faith must synthesize values and information; it must provide a basis for identity and outlook.

Stage 3 typically has its rise and ascendancy in adolescence, but for many adults it becomes a permanent place of equilibrium. It structures the ultimate environment in interpersonal terms. Its images of unifying value and power derive from the extension of qualities experienced in personal relationships. It is a "conformist" stage in the sense that it is acutely tuned to the expectations and judgments of significant others and as yet does not have a sure enough grasp on its own identity and autonomous judgment to construct and maintain an independent perspective. While beliefs and values are deeply felt, they typically are tacitly held—the person "dwells" in them and in the meaning world they mediate. But there has not been occasion to step outside them to reflect on or examine them explicitly or systematically. At Stage 3 a person has an "ideology," a more or less consistent clustering of values and beliefs, but he or she has not objectified it for examination and in a sense is unaware of having it. Differences of outlook with others are experienced as differences in "kind" of person. Authority is located in the incumbents of traditional authority roles (if perceived as personally worthy) or in the consensus of a valued, face-to-face group.

The emergent capacity of this stage is the forming of a personal myth—the myth of one's own becoming in identity and faith, incorporating one's past and anticipated future in an image of the ultimate environment unified by characteristics of personality.

The dangers or deficiencies in this stage are twofold. The expectations and evaluations of others can be so compellingly internalized (and sacralized) that later autonomy of judgment and action can be jeopardized; or interpersonal betrayals can give rise either to nihilistic despair about a personal principle of ultimate being or to a compensatory intimacy with God unrelated to mundane relations.

Factors contributing to the breakdown of Stage 3 and to readiness for transition may include: serious clashes or contradictions between valued authority sources; marked changes, by officially sanctioned leaders, or policies or practices previously deemed sacred and unbreachable (for example, in the Catholic church changing the mass from Latin to the vernacular, or no longer requiring abstinence from meat on Friday); the encounter with experiences or perspectives that lead to critical reflection on how one's beliefs and values have formed and changed, and on how "relative" they are to one's particular group or background. Frequently the experience of "leaving home"—emotionally or physically, or both—precipitates the kind of examination of self, background, and lifeguiding values that gives rise to stage transition at this point.

The movement from Stage 3 to Stage 4 Individuative-Reflective faith is particularly critical for it is in this transition that the late adolescent or adult must begin to take seriously the burden of responsibility for his or her own commitments, lifestyle, beliefs and attitudes. Where genuine movement toward stage 4 is underway the person must face certain unavoidable *tensions:* individuality versus being defined by a group or group membership; subjectivity and the power of one's strongly felt but unexamined feelings versus objectivity and the requirement of critical reflection; self-fulfillment or self-actualization as a primary concern versus service to and being for others; the question of being committed to the relative versus struggle with the possibility of an absolute.

Stage 4 most appropriately takes form in young adulthood (but let us remember that many adults do not construct it and that for a significant group it emerges only in the mid-thirties or forties). This stage is marked by a double development. The self, previously sustained in its identity and faith compositions by an interpersonal circle of significant others, now claims an identity no longer defined by the composite of one's roles or meanings to others. To sustain that new identity it composes a meaning frame conscious of its own boundaries and inner connections and aware of itself as a "world view." Self (identity) and outlook (world view) are differentiated from those of others and become acknowledged factors in the reactions, interpretations and judgments one makes on the actions of the self and others. It expresses its intuitions of coherence in an ultimate environment in terms of an explicit system of meanings. Stage 4 typically translates symbols into conceptual meanings. This is a "demythologizing" stage. It is likely to attend minimally to unconscious factors influencing its judgments and behavior.

Stage 4's ascendant strength has to do with its capacity for critical reflection on identity (self) and outlook (ideology). Its dangers inhere in its strengths: an excessive confidence in the conscious mind and in critical thought and a kind of second narcissism in which the now clearly bounded, reflective self overassimilates "reality" and the perspectives of others into its own world view.

Restless with the self-images and outlook maintained by Stage 4, the person ready for transition finds him- or herself attending to what may feel like anarchic and disturbing inner voices. Elements from a childish past, images and energies from a deeper self, a gnawing sense of the sterility and flatness of the meanings one serves— any or all of these may signal readiness for something new. Stories, symbols, myths and paradoxes from one's own or other traditions may insist on breaking in upon the neatness of the previous faith. Disillusionment with one's compromises and recognition that life is more complex than Stage 4's logic of clear distinctions and abstract concepts can comprehend, press one toward a more dialectical and multileveled approach to life truth.

Stage 5 Conjunctive faith involves the integration into self and outlook of much that was suppressed or unrecognized in the interest of Stage 4's self-certainty and conscious cognitive and affective adaptation to reality. This stage develops a "second naïveté" (Ricoeur) in which symbolic power is reunited with conceptual meanings. Here there must also be a new reclaiming and reworking of one's past. There must be an opening to the voices of one's "deeper self." Importantly, this involves a critical recognition of one's social unconscious—the myths, ideal images and prejudices built deeply into the self-system by virtue of one's nurture within a particular social class, religious tradition, ethnic group or the like.

Unusual before mid-life, Stage 5 knows the sacrament of defeat and the reality of irrevocable commitments and acts. What the previous stage struggled to clarify, in terms of the boundaries of self and outlook, this stage now makes porous and permeable. Alive to paradox and the truth in apparent contradictions, this stage strives to unify opposites in mind and experience. It generates and maintains vulnerability to the strange truths of those who are "other." Ready for closeness to that which is different and threatening to self and outlook (including new depths of experience in spirituality and religious revelation), this stage's commitment to justice is freed from the confines of tribe, class, religious community or nation. And with the seriousness that can arise when life is more than half over, this stage is ready to spend and be spent for the cause of conserving and cultivating the possibility of others' generating identity and meaning.

The new strength of this stage comes in the rise of the ironic imagination—a capacity to see and be in one's or one's group's most powerful meanings, while simultaneously recognizing that they are relative, partial and inevitably distorting apprehensions of transcendent reality. Its danger lies in the direction of a paralyzing passivity or inaction, giving rise to complacency or cynical withdrawal, due to its paradoxical understanding of truth.

Stage 5 can appreciate symbols, myths and rituals (its own and others') because it has been grasped, in some measure, by the depth of reality to which they refer. It also sees the divisions of the human family vividly because it has been apprehended by the possibility (and imperative) of an inclusive community of being. But this stage remains divided. It lives and acts between an untransformed world and a transforming vision and loyalties. In some few cases this division yields to the call of the radical actualization that we call Stage 6.

Stage 6 is exceedingly rare. The persons best described by it have generated faith compositions in which their felt sense of an ultimate environment is inclusive of all being. They have become incarnators and actualizers of the spirit of an inclusive and fulfilled human community.

They are "contagious" in the sense that they create zones of liberation from the social, political, economic and ideological shackles we place and endure on human futurity. Living with felt participation in a power that unifies and transforms the world, Universalizers are often experienced as subversive of the structures (including religious structures) by which we sustain our individual and corporate survival, security and significance. Many persons in this stage die at the hands of those whom they hope to change. Universalizers are often more honored and revered after death than during their lives. The rare persons who may be described by this stage have a special grace that makes them seem more lucid, more simple, and yet somehow more fully human than the rest of us. Their community is universal in extent. Particularities are cherished because they are vessels of the universal, and thereby valuable apart from any utilitarian considerations. Life is both loved and held to loosely. Such persons are ready for fellowship with persons at any of the other stages and from any other faith tradition.

Passionate Breakthrough—
The Passionate God

Rosemary Haughton

This essay has in its title not only the word 'God', but the word 'Passion', and the ordinary experience just mentioned is an example of the kind of experience from which the theology of this book takes its name and its symbols and its dynamics. For its thesis is that we can begin to make some sense of the way God loves people if we look very carefully at the way people love people, and in particular at the way of love we can refer to as 'passionate' because that kind of love tells us things about how love operates which we could not otherwise know. We can say 'love' and mean a restful, gentle and essentially kind experience. But if we say 'passion' we evoke something in motion—strong, wanting, needy, concentrated towards a very deep encounter. It is a violent word. Yet it has, in its roots, obviously a 'passive' sense. 'Passion' also implies a certain helplessness, a suffering and undergoing for the sake of what is desired and, implicitly, the possibility of a tragic outcome.

'Genuine' Romantic love does occur, in spite of the culture, because it is too basic a human occurrence to be altogether denied or explained away. And however it may be subsequently weakened or corrupted through lack of knowledge or courage, it has certain characteristics which are significant.

These characteristics are the following: 'particularity'; 'singleness'; a capacity for changing the 'face of reality'; a kind of 'halo' of obscure glory; and, also, painfulness. It has also a great potential for corruption, though this is less a characteristic than a possible direction of the entire experience. (There is also a final, but actually primary, thing to add about Romantic passion, which is what one *does* about it.) These characteristics need to be clarified.

The very obviousness of *particularity* can make its importance less noticeable. Because the Romantic experience is a fully physical experience, it is particular. It happens through one person, not just in relation to 'humanity'. It is this particular girl (whose hair and eyes are a special colour, who smiles just so) who is the gateway to a universal glory. She provides a direct encounter with a basic reality of the universe at a level far deeper than the intellectual but, by that fact, illuminating and strengthening the intellect which itself is rendered sensitive to such awareness by the experience.

Singleness is a less obvious characteristic. It happens once, with one person, but other encounters of a comparable kind may come later and raise problems which must be resolved. This does not alter the fact that, at the point of encounter, the passionate breakthrough is not only particular but single, for the whole energy of the lover is concentrated on this single point. There is a curious kind of proportion to this, whereby a relationship with more opportunity for the couple to meet and 'get to know' each other tends to have less violence of emotion. Common-sense advice given to parents whose children have fallen in love with the 'wrong' person is, often, to 'let them see more of each other', because this will probably dilute passion with experience, while opposition may make the lovers even more obsessed with each other. This is so because the passionate breakthrough does not, in fact, indicate any great degree of compatibility between two people. All it means is that *something* in one is able to release that in the other which, at that time, has reached the point at which the breakthrough is required if spiritual growth is to be possible. It will force a way at some point, and the concentration of the impulse at the single point of encounter, through lack of opportunity for wider acquaintance, actually gives it its 'passionate' character, though it also makes the chances of developing a full everyday relationship more remote. From the point of view of the Romantic encounter this does not matter, though there is another aspect of Romantic doctrine, that of fidelity, to which it matters a great deal. But at the point of encounter intensity matters, and intensity is increased by narrowness and by obstacles, as a river running through a narrow gorge is faster and stronger than one meandering through meadows.

Once the breakthrough has occurred the waters so released rapidly flood the mind and emotions. People in love may look different, they have a 'glow', they walk more lightly, move more delicately. But also the face of reality is changed, the world looks different to them. All kinds of people seem more lovable or more interesting; compassion is more easily aroused, generous and tender feeling is so near the surface as to be painful. There is also, often, a sense of daring, a longing to undertake difficult things for the sake of the beloved, even without her knowledge. And not only other human beings but other material things acquire a sense that they embody a secret which is so near the surface that it is about to become apparent. (The Romantic poet or artist, of course, tries actually to make it apparent.)

Everything, from the face of the beloved down to the neighbour's cat, acquires a greater and more precise reality, but at the same time, apparently contradicting this, there is *the 'halo' of glory*, Dante's 'stupor', a sense of not being able to perceive clearly what one sees. The clarity of things seen is set within an ambience of felt ignorance, a sense that there is more inclusive meaning, which *should* be understood but cannot be. It is not a feeling of general 'mystery', but rather a nostalgia for something which is precise in its nature yet elusive because un-remembered, like the atmosphere of a dream which flees as one wakes.

Finally, the Beatrician experience is *painful*. Even in its joy it has a quality of longing for a completeness which is not achieved nor, the lovers feel, even possible. The oneness which is experienced is, they feel, only a glimpse of an experience which is closed to them. Something gets in the way, and although this 'something' may present itself to them as other people's codes of behaviour, or the necessities of everydayness, these are mere symbols of the essential barrier within. The barrier has been breached by the thrust of passion, but the opening is too small and something which was before unseen can now be seen through the gap. That hurts, with a sense of ineffable 'wrongness', yet that 'wrongness' is the indication of something so 'right' that to be rid of the hurt would be unthinkably worse than bearing it.

All these characteristics of the Romantic breakthrough are matters of experience, though temperament, circumstances and above all the attitude of the particular culture, filtered through the mind that experiences passion, alter the proportions. For instance in some the experience may be so deeply happy that the lovers would be surprised to hear it suggested that it was painful, yet there is a pain which they accept and expect: of separation, of failure to understand each other totally, of need to be concerned with other things. Again, people whose character is very 'action-oriented' may not experience the changed 'look' of things in any appreciable way because they have little awareness of 'things' except as a field for the expression of love felt as a call to caring. But, intensely or barely felt, these characteristics are present.

Among human experiences Romantic passion is peculiarly open to corruption, and this opens up the discussion of the whole 'problem' of evil. The associations of the original Romance movement with gnostic heresy (and even with Satanism in some of the backwaters of Catharism) is not due purely to the fevered imaginations of celibate Inquisitors. The popular linking of the Romantic revival in the nineteenth century with 'decadence', opium, occultism and a cult of sensuality for its own sake is also an indication (however exaggerated by the suspicious) of the kind of path that passion can take. Recently we have seen an unprecedented flowering of interest in the occult, a renaissance of serious witchcraft, and finally the rise of the cult of a kind of sexual licence so idiotically degraded that it seems unsure whether to collapse into a ludicrous banality of adolescent viciousness or to take a hopeless dive beyond tragedy. There is something so extremely nasty about what happens to Romantic passion when it 'goes wrong' that it is not very surprising that Romance itself has generally been viewed with suspicion by both Church and State, and indeed by 'all sensible people'.

The last element of Romantic doctrine is so important that it should have been placed first, except that it could not make sense outside the context of all the rest. It is the element referred to in the French of its originators as *amour voulu*. To them, Romantic passion might seize on human beings unawares, but simply to submit to be swept away by emotion was unworthy. They had as profound a contempt for such *amour fol* as they had for the false lover, because the lover who betrayed love was not only one who was calculating or shallow but the one who was self-indulgent, surrendering not to *love* but to *emotion*. In contrast to this they asserted that the only proper response to the *revelation* of love was a *commitment* to love—absolute, unconditional and permanent. The painful and often humiliating 'service' rendered by the sworn knight to his Lady was the working out of this in practice. 'Let him who has found a constant lover prize her above rubies, and serve her with a loyal service, being altogether at her will,' admonished Marie de France.

Amour voulu is a 'giving back', in free but completely uncompromising dedication, of that which has been freely and undeservedly received. This concept, strange to a culture which sees Romantic passion not as 'willed love' but as 'dominating emotion', leads us to understand what Jesus meant when he spelt out the meaning of love not as mystical invasion but as acts of practical service. It is the basis of both mysticism and moral theology.

All these characteristics of Romantic breakthrough are part of a total human development. Therefore in order to understand the event itself as a theological paradigm, it is necessary to see also *how* it occurs. Why with *this* person? Why *then*? Why *thus*? These are questions which will have to be answered in detail in a number of different contexts throughout this book, and here it will be enough to establish a kind of sequence of events for Romantic breakthrough, to indicate what occurs, and why, and leave illustration to the memory of the reader. It must also be said that the sequence I describe here is established by hindsight only, and that the three questions I asked cannot, even then, always be answered with more than 'reasonable' assurance, for no human person or situation can yield all its elements to the outside observer.

The sequence goes like this: a *remote preparation* creates the situation in which an *immediate preparation* can make or discover the 'vulnerable point' for the *breakthrough* itself. Once the breakthrough has occurred it requires something else in order to be effective—*a language*.

The *remote preparation* means a probably lengthy process in which the person is inclined, by circumstances and by 'education' (conscious and unconscious), to recognize and *want* something at least vaguely corresponding to the Romantic experience. This is both likely and unlikely in our culture. We are culturally sodden with Romantic expectations, and the young are showered with the perfume of it regularly. But it is a less than authentic brand of Romance, too heavily scented with purely sexual connotations, so it may distort the experience when it comes.

There has to be this 'remote preparation' or nothing happens. (There are plenty of people around to whom, visibly, 'nothing' has happened.) Adolescence itself is such a preparation, and this shows that there is a process, not just a state. If 'nothing' happens in adolescence it is because growth has been, somehow, arrested. Growth happens under the influence of cultural expectations, and adaptations to them, which produce a variety of behaviour and ideas but within certain limits of personal spiritual 'reach'. Yet this reach is increasingly felt to be too narrow. There is a restlessness; obscure desires stir but are still obscure. So the remote preparation is 'inward' and spiritual, reacting ,to and with the 'outward' and cultural—but I say that with reluctance, merely to make clear two aspects, for in practice the distinction is false. The 'outward' activates and indeed 'creates' the inward, yet the 'inward' of each, touching other 'inner' persons, is what creates the culture which in turn bears so heavily on the developing 'inner' consciousness. I have put this account of 'remote preparation' in terms of individual people, yet it will have been clear to anyone who has read the previous chapter that the things which went on in France towards the end of the 'Dark Ages' provided just such a restlessness, a sense of obscure need, a grabbing at trappings of luxury or heroism or sensuality, expressive of a desire for something or other, without any clear notion of what is desired.

In this situation occurs the *immediate preparation*, something which creates a 'weak spot'. Something happens which shakes the person loose from normal expectations and settled attitudes. It can be a book, or a vacation, or a disaster, or simply an intensification of the influences which have created the 'remote preparation'. It can be, in practice, the encounter with the person who will be 'the' person, but in whom the 'Beatrician experience' has not yet appeared. It can be something quite small and apparently trivial, such as suddenly catching sight of one's face in a mirror. There is no longer simply a vague sense of need but a definite expectancy, which may be somewhat fearful. There is within the person *something* which is, as it were, on the lookout for *itself*. It cannot 'come out' until something opens the door, from 'outside'—and when something does open it, there is an immediate sense of recognition. All is new—yet this is 'home'. Is it fanciful to see in eleventh-century Provence elements like this? The strangeness of Crusading experience, the sudden increase in the status and influence of women, the comings and goings of landless knights living on 'chivalry', and of poor, bold, exciting 'jongleurs', the influence of a persuasive and officially abhorrent heresy? Any one of these might have been enough to challenge the 'new' love to recognize itself.

The response to this recognition is passion: the thrust of the whole personality towards the strange 'home' it perceives. It is accompanied by intense emotion, which varies in quality according to temperament from a gentle but strong and certain joy to a desperate violence which is afraid of losing that which is perceived. But something very odd precedes this: I can only describe it as a kind of 'gap', in which there is no feeling or 'movement' but a timeless instant of oneness. It is an experience of recognition so complete and profound that it is impossible to say what is recognized. That is why it is experienced as a 'gap', and it can be so content-less that the person recoils and takes refuge behind a hastily closed door. Passion, therefore, is the thrust which leaps that void; it is a leap of faith, without guarantees or even knowledge. The leap is, therefore, not primarily emotional, but powerful emotion is released by it. The breakthrough of passion is this self-giving towards a wholeness intensely desired, but across a gap of 'un-knowing'. This is what makes it passionate—it is difficult; it is, as we saw, painful.

When the breakthrough has occurred, all depends on something quite simple: What do we do about it? *Amour voulu* must have some guidelines if it is to do more than flounder. What people do *about* the passionate breakthrough depends on what they understand to have happened, and in consequence what their expectation is of themselves. Clearly, the reaction of a person who has learned that Romantic passion is a disgraceful lapse from proper emotional direction will be quite different from that of a person who views Romance as the high point of human experience, or again from that of a person who has been taught that it is a fleeting though exciting experience, to be indulged and enjoyed but not directed. So what a culture or group 'says' concerning the breakthrough event is obviously of quite crucial importance. On this 'language' depends whether the experience is to be fully lived as *amour voulu*, or dismissed as trivial, or rejected as sinful, or wallowed in, or surrendered to without thought, or evaded, or greedily grasped, or perverted.

'Language' is communal, it means a society. The breakthrough cannot be 'private' since its results depend on a shared 'language' about it. This is the origin of religious and spiritual movements. The desert Fathers, the Franciscans, the Lollards, the Jesuits, the Separatists who went to New England, the Shakers, the Salvation Army and modern communes and religious sects are (to name a few out of thousands) examples of how the passionate breakthrough in one person's life is articulated in a language which becomes that of a group who also respond to the vision they perceive in the founder. Hence the passionate breakthrough leads, somehow or other, to *community*, and also (if it is fully lived) it creates and recreates the community within which it is understood, illuminating for others, as well as for the lovers themselves, the reality which each has encountered. (This is as true of a community for evil, such as the Hitler Youth became, as of a community of love.) Clearly, Romantic passion did create a community in its historical beginnings. The 'language' we now use to understand and live it was made possible by that community and re-created by it.

Section IV

Revisioning the Tradition
of Christian Spirituality

Here are resources for a most comprehensive and challenging vision of women's spirituality. Earlier sections presented distinct issues for women (Section I), explained the model of human maturity that emerges when women's experience is valued equally with men's (Section II), and supported the conclusion that classical as well as contemporary Christian spirituality is compatible with the feminist vision of human maturity (Section III). Now we come to essays which move into the pioneering territory where feminist spirituality is not only compatible but also trying to be comfortable with Christian tradition. As I explain in the first essay of this book, Christian feminists are pioneers and not yet content with the tradition because the male-centered tradition still needs to be revisioned completely to include women's experience before it can be fully a resource for women's spirituality.

These essays present feminist Christian revisioning of the most basic aspects of the tradition. Johnson and Fiorenza reconstruct the Old and New Testament images of God. Cooke reinterprets salvation, freeing this theme from patriarchal distortions. FitzGerald links John of the Cross' image of darkness with the contemporary feminist experience of impasse in a patriarchal culture. My essays revision aspects of discernment in Ignatius of Loyola and autonomy in Thérèse of Lisieux.

Until this kind of revisioning becomes part of mainstream Christian teaching, pastoral counseling, preaching, and spiritual di-

241

rection, women's spirituality will be restricted. For Christian spirituality involves a communal witness to God's presence. When that witness speaks the language of women's experience as easily as it now speaks the language of men, then, and only then, will the entire community be an authentic resource for women's spirituality.

The Incomprehensibility of God
and the Image of God Male and Female

Elizabeth A. Johnson, C.S.J.

The holiness and utter transcendence of God over all of creation has always been an absolutely central affirmation of the Judeo-Christian tradition. God as God—source, redeemer, and goal of all—is illimitable mystery who, while immanently present, cannot be measured or controlled. The doctrine of divine incomprehensibility is a corollary of this divine transcendence. In essence, God's unlikeness to the corporal and spiritual finite world is total; hence we simply cannot understand God. No human concept, word, or image, all of which originate in experience of created reality, can circumscribe the divine reality, nor can any human construct express with any measure of adequacy the mystery of God, who is ineffable. This situation is due not to some reluctance on the part of God to self-reveal in a full way, nor to the sinful condition of the human race making reception of such a revelation impossible, nor even to our contemporary mentality of skepticism in religious matters. Rather, it is proper to God as God to transcend all direct similarity to creatures, and thus never to be known comprehensively or essentially as God. In Augustine's unforgettable echo of the insight of earlier Greek theologians, if we have comprehended, then what we have comprehended is not God. This sense of an unfathomable depth of mystery, of a vastness of God's glory too great for the human mind to grasp, undergirds the religious significance of speech about God; such speech never definitively possesses its subject but leads us ever more profoundly into attitudes of awe and adoration.[1]

243

It would be a serious mistake to think that God's self-revelation through powerful acts and inspired words in the Jewish tradition and through the history and destiny of Jesus Christ which give rise to the Christian tradition removes the ultimate unknowability of God. In the history of these traditions, revelation has in fact given rise to the "dangerous situation" in which the need to preach and interpret has resulted in words becoming too clear and ideas too distinct, almost as if they were direct transcripts of divine reality.[2] At times we have forgotten whom we are dealing with, and have created the impression that the unknown God is now available for inspection, caught within our narratives or metaphysical concepts. Revelation, however, cannot and does not dissolve the mystery of God; in its light we see ever more clearly the incomprehensibility of God as free and liberating love, love which chooses us without our deserving it, bears and removes our bondage, gathers us in. Even and especially in revelation God remains the wholly other, conceptually inapprehensible, and so God.

The contemporary challenge of atheism and the purification of the doctrine of God which meeting it entails has led theology in some measure to a new reappropriation of the insight of the best of the theological tradition that it is impossible to understand God. Now another challenge, from the perspective of believing women, holds the promise of deepening yet further this truth of the incomprehensibility of God, as well as promoting the human dignity of women— the two not being separable from one another.

The problem with the understanding of God which women theologians, out of personal experience of its debilitating effects, have identified is that it envisions God exclusively through analogy with the male human being, and does so with a pervasiveness and tenacity which at least raises the question of the success of the first commandment in eliciting obedience. Imagery for the divine throughout the Judeo-Christian tradition is taken predominantly from the roles and relations of men, God being named as lord, king, father, son. Likewise, male self-definition has shaped the metaphysical concept of God which developed from the encounter of biblical with Greek philosophical traditions. The latter had equated male reality with spirit, with mind and reason, and, most importantly, with act, reserving for female reality a contrasting intrinsic connection with matter, with body and instinct, and with potency. God as absolute being or pure act necessarily excluded all potency, passivity, and prime matter, and thus could be thought only in analogy with the human spiritually masculine to the exclusion of analogy with the feminine passive material principle. This assumption and its attendant androcentric presuppositions permeate the classical Christian philosophical doctrine of God as well as the specifically Christian doctrine of the Trinity.[3] In a strikingly honest discussion of the issue, John B. Cobb summarizes: "Historically, whatever God's true nature and identity may be, God has been experienced, conceived, and spoken of as masculine," and this is a statement as applicable to metaphysical thinking about God as it is to religious images.[4]

The critique brought by women theologians against the exclusive centrality of the male image and idea of God is not only that in stereotyping and then banning female reality as suitable reference points for God, androcentric thought has denigrated the human dignity of women. The critique also bears directly on the religious significance and ultimate truth of androcentric thought about God. The charge, quite simply, is that of idolatry.[5] Normative conceptualization of God in analogy with male reality alone is the equivalent of the graven image, a finite representation being taken for and worshiped as the whole. What is violated is both the creature's limitation and the unknowable transcendence of the true God. It is true that sophisticated thinkers will immediately deny that any maleness in image or concept of God is meant to be taken literally. Yet the association of God with maleness lingers on implicitly even in highly abstract discussions, as evidenced in statements such as "God is not male; He is Spirit." Such an association is also presumed to be normative, a point demonstrated empirically by the dismay often registered when and if God is referred to with feminine images or pronouns. If it is not meant that God is male when masculine imagery is used, why the objection when female images are used? But in fact an intrinsic connection between God and maleness is usually intended, however implicitly. In spite of the affirmation of divine transcendence, the predominant developments of the Judeo-Christian tradition have lifted up the male way of being human to functional equivalence with the divine. More solid than stone, more resistant to iconoclasm than bronze, seems to be the male substratum of the idea of God cast in theological language and engraved in public and private prayer. Thus the critique: "It is idolatrous to make males more 'like God' than females. It is blasphemous to use the image and name of the Holy to justify patriarchal domination. . . . The image of God as predominantly male is fundamentally idolatrous" (as would be the image of God as exclusively female).[6]

Those who do not abandon the tradition because of its pervasive androcentrism but wrestle with it for its own deeper liberating truth propose by contrast an understanding of the unknown God derived from analogy with both male and female reality. The biblical creation narrative which presents both male and female created in the image of God (Gen 1:26–27), and the early Christian baptismal hymn which sees that in the world re-created by God's redeeming love there is no more division by race, class, or sex but all are one in Christ Jesus (Gal 3:28), are taken as clues that male and female are identical in their capacity to be images of God. Hence God, who is beyond all imaging, is well presented by analogy with both, and not well conceived on the pattern of merely one. The very incomprehensibility of God demands a proliferation of images and a variety of names, each of which acts as a corrective against the tendency of any one to become reified and literal. Female images and concepts of God disclose the relative character of male images and bracingly restrict their claim to ultimacy. Use of "God-She" immediately indicates the inherent inadequacy of "God-He." The understanding that God lies beyond whatever is thought or said is realized in the use of diverse images which balance or negate each other and thus point profoundly to the mystery of the present God who remains unknown.

In my judgment, what is at stake in this issue is simultaneously the freeing of both women and men from constricting reality models and social roles, and the very viability of the Judeo-Christian tradition for present and coming generations. The challenge to male monotheism and/or male Trinitarian thought arising from new recognition of women's equality and human dignity is one of the strongest in the course of the Judeo-Christian tradition, presaging a real Copernican revolution. As Wolfhart Pannenberg has elucidated the dynamics of the history of religions, religions die when their lights fail, when they lose the power to interpret the full range of present experience in the light of their idea of God.[7] If God is worshiped as the all-determining reality, the power over all, then the truth of God is tested by the extent to which the idea of God takes account of currently accessible aspects of reality and by the ability of the idea of God to integrate the complexity of present experience into itself. If the idea of God does not keep pace with developing reality, the power of experience pulls people on and the god dies, fading from memory. Is the God of the Judeo-Christian tradition so true as to be able to take account of, illumine, and integrate the currently accessible experience of women? This is an absolutely critical question.

[A survey of biblical, early Christian, and medieval tradition is omitted.]

THREE APPROACHES TO REVISION

Feminine Traits

A first step taken toward the revision of the patriarchal God image is the introduction of gentle, nurturing traits traditionally associated with the mothering role of women. The symbol of God as Father particularly benefits from this move. Too often this predominant symbol has been interpreted through association with traits associated with ruling men in a male-oriented society: aggressiveness, competitiveness, desire for absolute power and control, and demand for obedience. This certainly is not the *Abba* to whom Jesus prayed, and widespread rejection of such a symbol from Marx, Nietzsche, and Freud onward has created a crisis for Christian consciousness. But it is also possible to see God the Father displaying feminine, maternal features which temper "His" overwhelmingness. William Visser 't Hooft, e.g., argues that while the fatherhood of God is and must remain the predominant Christian symbol, it is not a closed or exclusive symbol but is open to its own correction, enrichment, and completion from other symbols, such as mother.[30] Thus gentleness and compassion, unconditional love, reverence and care for the weak, sensitivity to our every need, and desire not to dominate but to be intimate companion and friend are predicated of the Father God and make "Him" more attractive.[31] A clue to the use of this approach is almost invariably the use of the word "traits": the Bible allows us to speak of maternal traits in God (Visser 't Hooft); we have forgotten it, but the God of revelation has feminine traits such as tenderness (Congar); to transform our overmasculinized culture, we need to relate to the feminine traits of God (O'Hanlon); God is not simply male but has matriarchal traits (Küng).[32] God remains Father, but in a way tempered by the ideal feminine, so that we do not have to be afraid or rebellious against a crushing paternalism.

While this approach is appearing in the work of a fair number of male theologians trying to address the problem, and while it has the advantage of moving counter to the misogynism which has so afflicted Christian anthropology and the doctrine of God, women theologians are virtually unanimous in calling attention to its deficiencies and in precluding it as a long-range option.[33] The reasons for this are several. Even with the introduction of presumably feminine features, the androcentric pattern remains: God is still envisioned as a masculine God, only now possessing feminine characteristics. This is clearly seen in statements such as: God is not exclusively masculine but the "feminine-maternal element must also be recognized in Him."[34] God remains "Him," but imaged as a more wholistic male person who has integrated His feminine side. The patriarchy of God in this symbol is now benevolent, but it is nonetheless still patriarchy. And while the image of God as male as well as real male persons made in "His" image benefit and grow from the opening of nurturing and compassionate qualities in themselves, there is no equivalent attribution to a female symbol or to real female persons of corresponding presumably male qualities of rationality, power, the authority of leadership, etc. Men gain their feminine side, but not women their masculine side (if such categories are even valid). The feminine is there for the enhancement of the male, but not vice versa. Real women are then seen as capable of representing only the feminine element of what is still the male-centered symbol of God, the fulness of which can thereby be represented only by a male person. The female can never appear as icon of God in all divine fulness equivalent to the male. Inequality is not redressed but subtly furthered, as the androcentric structure of anthropology and the image of God remains in place and is made more appealing through the subordinate inclusion of feminine traits.

A critical issue underlying both this approach and the one to be considered next is that of the legitimacy of the rigid stereotyping involved in designating certain human characteristics as predominantly masculine or feminine. With what right are compassionate love, reverence, and nurturing predicated as primordially feminine characteristics, rather than human ones? Why are strength, sovereignty, and rationality exclusive to the masculine? Could it not be, as Ruether formulates the fundamental question, that the very concept of the "feminine" is a creation out of patriarchy, an ideal projected onto women by men and vigorously defended because it functions so well to keep men in positions of power and women out of public roles?[35] Masculine and feminine are among the most culturally stereotyped words in the language. This is not to say that there are no differences between women and men, but it is to question the justification of the present division and distribution of human virtues and attributes. Such stereotyping serves the true humanity of neither women nor men and results in a dualism in anthropology almost impossible to overcome. It does not, then, serve well for the re-envisionment of God in a more inclusive direction.

A Feminine Dimension of the Divine

Rather than merely attribute stereotypical feminine qualities to a male-imaged God, a second approach seeks a more ontological footing for the existence of the feminine in God. Most frequently that inroad is found in the doctrine of the Holy Spirit, who in classical Trinitarian theology is coequal in nature with the Father and the Son. Biblically, the Spirit is of feminine character, as is seen not only by the feminine gender of the Hebrew *ruah*, but by the use of the female imagery of the mother bird hovering or brooding to bring forth life, imagery associated with the Spirit of God in creation (Gen 1:2) and at the baptism of Jesus (Lk 3:22) among other places. Semitic and Syrian early Christians continued to construe the Spirit as feminine, attributing to the Spirit the motherly character which certain parts of the Hebrew Scriptures had already found in God.[36] The Holy Spirit is the maternal aspect of God, who brings about the incarnation of Christ, new members of the Body of Christ in the waters of baptism, and the body of Christ through the epiclesis of the Eucharist. The custom of thinking of the Holy Spirit as feminine waned in the West along with the habit of thinking very extensively about the Holy Spirit at all. As Heribert Mühlen observes, when most of us say "God," the Holy Spirit never comes immediately to mind; rather, the Spirit seems like an edifying appendage to the doc-

trine of God.[37] Even Thomas Aquinas had difficulty with this, saying that the Holy Spirit suffers from a poverty of terminology, so
that the relation of Spirit to Father and Son must remain in some
way unnamed.[38] It is pointed out today that one source of Aquinas'
problem was the metaphysical concepts of person and being with
which he was operating. Being of patriarchal origin and predicating
less than full personhood of women, they could not bring the personality of the Holy Spirit, which is feminine, fully to expression.[39]

Theologians such as Congar in his trilogy on the Holy Spirit and
Moltmann in his works on the Trinity are now trying to retrieve the
full Trinitarian tradition while overcoming its inherent patriarchy
by emphasizing the Holy Spirit as the feminine principle of the God-
head. Congar argues that a pretrinitarian monotheism and/or a
Christomonism, with its forgetfulness of the Holy Spirit, always
leads to patriarchy and male domination; rediscovering the Holy
Spirit as maternal gift and love performs the double task of rebalancing the doctrine of God and promoting the value of women.[40]
Moltmann connects monotheism with patriarchy, and pantheism
with matriarchy, arguing that only panentheism with a corresponding Trinitarianism (including the feminine Holy Spirit) can lead to
true community of women and men without privilege or subjec-
tion.[41]

There is a sense in which this approach can be helpful, especially for those whose thought tends to begin within the dogmatic or
liturgical traditions. Indeed, when the full range of the theology of
the Spirit is brought to bear, the effect can be quite powerful. The
Spirit is equal to Father and Son. She goes forth so that the hidden
Pantocrator can be made known:

> In the divine ecomony it is not the feminine person who remains
> hidden and at home. She is God in the world, moving, stirring
> up, revealing, interceding. It is she who calls out, sanctifies, and
> animates the church. Hers is the water of the one baptism. The
> debt of sin is wiped away by her. She is the life-giver who raises
> men [sic] from the dead with the life of the coming age. Jesus
> himself left the earth so that she, the intercessor, might come.[42]

This amounts to a revaluation of the feminine both in God and in
humanity.

But it is not enough. The Spirit may be the feminine aspect of the divine, but the endemic difficulty of Spirit theology insures that she remains rather unclear and invisible. A deeper theology of the Holy Spirit, notes Walter Kasper in another connection, stands before the difficulty that unlike the Father and Son, the Holy Spirit is "faceless."[43] While the Son has appeared in human form and while we can at least make an image of the Father, the Spirit is not graphic and remains the most mysterious of the three divine persons. For all practical purposes, we end up with two males and an amorphous third. Furthermore, the overarching framework of this approach remains androcentric, with the male principle still dominant and sovereign. The Spirit even as God remains the "third" person, easily subordinated to the other two, since she proceeds from them and is sent by them to mediate their presence and bring to completion what they have initiated. The extent to which this can go can be seen in Franz Mayr's attempt to understand the Holy Spirit as mother on the analogy of family relationships: if we liberate motherhood from a naturalistic concept and see it in its existential-social reality, then we can indeed see how the mother comes from the father and son, that is, how she receives her existential stamp and identity from them within the family.[44] While intending to rehabilitate the feminine, Mayr has again accomplished its subordination in unequal relationships.

The problem of stereotyping discussed before also plagues this approach. More often than not, those who use it associate the feminine with unconscious dreams and fantasies (Bachiega), or with nature, instinct, and bodiliness (Schrey), or with prime matter (Mayr), all of which is then said to be both endemic to God and experienceable as divine through the doctrine of the Holy Spirit.[45] The equation is set up: male is to female as transcendence is to immanence, with the feminine Spirit made the bearer of the experience of God's interiority to us. This stereotyping appears even in the creative attempt of process theologian John B. Cobb to come to terms with the charge of male idolatry in worship and thought. While acknowledging that "currently the received polarity of feminine and masculine is under consideration,"[46] he goes on to identify the Logos, the masculine aspect of God, with order, novelty, demand, agency, transformation; and the kingdom, or the feminine aspect of God equivalent to the Holy Spirit, with receptivity, empathy, suffering, preservation. The lines are drawn: the Logos provides ever-new initial aims and lures us always forward, while the feminine aspect of God responds tenderly to our failures and successes, assures us that whatever happens we are loved, and achieves in her whole life a harmonious wholeness of all that is. Besides the very real question of whether nature or culture shapes this description of roles, their effect on the perception of the being and function of real women is deleterious and restrictive. Nurturing and tenderness simply do not exhaust the capacities of women, nor do bodiliness and instinct define women's nature, nor is creative transformative agency beyond the scope of women's power. Ruether's question returns again in force, as to whether the very concept of the "feminine" which supposedly defines the essence of real women is not a patriarchal creation, useful insofar as it relegates women to the realm of the private and the role of succoring the male. Understanding the Holy Spirit as the bearer of the feminine is no final solution. Even at its best, it does not exhaust the possibilities for discovering the fulness of God or humanity.

The Image of God Male and Female

While both the "traits" and the "dimension" approach are inadequate for the reinterpretation of the doctrine of God in the light of women's dignity and freedom, since in both an androcentric focus remains dominant, a third approach images God equivalently as male and female. This approach shares with the other two the fundamental assumption that language about God as personal has a special appropriateness. Behaviorism notwithstanding, human persons are the most mysterious and attractive reality that we experience, and the highest order of being on this earth according to the metaphysical tradition. God is not a person as anyone else we know, but the language of person evokes in a unique way the mysteriousness, nonmanipulability, and freedom of action associated with God.

Predicating personality of God, however, immediately involves us in the question of gender, for all the persons we know are either male or female. God is properly understood as neither male nor female. But insofar as God created both male and female in the divine image and is therefore the source of the perfection of both, God can be represented equally well by images of either. Both are needed for a less inadequate imaging of God, in whose image the human race is created. This "clue"[47] for speaking of God in the image of male and female has the advantage of making clear at the outset that women enjoy the dignity of being made in God's image and are therefore capable as women of representing God. Simultaneously, it relativizes undue emphasis on any one image, since pressing the fulness of imagery shows the partiality of images of one sex alone. The incomprehensible mystery of God is brought to light and deepened in our consciousness through the imaging of God male and female, beyond any person we know.[48]

It has already been noted how the biblical, early Christian theological, and mystical traditions, though drawing a predominance of God imagery from male reality, also use female images of God without embarrassment or explanation. These images and personifications are not considered feminine aspects or features of the divine, to be interpreted in dualistic tension with masculine dimensions or traits, but representations of the fulness of God in creating and redeeming. Since it brings us into a world of thought different from our customary one, reference to ancient religions that worshiped gods and goddesses may be helpful in clarifying this thrust of the third approach (although in no way is it being suggested that monotheism be compromised). In those religions, as evidenced in their psalms and prayers, the gods and goddesses were not stereotyped according to the later idea of masculine and feminine, but each could represent the fulness of divine attributes and activity. In them "gender division is not yet the primary metaphor for imaging the dialectics of human existence,"[49] nor is the idea of "gender complementarity" present in the ancient myths. Rather, male and female are equivalent images of the divine. A goddess such as Ishtar, e.g., is addressed as the expression of divine power and sovereignty in female form, a deity who performs the divine works of dividing heaven from earth, setting captives free, waging war, establishing peace, administering justice, exercising judgment, and enlightening human beings with the truth—as well as presiding over birth, healing the sick, and nurturing the little ones.[50] When a god (e.g., Horus) is addressed, he has similar functions. Both male and female are powerful in the private and public spheres.

The point for our interest is that the goddess is not the expression of the feminine dimension of the divine, but the expression of the fulness of divine power and care shown in a female image. A case can be made for a similar implicit understanding present in the Christian Gospels in the parallel parables of the shepherd looking for the sheep and the woman searching for the lost coin (Lk 15:4–7, 8–10). In both stories God vigorously seeks what is lost and rejoices when it is found. Neither story discloses anything about God that the other hides. Using traditional men's and women's work, both parables orient us to God's redeeming action in images that are equivalently male and female. The woman and the coin image, while not portrayed in Christian art as frequently as the shepherd, is essentially as legitimate a reference to God as is the latter. Conversely, God imaged this way cannot be used to validate role stereotyping, wherein the major redeeming work in the world is done by men to the exclusion of women.

The understanding of the power of equivalent images for God is applicable as well to the specifically Christian doctrine of the Trinity. While this doctrine took shape under the hegemony of a patriarchal understanding of God and humanity, exclusively male imaging is not essential for understanding the inner-Trinitarian relations or the missions *ad extra*. Starting with Paul Tillich, a number of theologians have combed the tradition for elements usable in re-envisioning not only the Holy Spirit but all three "persons" in God in nonmasculine ways.[51] The unoriginate creator and continuing source of life can be named Mother as well as Father; neither image is sufficient but either is appropriate. As Moltmann struggles to express it, God is both "motherly Father" and "fatherly Mother."[52] Using both renders the unoriginate Creator God more intelligible in a culture which no longer sees the sole active principle in human generation as male, and more believable in a time which begins to recognize how the Father God symbol has been used to reinforce patriarchy and male dominance to the distortion of both male and female humanity. The first person generates the second, self-expressing the fulness of divine life in the eternal Word. The Father-Son imagery traditionally used to express this relation within God can be shifted to Mother-Daughter without proportionally changing the relation. Furthermore, an understanding of how the Hebraic female Sophia theology shaped and penetrated the Logos doctrine brings to light the fluidity of gender symbolism already present in expressions of the second person. The undoubted human maleness of Jesus, without whom there would be no Christian doctrine of the Trinity, is not an obstacle to this reenvisionment unless it is interpreted naively as revelatory of the maleness of God. Wisdom Christologies attest to Jesus Christ as child of Sophia-God, sent to gather the lost and broken under her merciful wings, and even as Sophia herself. In a paradoxical way, the union of female divine Wisdom and male humanity in Jesus can appear as a most intimate marriage of all being. Identifying the Wisdom elements in Christology leads in fact to a healthy blend of male and female imagery that empowers everyone and works to signify the self-expression of the one redeeming God who is neither male nor female.

As for the bond of mutual love between the first and second persons, the Holy Spirit is quite susceptible to female imaging, as has already been shown. The point is, all "three persons" of the Trinity transcend categories of male and female; yet all can be spoken of in human metaphors drawn from either. The cautions to be sounded in using female imagery of the triune God are the same as for using male imagery: not to lose sight of the unity of God, forgetting that the language of "three" is analogical and not meant in a mathematical sense; not to utilize restrictive stereotypes; not to forget the radical limitations of any imagery of God, female ones to be sure, but also Father and Son, Word or Wisdom, or memory, understanding, and will.

Beyond particular images for each of the divine persons, the Trinity in a formal way gives a model of relationship marked by total equality and reciprocity rather than dominance and subordination. All that the first person is is communicated to the second; all that the second person receives is returned to the first; and the life of mutuality which they share is the third person, powerful Spirit of love. All uniquely give, all uniquely receive, all hold together a shared life. Creator, Word, and Spirit are simply mutually one. This is the ideal of human interrelationship, made more effective by the use of images taken from both genders.

Was John Paul I a heretic when he addressed God as our Father and Mother? After a review of the biblical and theological tradition, one thinker answered "no" to that question.[53] While the Pope's use of both genders was "daring," God goes beyond all images and can be named in concepts taken from male or female reality. The third approach examined here proceeds with the insight that only if God is so named, only if the full reality of woman as well as man enters into the conceptualization of God, can the idolatrous fixation on one image be broken and the truth of the mystery of God, in tandem with the liberation of human beings in all of our mystery, emerge for our time.

CONCLUSION

It is beyond dispute that we have no completely adequate name for God. Nevertheless, at first hearing, inclusive naming of God in the image of male and female may seem strange. Exclusively male naming of God has predominated in the tradition and is deeply rooted, so that the shift of usage being envisioned here is indeed "seismic" in quality.[54] Given the new situation in which we find ourselves, however, this issue is ignored at peril of losing the relevance and, even more, the long-range credibility of the faith. There is a psychological inevitability of at least a degree of anthropomorphism in our idea of God. Even the sharpest, most self-critical mind can avoid only with difficulty (and then not always) the inclination to invest God with qualities of human personal reality with which one is well acquainted, among which gender is essential. God, however, is utterly transcendent, neither male nor female, yet creator of both in the divine image. Focusing on one to the exclusion of the other and clinging to that image has the religious effect of making God less God, at once restrictively expressed and too well known.

Since the concept of God defines and orients a whole way of life and understanding, sustaining a moral universe, the exclusive masculinity presumed in the traditional doctrine of God has also had profound consequences beyond the idea of God.[55] It has led to a distortion in Christian anthropology whereby men have theorized that the fulness of the divine image resides only or primarily in themselves, while women are derivatively or secondarily made in the image and likeness of God and thus subordinate. It has correspondingly sustained and legitimated institutional structures and personal interrelationships which are patriarchal in form, in which men alone by virtue of their maleness as representative of God may serve in positions of leadership and authority. Insofar as the systematic denigration of the human dignity of any one group of persons by any other group is considered to be morally reprehensible, in this inherited male-oriented concept of God intrinsically linked with such theory and practice there is at the very least a profound ambiguity.[56]

Image-breaking is a part of religious traditions, because focusing on a fixed image not only compromises the transcendence of God, but petrifies and stultifies human beings into the likeness of the image worshiped, inhibiting growth by preventing further searching for knowledge of God. Calling into question the exclusively male idea of God does not spell the end of male imagery used for God; what has been destroyed as an idol can return as an icon, evoking the presence of God. Using female imagery for God does not introduce a distraction from belief in the one God of the Judeo-Christian tradition; the use of startling metaphors opens up the possibility of new religious experience of the one Holy Mystery. The proposal to name God in the image of male and female holds the promise of renewing the tradition in line with one of its own best insights into the mystery of God, at the same time that it allies itself with emerging understanding of the human dignity of women. Our speech about God becomes more truly analogical at the same time that we slip the bonds of the stereotyping and subordination of persons. To paraphrase a Rahnerian axiom used with great beneficial effect in Christology,[57] the truth of the mystery of God and the liberation of human beings grow in direct and not inverse proportion.

NOTES

1. See developments of the theme of divine incomprehensibility in Victor White, *God the Unknown* (New York: Harper, 1956); Charles Bent, *Interpreting the Doctrine of God* (New York: Paulist, 1968); Gordon Kaufman, *God the Problem* (Cambridge, Mass.: Harvard University, 1972), esp. "God as Symbol" 82–115.

2. Hans Urs von Balthasar, "The Unknown God," *The von Balthasar Reader*, ed. M. Kehl and W. Löser (New York: Crossroad, 1982) 184. Balthasar queries where one can find a work of dogmatics which gives the incomprehensibility of God significant expression; theological textbooks have forgotten it; even Barth does not hold on to it to the end. Research for this study has convinced me that he is right; material on incomprehensibility is not plentiful. For the relation of God's incomprehensibility to

revelation, see also William Hill, *Knowing the Unknown God* (New York: Philosophical Library, 1971) ii; Leo Scheffczyk, "God," *Sacramentum mundi* 2 (New York: Herder & Herder, 1968) 382–87.

3. See development of this thesis with focus on Augustine and Aquinas by Franz Mayr, "Patriarchalisches Gottesverständnis?" *Theologische Quartalschrift* 152 (1972) 224–55, and "Trinitatstheologie und theologische Anthropologie," *Zeitschrift für Theologie und Kirche* 68 (1971) 427–77; also Rosemary Radford Ruether, "Misogynism and Virginal Feminism," *Religion and Sexism,* ed. R. Ruether (New York: Simon and Schuster, 1974) 150–83.

4. John B. Cobb, "God and Feminism," *Talking about God,* ed. J. B. Cobb and David Tracy (New York: Seabury, 1983) 79.

5. For expatiations on the charge of idolatry, from which the following section draws, see Rosemary Radford Ruether, *Sexism and God-Talk: Toward a Feminist Theology* (Boston: Beacon, 1983) 22–27; also her "The Female Nature of God," *God as Father?* (*Concilium* 143; New York: Seabury, 1981) 66; Mary Daly, *Beyond God the Father* (Boston: Beacon, 1973); Elisabeth Schüssler Fiorenza, "Feminist Spirituality, Christian Identity, and Catholic Vision," *Womanspirit Rising,* ed. C. Christ and J. Plaskow (San Francisco: Harper & Row, 1979) 139; Rita Gross, "Female God Language in a Jewish Context," ibid. 169–70; Anne Carr, "Is a Christian Feminist Theology Possible?" *TS* 43 (1982) 296; Gail Ramshaw Schmidt, "De divinis nominibus: The Gender of God," *Worship* 56 (1982) 117–31.

6. Ruether, *Sexism and God-Talk* 23.

7. Wolfhart Pannenberg, "Toward a Theology of the History of Religions," *Basic Questions in Theology* 2 (Philadelphia: Fortress, 1971) 65–118; also his "Anthropology and the Question of God," *The Idea of God and Human Freedom* (Philadelphia: Westminster, 1973) 94–98; and his *Theology and the Philosophy of Science* (Philadelphia: Westminster, 1976) 301–26.

30. W. A. Visser 't Hooft, *The Fatherhood of God in an Age of Emancipation* (Geneva: World Council of Churches, 1982) 133.

31. List of characteristics of the feminine offered by Daniel O'Hanlon, "The Future of Theism," *Catholic Theological Society of America Proceedings* 38 (1983) 8.

32. Visser 't Hooft, *Fatherhead of God* 133; Congar, *Je crois* 3, 207; O'Hanlon, "Future of Theism" 7–8; Hans Küng, *Does God Exist?* (Garden City, N.Y.: Doubleday, 1980) 673.

33. E.g., Ruether, *Sexism and God-Talk* 69, 128–32; Schmidt, "De divinis nominibus" 125; Borresen, "L'Usage patristique" 219.

34. Küng, *Does God Exist?* 673.

35. Ruether, "The Female Nature of God" 65. Contemporary use of

the concept of the feminine is usually related to the categories codified by Carl Jung; cf. Naomi Goldenberg, "A Feminist Critique of Jung," *Signs*, Winter 1976, 443–49, and her unpublished dissertation at Yale University, 1976, *Important Directions for a Feminist Critique of Religion in the Works of Sigmund Freud and Carl Jung*.

36. Cf. Robert Murray, "The Holy Spirit as Mother," *Symbols of Church and Kingdom* (London: Cambridge University, 1975) 312–20; P. A. De Boer, *Fatherhood and Motherhood in Israelite and Judean Piety* (Leiden: Brill, 1974).

37. Heribert Mühlen, "The Person of the Holy Spirit," *The Holy Spirit and Power*, ed. Kilian McDonnell (Garden City, N.Y.: Doubleday, 1975) 12.

38. Aquinas, *Summa theologiae* 1, q. 37, a. 1.

39. Mayr, "Trinitätstheologie" 471.

40. Congar, *Je crois* 3, 215–17.

41. Jürgen Moltmann, *The Trinity and the Kingdom* (San Francisco: Harper & Row, 1981) 57, 164–65.

42. Jay G. Williams, "Yahweh, Women and the Trinity," *Theology Today* 32 (1975) 240.

43. Walter Kasper, *Der Gott Jesu Christi* (Mainz: Grünewald, 1982) 246, 273–74. Kasper does not deal with the Holy Spirit as feminine or any other aspect of our question in this book.

44. Mayr, "Trinitätstheologie" 474. This is reminiscent of Basil of Caesarea, who at one point held that the Holy Spirit was equal in nature but not in rank or dignity with the Father and the Son (*Contra Eunomium* 3, 2 [PG 29, 657c]). While he later changed his position, the whole incident is illustrative of the tendency to subordination connected with the Holy Spirit.

45. Mario Bachiega, *Dio Padre o Dea Madre?* (Florence, 1976) 125; H. H. Schrey, "Ist Gott ein Mann?" *Theologische Rundschau* 44 (1979) 233; Mayr, "Trinitätstheologie" 469.

46. John B. Cobb, "The Trinity and Sexist Language," *Christ in a Pluralistic Age* (Philadelphia: Westminster, 1975) 264. George Tavard sets up the same polarity in *Woman in Christian Tradition* (Notre Dame: University of Notre Dame, 1973) 195–99, but then questions it on the basis of the difficulties it presents.

47. Phyllis Trible's expression, used throughout *God and the Rhetoric of Sexuality*.

48. Herbert Richardson recounts the following personal recollection. As a child he was taught to say a bedtime prayer "Father-Mother God, loving me, guard me while I sleep, guide my little feet up to thee." It was thereby borne in upon his young mind that if God is both Father and

Mother, God is different from any one thing he experienced around him (*Women and Religion*, ed. E. Clark and H. Richardson [New York: Harper & Row, 1977] 164–65).

49. Ruether, *Sexism and God-Talk* 52.

50. In Frederick Grant, *Hellenistic Religions: The Age of Syncretism* (New York: Liberal Arts, 1953) 131–33.

51. See Paul Tillich, *Systematic Theology* 3 (Chicago: University of Chicago, 1963) 293–94; Margaret Farley, "Sources of Inequality in Christian Thought," *Journal of Religion* 56 (1976) 173–74, and "New Patterns of Relationship," *TS* 36 (1975) 640–42; Letty Russell, *Human Liberation in a Feminist Perspective* (Philadelphia: Westminster, 1974) 100–103; Wilson Kastner, "Faith" 92–97, 133–34; Moltmann, *The Trinity and the Kingdom* 57, 164–65.

52. Moltmann, ibid. 164. Jesus' use of *Abba* for God does not bind Christians to exclusive use of the word "Father" for God, insofar as Jesus envisioned God in other ways as well (cf. the parables); insofar as the English word "Father" is questionable as an accurate translation of *Abba* (cf. Schmidt, "De divinis nominibus" 122, and H. Paul Santmire, "Retranslating 'Our Father': The Urgency and the Possibility," *Dialog* 16 [1977] 102, 104); and insofar as it is debatable whether fatherhood or the feminine *basileia* (reign of God) is the key image co-ordinating all others in Jesus' speech (Philip Harner, *Understanding the Lord's Prayer* [Philadelphia: Fortress, 1975] vs. Robert Hammerton-Kelly, *God the Father: Theology and Patriarchy in the Teaching of Jesus* [Philadelphia: Fortress, 1979]).

53. Hans Dietschy, "God Is Father and Mother," *Theology Digest* 30 (1982) 132–33; from *Reformatio* 30 (1981) 425–32.

54. Daniel Maguire, "The Feminization of God and Ethics," *Annual of the Society of Christian Ethics* 1982, 3; also Cobb, *Talking about God* 79–80.

55. Functions of the concept of God are discussed in Kaufman, *God the Problem* 89–113, 169; Farley, "Sources of Inequality" 164–68; Kari Elisabeth Børresen, "The Imago Dei: Two Historical Contexts," *Mid-Stream* 21 (1982) 359–63; Juan Luis Segundo, *Our Idea of God* (Maryknoll, N.Y.: Orbis, 1974) 7–10.

56. Kaufman, in *God the Problem* 112, n. 31, deals with the relation of the image of God to militarism; his insights apply equally well to sexism.

57. Rahner's original principle, expressed in a variety of synonymous ways, holds that nearness to God and genuine human autonomy grow in direct and not in inverse proportion; cf. "Jesus Christ," *Sacramentum mundi* 3 (New York: Herder & Herder, 1968) 206.

The Sophia-God of Jesus
and the Discipleship of Women

Elisabeth Schüssler Fiorenza

The Jesus movement articulates a quite different understanding of God because it had experienced in the praxis of Jesus a God who called not Israel's righteous and pious but its religiously deficient and its social underdogs. In the ministry of Jesus God is experienced as all-inclusive love, letting the sun shine and the rain fall equally on the righteous and on sinners (Matt 5:45). This God is a God of graciousness and goodness who accepts everyone and brings about justice and well-being for everyone without exception.[71] The creator God accepts all members of Israel, and especially the impoverished, the crippled, the outcast, the sinners and prostitutes, as long as they are prepared to engage in the perspective and power of the *basileia*. Conversely, it is stressed: "No one is good but God alone" (Mark 10:18b; Luke 18:19b).

1. This inclusive graciousness and goodness of God is spelled out again and again in the parables.[72] It has already been shown that the parable of the creditor who freely remits the debts of those who cannot pay articulates this gracious goodness of God by stressing that women, even public sinners, can be admitted to the Jesus movement in the conviction that "they will love more." The double simile of the shepherd searching for the lost sheep and of the woman searching for her lost silver coin, in all likelihood was already taken over by Luke from Q in its present form.[73] The Q community used these similes to reply to the accusation that "Jesus receives sinners and eats with them" (Luke 15:2; cf. Mark 2:16b for a similar ac-

cusation), justifying it with the application that "in heaven there is joy over the sinner who repents." The original form of the double story was probably parable rather than simile, since it did not include this explicit "application" to the situation of the community. Like the original story, this application stresses the joy of "finding the lost" but no longer emphasizes the search. As Jesus might have told this parable, it would have jolted the hearer into recognition: this is how God acts—like the man searching for his lost sheep, like the woman tirelessly sweeping for her lost coin. Jesus thus images God as a woman searching for one of her ten coins, as a woman looking for money that is terribly important to her. In telling the parable of the woman desperately searching for her money, Jesus articulates God's own concern, a concern that determines Jesus' own praxis for table community with sinners and outcasts. The parable then challenges the hearer: do you agree with the attitude of God expressed in the woman's search for her lost "capital"?

The *basileia* parable of "the laborers in the vineyard" (Matt 20:1–16) articulates the equality of all rooted in the gracious goodness of God.[74] Its *Sitz im Leben* is similar to that of the parable of the lost sheep and the lost coin, namely, the Jesus movement's table sharing with outcasts. The social world of the parable is that of a first-century Palestinian landowner who, in order to save money, hired laborers day by day and hour by hour during the harvest. To a contemporary hearer of this parable the householder would clearly be God, and the vineyard, Israel. The contrast between the parable's world and the actual labor practices and exploitation of the poor laborers—daily or hourly—underlines the gracious goodness and justice of God. Those who are last receive a whole day's payment. Yet the story does not end here, for it also expresses the offense taken by some of the first hired. The householder had treated them justly in giving them the promised payment for the day's work. If the last had received less they would have been satisfied. But instead of arguing for "just wages" and labor practices for all, those first hired grumble because the householder "has made the last equal to themselves." Jesus' parable thus startles his hearers into the recognition that God's gracious goodness establishes equality among all of us, righteous and sinner, rich and poor, men and women, Pharisees and Jesus' disciples. It challenges the hearer to solidarity and equality with "the last" in Israel. The all-inclusive goodness of Israel's God calls forth human equality and solidarity. The tensive symbol *basileia* of God evokes in ever new images a realization of the gracious goodness of Israel's God and the equality and solidarity of the people of God. A very similar understanding of equality is expressed in one of the earliest statements of the contemporary women's liberation movement:

> We define the best interests of women as the best interests of the poorest, most insulted, most despised, most abused woman on earth. . . . Until Everywoman is free, no woman will be free.[75]

Radical feminism has rediscovered the "equality from below" espoused by the Jesus movement in Palestine without recognizing its religious roots.

The earliest Jesus traditions perceive this God of gracious goodness in a woman's *Gestalt* as divine *Sophia* (wisdom).[76] The very old saying, "Sophia is justified [or vindicated] by all her children" (Luke 7:35[Q]) probably had its setting in Jesus' table community with tax collectors, prostitutes, and sinners, as well. The Sophia-God of Jesus recognizes all Israelites as her children and she is proven "right" by all of them. The Q community qualifies this saying by stressing that the most eminent of the children of Sophia are John and Jesus. Only Matthew identifies Sophia with Jesus.[77] It is now Jesus-Sophia who becomes justified by her deeds.

Jewish wisdom theology developed in Egypt, but it also permeated apocalyptic literature and can be found in Qumran theology. From the third century B.C.E. on, Jewish wisdom theology celebrated God's gracious goodness in creating the world and electing Israel as the people among whom the divine presence dwells in the female *Gestalt* of divine *Sophia*. Although Jewish (and Christian) theology speaks about God in male language and images, it nevertheless insists that such language and images are not adequate "pictures" of the divine, and that human language and experience are not capable of beholding or expressing God's reality. The second commandment and the unspeakable holiness of God's name are very concrete expressions of this insistence. To fix God to a definite form and man-made image would mean idolatry. Classical prophetic theology, often in abusive language, polemicized against the pagan idols and thus rejected goddess worship, but it did not do so in defense

of a male God and a patriarchal idol. By rejecting all other gods, prophetic theology insisted on the *oneness* of Israel's God and of God's
creation. It therefore rejected the myth of the "divine couple," and
thus repudiated masculinity and feminity as ultimate, absolute principles. But in doing so, it did not quite escape the patriarchal understanding of God, insofar as it transferred the image of the divine
marriage to the relationship of Yahweh and Israel who is seen as his
wife or bride.

Unlike classical prophecy, wisdom theology is not characterized by fear of the goddess in its apologetic "defense" of monotheism.[78] Rather, it is inspired by a positive attempt to speak in the
language of its own culture and to integrate elements of its "goddess
cult," especially of Isis worship, into Jewish monotheism. As such
it does theology as "reflective mythology," that is, it uses elements
of goddess-language in order to speak of the gracious goodness of
Israel's God. A well-known prayer to Isis proclaims that all the different nations and peoples use divine names familiar to them. They
call on the goddess, doing so because they know that Isis, being *one*,
is all.

Divine Sophia is Israel's God in the language and *Gestalt* of the
goddess.[79] Sophia is called sister, wife, mother, beloved, and
teacher. She is the leader on the way, the preacher in Israel, the task-
master and creator God. She seeks people, finds them on the road,
invites them to dinner. She offers life, rest, knowledge, and salvation to those who accept her. She dwells in Israel and officiates in
the sanctuary. She sends prophets and apostles and makes those who
accept her "friends of God." "She is but one but yet can do everything, herself unchanging. She makes all things new" (Wis 7:27).
Wisdom sought a dwelling place among humanity, but found none.
Therefore she has withdrawn again and "has taken her seat among
the angels" (*1 Enoch* 42:1–2). Sophia is described as "all-powerful,
intelligent, unique" (Wis 7:22). She is a people-loving spirit (*phi-
lanthrōpon pneuma*, 1:6) who shares the throne of God (9:10). She is
an initiate (*mystis*) of God's knowledge, an associate in God's works,
and emanation of the God of light, who lives in *symbiōsis* with God
(8:3–4), an image of God's goodness (7:26). One can sense here how
much the language struggles to describe Sophia as divine (without
falling prey to ditheism). Goddess-language is employed to speak
about the *one* God of Israel whose gracious goodness is divine So-

phia. Jewish wisdom theology, as distinct from gnostic theology, has successfully struggled against the danger of divine dimorphism. It did not, however, avoid anthropological dualism, as the negative characterization of women in wisdom and apocalyptic writings indicates. It thereby opened up the possibility for projecting such anthropological dualism into divine reality and for rejecting the creator God of Judaism.

While cosmological wisdom mythology has influenced the earliest christological expressions of the Christian missionary movement, its traces—though significant—are scant in the traditions of the Jesus movement. The earliest Palestinian theological remembrances and interpretations of Jesus' life and death understand him as Sophia's messenger and later as Sophia herself. The earliest Christian theology is sophialogy. It was possible to understand Jesus' ministry and death in terms of God-Sophia, because Jesus probably understood himself as the prophet and child of Sophia. As Sophia's messenger he calls "all who labor hard and are heavy laden" and promises them rest and *shalom*. He proclaims that the discipleship (the "yoke") of Sophia is easy and her load light to bear (Matt 11:28–30). Such a sophialogical context also makes more comprehensible the difficult saying of Q (Matt 12:32; Luke 12:10) that blasphemy against Jesus, the paradigmatic Human Being, will be forgiven, but not blasphemy against the Holy Spirit. A statement against Jesus can be forgiven, but a statement against the "child" or messenger of Sophia-Spirit cannot, because it means a rejection of the gracious goodness of God.

This theological reflection understood John and Jesus as the prophets and apostles who stand in the succession of Sophia's messengers. Like these others, they are persecuted and killed: "Therefore also the Wisdom of God said: 'I will send them prophets and apostles, some of whom they will kill and persecute' " (Luke 11:49 [Q?]). In a moving passage Sophia laments the murder of her envoys, her prophets, who are sent in every generation to proclaim the gracious goodness and justice of God to the people of Israel:

O Jerusalem, Jerusalem, you slay the prophets and stone those who are sent to you. How often have I wanted to gather your children as a mother bird collects her young under her wings, but you refused me. [Luke 13:34 (Q)][80]

This saying likens the ministry of Sophia-Jesus to that of a hen gathering her very own brood under her wings. But the gentleness and care of Sophia is rejected.

To sum up, the Palestinian Jesus movement understands the ministry and mission of Jesus as that of the prophet and child of Sophia sent to announce that God is the God of the poor and heavy laden, of the outcasts and those who suffer injustice. As child of Sophia he stands in a long line and succession of prophets sent to gather the children of Israel to their gracious Sophia-God. Jesus' execution, like John's, results from his mission and commitment as prophet and emissary of the Sophia-God who holds open a future for the poor and outcast and offers God's gracious goodness to *all* children of Israel without exception. The Sophia-God of Jesus does not need atonement or sacrifices. Jesus' death is not willed by God but is the result of his all-inclusive praxis as Sophia's prophet. This understanding of the suffering and execution of Jesus in terms of prophetic sophialogy is expressed in the difficult saying which integrates the wisdom and *basileia* traditions of the Jesus movement: "The *basileia* of God suffers violence from the days of John the Baptist until now and is hindered by men of violence" (Matt 11:12). The suffering and death of Jesus, like that of John and all the other prophets sent to Israel before him, are not required in order to atone for the sins of the people in the face of an absolute God, but are the result of violence against the envoys of Sophia who proclaim God's unlimited goodness and the equality and election of *all* her children in Israel.

2. This reality of God-Sophia spelled out in the preaching, healings, exorcisms, and inclusive table community of Jesus called forth a circle of disciples who were to continue what Jesus did. Sophia, the God of Jesus, wills the wholeness and humanity of everyone and therefore enables the Jesus movement to become a "discipleship of equals." They are called to one and the same praxis of inclusiveness and equality lived by Jesus-Sophia. Like Jesus, they are sent to announce to everyone in Israel the presence of the *basileia*, as God's gracious future, among the impoverished, the starving, the tax collectors, sinners, and prostitutes. Like Jesus, his disciples are sent to make the *basileia* experientially available in their healings and exorcisms, by restoring the humanity and wholeness of Sophia-God's children. The majority of them were not rich, like the

Cynic philosophers who could reject property and cultural positions in order "to become free from possessions." Rather, they were called from the impoverished, starving, and "heavy laden" country-people. They were tax collectors, sinners, women, children, fishers, housewives, those who had been healed from their infirmities or set free from bondage to their evil spirits. What they offered was not an alternative lifestyle but an alternative ethos: they were those without a future, but now they had hope again; they were the "outcast" and marginal people in their society, but now they had community again; they were despised and downtrodden, but now they had dignity and self-confidence as God-Sophia's beloved children; they were, because of life's circumstances and social injustices, sinners with no hope to share in the holiness and presence of God, but now they were heirs of the *basileia*, experiencing the gracious goodness of God who had made them equal to the holy and righteous in Israel. As such they came together in the discipleship of equals and shared their meager bread with those who came to hear the gospel. (The stories about the miraculous feedings of the multitudes not only have eucharistic overtones but also speak of the worry and concern of Jesus' disciples that they had so little food to share.) They stand in the succession of Sophia-prophets, announcing *shalom* to Israel. As the disciples of Jesus-Sophia they continue what Jesus did, namely, making the reality of God's *basileia* and the all-inclusive goodness of the Sophia-God of Jesus experientially available.[81]

Whereas the Q traditions limit the prophetic ministry of Jesus and his movement to the people of Israel, the Galilean Jesus movement seems to have accepted gentiles at a very early date. The pre-Markan controversy dialogues Mark 2:1–3:6, as well as the pre-Markan miracle collection utilized in Mark 4:35–8:10, seem to address the question of inclusive table community with gentiles as an inner-Christian problem. The Galilean "missionaries" stress that many sinners were sitting down at table with Jesus and his disciples "for there were many who followed him" (Mark 2:15).[82] Sinners now meant not those Jews who in one way or the other had committed an offense against the Torah, but, as is often the case in Jewish discourse, it meant "pagans." Thus at an early stage some members of the Galilean Jesus movement justified their inclusive table community with pagans by reference to Jesus' own praxis and the fact that many non-Jews had become disciples of Jesus.

They do this, not so much as a defense against the Pharisees but rather against the criticism of other Christians, since the controversy collection evidences an inner-Christian debate. That such an inclusive table sharing of both Jews and gentiles was very controversial among Christians is obvious from Paul's statement (Gal 2:11–14) that Peter the Galilean had table community with gentile Christians in Antioch but ceased to do so when he was attacked. He and other Jewish Christians reversed themselves when they were under attack by some followers of James from Jerusalem. The conversion of the centurion Cornelius in Acts 10:1–11:18 reflects the same debate about ritual uncleanliness. After Peter had baptized the Roman's whole house he went up to Jerusalem and was attacked by the "circumcision party" (Acts 11:2f): "Why did you go to the uncircumcised [i.e., pagans] and eat with them?" Peter justifies his table sharing with gentile Christians by citing a heavenly vision in which he was directed to eat unclean food.

The pre-Markan story about the healing of the Gerasene demoniac (Mark 5:1–20) makes the same point but with a different theological-historical argument: it was Jesus himself who liberated the gentiles from their "unclean" spirits. Jesus did not ask him to stay "with him" but commanded him to proclaim to his friends the "great mercy" of the Lord (5:18–20). The *Sitz im Leben* of this strange exorcism story is, therefore, not the missionary preaching to gentiles but the inner-Christian debate over the mission to pagans and table sharing between them and Jewish Christians.

The same difficult problem is discussed theologically in the pre-Markan miracle story in Mark 7:24–30.[83] Surprisingly, the major theologian and spokesperson for such a table sharing with gentiles is a woman. As distinct from all other controversy dialogues, Jesus does not have the last word. Rather, the woman's argument prevails over that of Jesus. The parabolic saying of Jesus against the admission of gentiles to the community of Jesus provokes the intelligent retort of the woman. She takes up Jesus' parabolic image of the "table-children-housedogs" and uses it to argue against him. The woman "wins" the contest because Jesus, convinced by her argument (*dia touton ton logon*), liberates her daughter from the demon.

Except for the introduction in v. 24a and the addition in v. 27 (the children *first*), the story is a unified pre-Markan composition. If it was told together with the exorcism story of the unclean Gerasene demoniac, then these stories use the *example* of Jesus against those who use a *saying* of Jesus to justify a strict prohibition against the gentile mission. Thus the enigmatic saying in Matt 7:6 warns not to give food offered in sacrifice (and therefore holy) to dogs, and not to give pearls to swine. Since dogs and swine were considered unclean animals they could be used figuratively to characterize pagans. This saying ascribed to Jesus, then, argues that the gospel of the *basileia* which is compared to a pearl in Matt 13:45 (and the "holy" table sharing among Christians) should not be given to gentiles for fear they might misuse it.

If Mark 7:24a is Markan redactional introduction, then the original story is located in Galilee. The woman is characterized ethically and culturally as a gentile. Her daughter (her future?) is in bondage to evil and she expects liberation from Jesus. The Greek verb *chortasthēnai* ("become satisfied") connects the story with the two messianic pre-Markan feeding miracles, insofar as this verb is only found in Mark here and in 6:42; 8:4, 8).[84] The feeding miracles have strong eucharistic overtones which are toned down by Mark. The argument, then, that the children (Israel) should be fed and that their food should not be taken from them and given to the dogs (gentiles) is countered by the woman by referring to the messianic abundance of Christian table community. The gracious goodness of the God of Jesus is abundant enough to satisfy not only the Jews but also the gentiles. The power of the *basileia* liberates not only the "children" of Israel but also the woman-child who, as a female and as a gentile, is doubly polluted and subject to the "bondage" of ritual impurity.

If John 4:1–42 reworks a traditional mission legend about a woman's primary role in the beginnings of the Christian community in Samaria,[85] then there is evidence from two different strata of the gospel tradition that women were determinative for the extension of the Jesus movement to non-Israelites. Women were the first non-Jews to become members of the Jesus movement. Although the Syrophoenician respects the primacy of the "children of Israel," she nevertheless makes a theological argument against limiting the inclusive messianic table community of Jesus to Israel alone. That such a theological argument is placed in the mouth of a woman is a sign of the historical leadership women had in opening up Jesus' movement and community to "gentile 'sinners' " (Gal 2:15b).

This historical development was of utmost significance for the beginnings of Christianity. Women who had experienced the gracious goodness of Jesus' God were leaders in expanding the Jesus movement in Galilee and in developing a theological argument from the Jesus traditions for why pagans should have access to the power of Jesus' God and a share in the superabundance of the messianic table community. By challenging the Galilean Jesus movement to extend its table sharing and make the *basileia's* power and future experientially available also to gentiles, these women safeguarded the inclusive discipleship of equals called forth by Jesus. The Syrophoenician woman whose adroit argument opened up a future of freedom and wholeness for her daughter has also become the historically-still-visible advocate of such a future for gentiles. She has become the apostolic "foremother" of all gentile Christians.

3. Galilean women were not only decisive for the extension of the Jesus movement to gentiles but also for the very continuation of this movement after Jesus' arrest and execution. Jesus' Galilean women disciples did not flee after his arrest but stayed in Jerusalem for his execution and burial. These Galilean women were also the first to articulate their experience of the powerful goodness of God who did not leave the crucified Jesus in the grave but raised him from the dead. The early Christian confession that "Jesus the Nazarene who was executed on the cross was raised" is, according to the pre-Markan resurrection story of Mark 16:1–6, 8a,[86] revealed in a vision first to the Galilean women disciples of Jesus.

In all likelihood, the Galilean disciples of Jesus fled after his arrest from Jerusalem and went back home to Galilee. Because of their visionary-ecstatic experiences, the women who remained in the capital came to the conviction that God had vindicated Jesus and his ministry. They, therefore, were empowered to continue the movement and work of Jesus, the risen Lord.[87] They probably sought to gather together the dispersed disciples and friends of Jesus who lived in and around Jerusalem—women disciples like Mary, Martha of Bethany, the woman who had anointed Jesus, the mother of John Mark who had a house in Jerusalem, or Mary, the mother of Jesus, as well as such male disciples as Lazarus, Nicodemus, or the "beloved" disciple. Some of these women probably also moved back, very soon, to Galilee, their native country. Such a reconstruction of the events after the death and resurrection of Jesus is historically plausible, since it might have been easier for the women of the Jesus movement to go "underground" than the men. By keeping alive the good news about the manifestation of God's life-giving power in Jesus of Nazareth, among the followers and friends of Jesus, the Galilean women continued the movement initiated by Jesus. Mary of Magdala was the most prominent of the Galilean disciples, because according to tradition she was the first one to receive a vision of the resurrected Lord.

Two different pre-Gospel traditions transmit names of Galilean women disciples. Although their names differ, Mary of Magdala seems to have been the leader among them, since she is usually mentioned first. The names vary in both the Palestinian (?) pre-Lukan and pre-Markan lists. However, Hengel has observed the tendency to group the women's names into groups of three, similar to the special groups of three among the twelve (Peter, James, John) and the leaders of the Jerusalem community (James the brother of the Lord, Cephas, and John). The membership in such a group of three, and the sequence of the names in it, indicates a preeminence in the latter community.[88] In Luke 8:3 the special Lukan source mentions Joanna, the wife of Herod's steward, who is characterized as a woman with higher social standing. How important she was for Luke is evident from his insertion of her name into the Markan list in Luke 24:10. Yet it is likely that Luke added her name to the original list because of his interest in wealthy women, as evident in Luke 8:1–3 and Acts.

Hengel concludes his article by noting that "the message of Jesus must have had a special impact on the women in Israel,"[89] but he does not explain why this was the case. We have seen that the Sophia-God of Jesus made possible the invitation of women to the discipleship of equals. However, one could object that the Q traditions not only image the gracious goodness of the God of Jesus as divine Sophia but also call this God "father." Do they thereby indirectly legitimize patriarchal structures and the "second class" status of women in such structures, or does their androcentric language have a critical impulse that radically denies any religious authority and power for the structures of patriarchy? To raise such a question is not to raise a modern question alien to the New Testament text, but to explore the Jesus traditions in terms of social-political structures. We have seen that, in the first century, patriarchy was well established as a social institution but also that it was undermined by religious practices and legal conventions that gave women more freedom and economic powers.

NOTES

71. Müller, "Vision und Botschaft," p. 447.

72. See Perrin's review in his *Jesus and the Language of the Kingdom*, pp. 89–193; P. Perkins, *Hearing the Parables of Jesus* (New York: Paulist Press, 1981).

73. J. Lambrecht, *Once More Astonished: The Parables of Jesus* (New York: Crossroad, 1981), pp. 24–56.

74. L. Schottroff, "Die Güte Gottes und die Solidarität von Menschen: Das Gleichnis von den Arbeitern im Weinberg," in Schottroff and Stegemann, *Der Gott der kleinen Leute*, pp. 71–93.

75. "Redstockings, April 1969," in *Feminist Revolution* (New York: Random House, 1975), p. 205.

76. F. Christ, *Jesus Sophia: Die Sophia Christologie bei den Synoptikern* (Zurich: Zwingli Verlag, 1970); J. M. Robinson, "Jesus as Sophos and Sophia: Wisdom Tradition and the Gospels," in R. Wilken, ed., *Aspects of Wisdom in Judaism and Early Christianity* (Notre Dame: University of Notre Dame Press, 1975), pp. 1–16.

77. M. J. Suggs, *Wisdom, Christology and Law in Matthew's Gospel* (Cambridge, Mass.: Harvard University Press, 1970), pp. 31–62.

78. For a fuller development and discussion of the literature, cf. my article "Wisdom Mythology and the Christological Hymns of the New Testament," in Wilken, *Aspects of Wisdom*, pp. 17–42.

79. For a different "archetypal" interpretation, cf. J. Chamberlain Engelsman, *The Feminine Dimension of the Divine* (Philadelphia: Westminster, 1979), pp. 106–18.

80. S. Schulz, *Die Spruchquelle der Evangelien* (Zurich: Theologischer Verlag, 1972), pp. 336–45, for bibliography.

81. P. Hoffmann, *Studien zur Theologie der Logienquelle* (Münster: Aschendorff, 1972), pp. 287–311: esp. 296ff.

82. U. B. Müller, "Zur Rezeption gesetzeskritischer Jesusüberlieferung im frühen Christentum," *NTS* 27 (1981) 158–85; U. Luz, "Das Jesusbild der vormarkinischen Tradition," in G. Strecker, ed., *Jesus Christus in Historie und Theologie* (Tübingen: Mohr-Siebeck, 1975), pp. 347–74.

83. Cf. the discussion and literature in Alice Dermience, "Tradition

et rédaction dans la péricope de la Syrophénicienne: Marc 7,24–30," *Revue Théologique de Louvain* 53 (1977) 15–29.

84. B. Flammer, "Die Syrophoenizerin," *Theologische Quartalschrift* 148 (1968) 463–78:468.

85. R. Bultmann, *The Gospel of John* (Philadelphia: Westminster, 1971), pp. 175f.

86. For a review and discussion, cf. H. Paulsen, "Mk xvi 1–8," *NovT* 22 (1980) 138–75; A. Lindemann, "Die Osterbotschaft des Markus: Zur theologischen Interpretation von Mark 16.1–8," *NTS* 26 (1980) 298–317.

87. This is completely neglected in the discussion of G. O'Collins, "Peter as Easter Witness," *Heythrop Journal* 22 (1981) 1–18.

88. M. Hengel, "Maria Magdalena und die Frauen als Zeugen," in P. Schmid, ed., *Abraham unser Vater* (Leiden: Brill, 1963), pp. 243–56:248.

89. Ibid., p. 256.

Non-Patriarchal Salvation

Bernard Cooke

Among the more fundamental—and for that very reason more complex—elements in the present reassessing of women's role in Christianity is the issue of the "masculinity" of God and the masculinity of Jesus. How are women, without conforming to the discriminations inherent in a patriarchal culture, to relate to God as a "he" or to accept as their savior a Christ who has never shared their femininity?[1]

One of the key aspects of this issue, though by no means the only one, is the theological: how does Christian belief address itself to this issue, suggest "solutions," or perhaps limit the range of acceptable feminist understandings of God? The present essay is meant to explore this theological dimension by relating New Testament understandings of Jesus' "Abba" experience (I) to two questions: How did Jesus' masculinity and his experience of God affect one another? (II) and In Christianity how appropriate is the name "Father" for God? (III).

I. JESUS' "ABBA" EXPERIENCE

Without rehearsing all the complexities regarding the nature of Jesus' unique experience of the divine, complexities that a number of recent studies have detailed,[2] we can begin with the Gospel indications that Jesus' reference to God as his "Abba" points to some distinctive exposure of his consciousness to God. Unless Jesus had some such unique and immediate awareness of God, there would be no basis for talking about "Christian revelation" and there would ultimately be nothing irreducibly distinctive about Christianity as a faith and a religion.[3]

If Christianity has any distinctive insight regarding the salvation (i.e., the liberation) of women, it is rooted in this experience Jesus has of God. At first blush, however, this only seems to intensify the difficulty many Christian women now feel, for the very term that Jesus uses to name God is "Abba," i.e., "Father." Does not this require any Christian, woman or man, to think of and pray to the transcendent as somehow "masculine"?

One element of New Testament description of Jesus may help: Jesus and the experience he has of God are clearly depicted as "prophetic." He is the eschatological prophet, come to inaugurate the final stage of God's kingdom;[4] and the religious experience that launches his public prophecy is related to those of other charismatic prophets in Israel. In the case of such prophetic "vocation experiences," and a fortiori in Jesus' case, what seems to occur is a "swamping" of the prophet's consciousness by the reality of the presence of God.[5] God is known, inescapably known, and known to be present, but the knowing involved fits none of the images already in the prophet's memory, fits none of the categories that up to this point have structured the prophet's understanding. Yet, this experience, though immediate and in itself categorically unstructured, will inevitably relate to and "trigger" those images and categories by which the prophet had previously thought about God—but rather than fit into these, it will challenge and "shatter" them, demanding that the prophet somehow reach towards a *radically new* way of thinking about and therefore "naming" God. The new name may well sound like the "old name," but for the prophet and for those who listen to him or her, the same-sounding name now has a different content, a content that may run directly counter to the meaning most people attach to the name.

II. "ABBA" AND JESUS' MASCULINITY

Now to apply this to Jesus, whose experience on the occasion of baptism by John is described by the Gospels as such a prophetic awareness of the divine. Several things can be said.

1. Jesus comes to this baptismal experience with the images and understandings about God that would have belonged to a young Galilean male of his day.[6] This shaping of his religious consciousness came from the instruction provided by Mary and Joseph, from his hearing of the biblical texts in the synagogue, from conversations with his contemporaries, from his praying the Psalms. In the context of such Jewish modes of religious awareness he (like any other Jew) would have used the term "father" *metaphorically* to describe the God of Israel; in so doing, he would have been extrapolating from his human experience and understanding of fatherhood—experience and understanding that took place within the presuppositions and outlooks of the patriarchal Jewish culture. And in so applying the term "father" to God, and seeing this application as somewhat appropriate, there would have been a subtle but real reinforcing and justification of those cultural outlooks and presuppositions.

2. However, the consciousness of God to which Jesus attaches the term "Abba" is radically different—and the term "Abba" is *not a naming of God by way of metaphor.* Just the opposite. Even if it were nothing more than the experience of a prophet like Jeremias—and Christian faith believes that it was qualitatively beyond such Old Testament prophetic experience—the awareness Jesus had of the transcendent was immediate and personally intimate, so intimate that it was *the* foundation for his own self-identity. As such, it defied "insertion into" or "translation by" any of the religious images or categories Jesus would have acquired from his experience and education as a devout Jew. What Jesus experienced was "the limitless," "the ineffable," "the other-than-created"; and this experience was one of unmediated exposure to this divine reality. At the same time, this awareness of God was not walled off from the rest of Jesus' human consciousness—especially since it was intrinsic to his very self-awareness—and it resonated with the psychological structures already present.[7]

3. Quite logically, this God-consciousness would trigger in a special way whatever was most congruent or most incongruent; it would most clearly challenge whatever categories were being inappropriately applied to structure it. Since "father" as a root summation of the authority structures and values system of a patriarchal theocratic culture was applied in the Judaism of Jesus' day to the God of Old Testament revelation, Jesus' immediacy experience of

God would have clashed specially with this notion. The clash, however, would not have been total, since the Israelitic *religious* view of Yahweh was itself not basically assimilable to the legitimating usage attempted by the patriarchal elements of Israelitic culture. Thus, the immediacy-experience of Jesus could "feel comfortable" with the deeper insights involved in Old Testament usage of "God as father" (which incidentally were paralleled by other usage of "God as mother") but rejected the elements of God's "fatherhood" that were rooted in patriarchal (and therefore discriminating) understandings of male superiority, of authority as dominating and rooted in physical power, and of reality as hierarchically structured.

4. While such an immediate "prophetic" experience would have interacted in this complex way with the consciousness of any Jew of Jesus' time, man or woman, the impact and the radicality of the "challenge" would have been greater in a man, for the very reason that his own self-identity as "masculine" was more basically tied into positive agreement with these presuppositions: he would have been socialized into "masculinity" by receiving from his culture these patriarchal values as something to be assimilated and affirmed as his own. As a man, he could not only learn that God was the ultimate "patriarch"; he could experience this patriarchal God as a subtle confirmation that his own masculinity was the better of two ways of being human. From a purely human cultural point of view, such a patriarchal God would have been more agreeable to a Jewish male than to his female counterpart because this *affirmed* him while *demeaning her*. So, an immediacy experience of God would have been more of a "shock" to a Jewish male like Jesus.

This would seem to say that the reality of God could not have challenged those illegitimate understandings of the divine which characterize patriarchy as deeply as it did if the experience which Jesus had had come to a woman. For this reason, it does not seem arbitrary that the saving revelation of the divine came through a man; because the religious experience of this Jewish male was not the confirmation of patriarchal prejudice but the most profound negation of such prejudice. *Jesus' experience of God does not allow him to think of himself as masculine in patriarchal terms.* Beginning with the challenge to Jesus' own culturally-acquired understandings, the God known by Jesus refuses any claims made upon him by the negativities of a patriarchy that seeks divine legitimation.

One can begin to understand better, then, the depth of the resistance to Jesus' teaching on the part of the Jewish religious establishment. The central issue in the opposition to Jesus' teaching was
not this or that element of religious practice (e.g., the sabbath), it
was not even his audacity in publicly teaching without official validation, it was *the kind of God* he was proclaiming which constituted
the threat to the religious power structure of his day. If, indeed, God
was as Jesus described, a very new day had dawned, a new humanity
was being initiated by this "new Adam"—for in the mystery of this
Jesus as the Christ the old patriarchal discriminations could no
longer lay claim to God: "neither Jew nor Gentile, neither master
nor slave, neither male nor female."

All of this placed Jesus in a very perilous human situation: he
did not fit, and because he did not fit he was seen as dangerous—
which, of course, he was. He threatened, not only the social power
structure of his world, but the very notion of "society"; for, on the
basis of his experience of God, he proposed and embodied a new
approach to human relationships and human community, a new understanding of what it meant for a human to be a person, a new foundation for evaluating humans and their behavior.

5. It is the Greek word *agapetos* as used in the Synoptic Gospel
descriptions of Jesus' experience of God (immediately after his baptism by John) that gives us, perhaps, the deepest insight into this
"newness" that has occurred in Jesus. The word itself means "beloved one"; it probably is meant to remind us of the first of the Isaian
Servant Songs in which the "servant of God" is called (in the Sep-
tuagint translation) *agapetos*.[8]

But it also points to what was the most fundamental and pervading element in Jesus' awareness of the divine, an element that
could exist prior to and beyond all categorizing: he, Jesus, was *un-
conditionally and intimately loved by the transcendent,* beyond what any
child was by a parent or any person by his or her lover. This is what
the name "Abba" is all about—it was the one word available to challenge "father" in so far as this term had been misused and misunderstood in a patriarchal world and to suggest what "father" might
truly mean. Jesus' experience of being loved by God, his "Abba,"
forces him out of any of the patriarchal prejudices of his culture and
grounds his scandalous attitude towards women and non-Jews.[9] Experiencing this "Abba" as transcendent lover reveals to Jesus the

extent to which this God's creative love for all humans wipes out the inequalities and stratifications that humans have introduced into human society. Were there time, it would be fascinating to examine the manner in which this radically personal character of Jesus' experience of reality affected those implicitly cognized metaphysical principles of understanding that underpin all human perception of reality.

6. Jesus not only had this awareness of God's "attitude" towards humans; he had (as is typical of authentic prophetic experience) the abiding sense of "being sent" as the expression and implementation of this liberating divine love.[10] His regard for people was simultaneously his Father's regard; his "Abba" would have him deal with women and men and children in this maturely compassionate manner, in a way that took cognizance of the human frailty and needs he shared with them but also of the personal dignity they had as humans, so that in encountering Jesus' love for them people could come to know and accept the true God—and be freed from the "God" distorted by cultural and political legitimation. To put it succinctly: *Jesus sacramentalized a non-patriarchal God.*

At the risk of unduly complicating our discussion it does seem necessary to add one element to this explanation. When we talk about the saving work effected by Jesus as the Christ, we must not lose sight of the fact that he does not accomplish this as an isolated historical individual. Rather, his saving work is carried on in relation to others and through their cooperation, i.e., their discipleship. This is particularly true when one is dealing with the continuing sacramentality of Jesus' death and resurrection: it is the Christian community, and in somewhat differing fashion all humans of good will, that extends and fleshes out the sacramentality of Jesus himself as the risen one. Thus, "Christ as savior" refers to what sometimes is called "the whole Christ," the risen Jesus and those who with him take up one body which is the Church.[11] The implication of this for our present discussion is that women members as well as men share in the salvation being accomplished by "the whole Christ"; what they sacramentalize as women Christians is intrinsic to Christ's sacramentalizing a non-patriarchal God.

So, the masculinity of Jesus does seem to have played an intrinsic and soteriologically effective role in his experience of God. At the same time, the experience of God as "Abba" transformed in Jesus' case the human experience of being masculine. Without going into any detail, for that would be the matter of another and fairly lengthy essay, we can only suggest some of the questions raised by this situation. How does a man differentiate himself from women in a world where God does not expect males to be more responsible and more directive in society, even in the marriage and family relationship? How does a man image God (and himself) if he accepts women as equally though distinctively imaging the divine? How does he admit this radical symbolic equality of women without denying the fellowship he has with other males? How does he experience women— and therefore himself as a man in relationship to them—as fellow humans who possess a range of *personal* generativity comparable to and interacting with his own, and therefore as truly sacramental of the divine creativity?

Obviously, a parallel set of questions arises about the manner in which women's perception of their distinctiveness as feminine is altered by the knowledge of God as non-patriarchal. Given the immense task of freeing ourselves from cultural presuppositions and stereotypes regarding "masculine" and "feminine," we cannot realistically hope to do much more today than help free up the next couple generations, so that their experience and insights can better fit them to discover the personal dialectic intrinsic to the human distinction of the sexes.

Jesus, A Non-Patriarchal Savior

Without waiting for such future clarification, raising questions of the kind we have about Jesus' experience of being masculine may help pave the way for addressing the difficulty some Christian women find today in accepting a human savior who is masculine.

First of all, both women and men should regard Jesus *primarily as a fellow human* who shared the same basic human experiences but lived these experiences with a new depth because of living them in immediate exposure to the divine—Jesus may be a revelation of what it should mean to be masculine, but he is more basically a revelation of what it means to be human. Secondly, Jesus does undermine the forces which historically have oppressed women, because his own sacramental anti-patriarchalism shatters the claims to divine legitimation by any oppressive patriarchal situation. Thirdly, by being a man who does not exist or relate to others patriarchally, i.e., whose own self-identification and self-expression are in no way grounded in assumptions of male priority, Jesus challenges in any Christian woman who relates to him in faith those elements of patriarchal culture that she herself has assimilated—and thus frees her from her "inner oppressor." Fourthly, by being able to relate to this man Jesus (and hopefully also to some Christian men) in a non-patriarchal context a Christian woman now has the opportunity to discover that genuine dialectic between masculinity and femininity which is meant to be part of the personal psychological development of any mature human—a dialectic that has been so distorted that it could be referred to as "the war between the sexes." (Parenthetically, we might remark that any Christian man who establishes a faith relationship with the risen Christ, who understands and embraces real discipleship, is challenged to shed his patriarchalism and to discover a new meaning for his masculinity.)

Before leaving the question of Jesus serving as a savior for women, it might be good to examine quickly the term "salvation" as it is meant to be understood in Christianity: God's act of salvation, as it finds a focus in Jesus as the Christ, is not so much a matter of God *doing something to* humans as it is a matter of "inviting" humans to reach for their own intrinsic self-fulfillment. God's saving act in Christ does not treat us as children and supply for what we ourselves should be doing; rather, it is challenging us to be what we are capable of becoming, making us aware of potentialities we never dreamt we had, and providing resources of personal growth that by ourselves alone we would not have.[12] There is an element of dependence in our being saved by God, but it is the kind of dependence that one freely accepts in deciding to go ahead with any genuine personal friendship—one accepts being loved and *in the context of the friendship* needing the other person. Such a dependence involves no subordination; rather, it is one half of the most radical kind of personal equality. The ways in which we have described Jesus serving as savior relative to women clearly fits this "person-respecting" model of salvation.

III. GOD AS "FATHER"

In some ways our second main area of reflection, the use of "father" to refer to God, appears easier to handle—since the monotheism of Christian faith implies that the transcendent reality it calls "God" is totally beyond anything like gender characteristics. Any reference to this transcendent reality by use of masculine terms is metaphorical, and scripture itself suggests that it is just as appropriate to apply feminine metaphors to the divine.[13] Granting all this, there is still a psychological resonance of "male superiority" when "Father" is seen as the preferred way of referring to God in Christianity, when this name seems to be enshrined in the prayer that Jesus himself is described as giving to his disciples.[14] To avoid this subtle but constant assertion that somehow masculinity is more appropriate to God, to avoid placing Christian women in the situation of dealing with a God who always "stands over against" their identity as women, would it not be better to drop "God the Father" from our Christian vocabulary?

In response, the contention of this essay is two-fold: (1) "God the Father" is neither the proper nor the appropriate Christian name for the God revealed in Jesus, and (2) to drop the name "God the Father of our Lord Jesus Christ," which is the proper Christian way of naming God, would be to lose the ultimate source of freeing us, both men and women, from the prejudices and oppressions of patriarchalism. So, to expand these two statements.

1. It is critical to the position taken in this essay to distinguish *two ways* of naming the transcendent. *One way* is to see the transcendent reality as the prime analogate whose creative perfection is reflected in the created realities of our experienced world: the creator is existent beyond any particular existents, is beautiful beyond any created beauty, is good beyond anything in the world that could be called "good," is personal beyond what it means for us humans to be personal, etc. While it may well be legitimate to proceed in this fashion, the legitimacy rests on our recognition that we are using *metaphor;* the name we are applying is not a proper name. This is what occurs in all "natural" religions as humans struggle to explain the forces that operate in their life experience.

A second way, based on the religious belief that the transcendent has intervened in more direct and "unusual" fashion in people's experience, names the transcendent in terms of these "special events." Thus, the most proper naming of God in Israelitic faith is "I am the God who brought your ancestors out of Egypt." The name "Yahweh" points to this God but for practical purposes is without content; what tells us something about this God is his saving activity on Israel's behalf—this is not an *essential* but an *historical* way of naming God.

It is this historical manner of naming God that is applicable to the Christian name for God. The God who is worshipped in Christianity is the God experienced by Jesus—*named and known by Christians in terms of that experience.* If this meaning is true, it gets at the divine in a way that metaphor cannot, it gets at God somewhat the way we directly perceive reality. But the name for God that is involved in this mode of religious knowledge is not "God the Father"; rather, it is "God the Father of our Lord Jesus Christ," i.e., the God experienced by Jesus.[15]

Because it is this kind of a name, "God the Father of our Lord Jesus Christ" is not an extrapolation of some elements of fatherhood derived from our human experience. It does not, then, confirm whichever of those elements are intrinsic to patriarchy. God as known by Jesus cannot be appealed to as legitimation for patriarchy; rather, as we have already argued, such a view of the transcendent challenges whatever, in any human situation, denies the dignity and equality and "created transcendence" that is proper to human persons.

2. We can agree, then, that it may be misleading to name the transcendent "God, the Father." But conversely, it may be an irreparable mistake to abandon the much different name "God, the Father of our Lord Jesus Christ." This name has as its referent the patriarchy-challenging knowledge that Jesus has of the divine; it is the name that says that God is not "super-patriarch," but just the opposite; it is the name which relates us to a God who demands the rejection in both men and women of those humanly-demeaning prejudices and injustices which have marked patriarchal cultures historically. To drop this name—and the insight it is meant to bear—would mean the loss of the very force that is meant to help liberate us from these prejudices and injustices.

Obviously, it is not enough to argue in this way, even if the argument is theoretically valid. Most Christians certainly do not now use the term "God, the Father of our Lord Jesus Christ," nor do they realize that this is the name that is really involved in the "Our Father" that they pray. Instead, they use the term "God, the Father" without realizing its Christian inadequacy. We need a massive conversion of understanding to underpin a more correct use of Christian religious language. But if such a shift in understanding and language does occur, it will represent a most important step forward in the clarification of Christian belief and in the process of salvation, a most important contribution of Christianity to the establishment of the kingdom of God.

NOTES

1. Though not the first to mention the issue, Mary Daly's *Beyond God the Father* (Boston: Beacon, 1973) was a major influence in highlighting the problem of calling God "Father." Since its appearance in 1973, there have been a number of substantial discussions of the topic, such as Robert Hamerton-Kelly, *God the Father, Theology and Patriarchy in the Teaching of Jesus* (Philadelphia: Fortress, 1979); William Visser't Hooft, *The Fatherhood of God in an Age of Emancipation* (Geneva: World Council of Churches, 1982); or the Concilium volume, Johannes Baptist Metz and Edward Schillebeeckx, eds., *God as Father?* (New York: Seabury, 1981). The cutting edge of the debate is to be found, however, in feminist theological writing, e.g., several of the essays in Carol Christ and Judith Plaskow, eds., *Womanspirit Rising* (New York: Harper & Row, 1979) or Rosemary Ruether, *New Woman, New Earth* (New York: Seabury, 1978).

Questions about Jesus as appropriate savior figure for women surfaced slightly later, but not in less acute form. ". . . [A] feminist theologian must question whether the historical man Jesus of Nazareth can be a role model for contemporary women, since feminine psychological liberation means exactly the struggle of women to free themselves from all male internalized norms and models" (Elisabeth Schüssler-Fiorenza, "Towards a Feminist Biblical Hermeneutic" in Brian Mahan and L.Dale Richesin, eds. *The Challenge of Liberation Theology* [Maryknoll, NY: Orbis, 1981], pp. 91–112, at 107).

2. See John Galvin, "The Uniqueness of Jesus and His 'Abba Experience' in the Theology of Edward Schillebeeckx," *CTSA Proceedings* 35 (1980), 309–14; Edward Schillebeeckx, *Jesus* (New York: Seabury, 1979), pp. 256–71, 472–515; Michael Cook, *The Jesus of Faith* (New York: Paul-

ist, 1981), pp. 36–51, which links the "Abba experience" with Jesus' awareness of being the eschatological prophet.

3. Schillebeeckx, pp. 268–69, carries the point one step further back, arguing that Jesus' career and teaching is inexplicable with such an experience.

4. See Schillebeeckx, pp. 140–78; Reginald Fuller, *Foundations of New Testament Christology* (New York: Scribner's, 1965), pp. 125–31; Joachim Jeremias, *New Testament Theology* (New York: Scribner's, 1971), which focuses on Jesus' prophetic identity and activity.

5. See Johannes Lindblom, *Prophecy in Ancient Israel* (Oxford: Blackwell, 1963) which compares and distinguishes the prophetic experience from that of the mystic.

6. For purposes of simplifying the discussion, no account is being taken of the extent to which a distinctive experience of God was present prior to the baptism by John and therefore already shaping Jesus' religious awareness. For one thing, scripture texts give us no guidance in this regard; we can only argue to such experience theologically.

7. Giving any such priority to Jesus' ordinary human learning relative to his Abba-awareness is, of course, artificial. If there was an "Abba experience" of the kind we are suggesting, it provided for Jesus the very root of the process of personal self-identification, and as such it must somehow have been operative from the beginnings of that process.

8. Isaiah 42:1. See Walter Zimmerli and Joachim Jeremias, *The Servant of God* (Naperville, IL: Allenson, 1965).

9. On Jesus' "revolutionary" attitude and behavior towards women, see Leonard Swidler, *Biblical Affirmations of Woman* (Philadelphia: Westminster, 1979), pp. 163–290.

10. On the "mission impulse" intrinsic to the prophetic charism, see Lindblom, pp. 182–97.

11. Besides the classic works of Emile Mersch, *The Whole Christ* (Milwaukee: Bruce, 1938) and *Theology of the Mystical Body* (St. Louis: Herder, 1951), see Alfred Wikenhauser, *Pauline Mysticism* (New York: Herder & Herder, 1960); and *The Church as the Body of Christ* (edit. R. Pelton) (Notre Dame, IN: University of Notre Dame Press, 1963).

12. This soteriological shift in model is part of the present re-assessment of "divine providence," a notion that is obviously linked with any "paternalistic" understanding of God.

13. Considerable work has been done on uncovering the "feminine dimension" of the Bible, especially description of God by use of feminine metaphors. For a listing of such usages, see Swidler. Reinforcing this, studies like those of Walter Brueggeman, "Israel's Social Criticism and Yahweh's Sexuality," *Journal of the American Academy of Religion* 45 (1977),

Supplement, 739–72; and Phyllis Trible, *God and the Rhetoric of Sexuality* (Philadelphia: Fortress, 1978) have drawn attention to the depatriarchalizing elements already present in the Old Testament traditions.

14. We say *"seems* to be enshrined . . .", because study of early Christian use of "Father" to refer to God indicates that it is the term "Abba," with the special implications of this term to which we referred earlier, which stands behind this use.

15. So, for example, the doxological introductions of the Pauline letters speak of "praising the Father of our Lord Jesus Christ. . . . "

Impasse and Dark Night

Constance FitzGerald, O.C.D.

A number of issues in contemporary Christian spirituality underpin and influence the theological interpretation developed in this chapter. Today our spirituality is rooted in experience and in story: the experience and story of women (poor women, black women, white women, exploited women, Asian women, Native American women, etc.); the experience of the poor and oppressed of the world; the experience of the aging; the experience of the fear of nuclear holocaust and the far-reaching evils of nuclear buildup for the sake of national security, power, and domination; the experience of the woundedness of the earth and the environment.

This experience is nourished with meaning by history. It values, therefore, the interpretation of and dialogue with classical sources, with the story of the tradition. Within this framework, Christian spirituality remains attentive to the centrality of the self—to stages of faith development, to passages, to crises of growth—in one's search for God and human wholeness. It reaches, moreover, with particular urgency in our own time for the integration of contemplation and social commitment.

Against this background, I hope to interpret John of the Cross' concept and symbolism of "dark night" (including his classical signs concerning the passage from meditation to contemplation) to show what new understanding it brings to the contemporary experience of what I would call impasse, which insinuates itself inescapably and uninvited into one's inner life and growth and into one's relationships.[1] What is even more significant today is that many of our *so-*

287

cietal experiences open into profound impasse, for which we are not educated, particularly as Americans.

This brings me to two assumptions. First, our experience of God and our spirituality must emerge from our concrete, historical situation and must return to that situation to feed it and enliven it. Second, I find a great number of dark night or impasse experiences, personal and societal, that cry out for meaning. There is not only the so-called dark night of the soul but the dark night of the world. What if, by chance, our time in evolution is a dark-night time—a time of crisis and transition that must be understood if it is to be part of learning a new vision and harmony for the human species and the planet?

To discover meaning, there is value in bringing contemporary impasse into dialogue with the classical text of John.[2] In unfolding the mystery of dark night and unpacking its symbolism in response to the experience of impasse, I would hope to help others understand, name, and claim this experience of God and thereby direct their own creative and affective energy.

IMPASSE

By impasse, I mean that there is no way out of, no way around, no rational escape from, what imprisons one, no possibilities in the situation. In a true impasse, every normal manner of acting is brought to a standstill, and ironically, impasse is experienced not only in the problem itself but also in any solution rationally attempted. Every logical solution remains unsatisfying, at the very least. The whole life situation suffers a depletion, has the word *limits* written upon it. Dorothée Soelle describes it as "unavoidable suffering," an apt symbol of which is physical imprisonment, with its experience of being squeezed into a confined space. Any movement out, any next step, is canceled, and the most dangerous temptation is to give up, to quit, to surrender to cynicism and despair, in the face of the disappointment, disenchantment, hopelessness, and loss of meaning that encompass one.

It is not difficult to imagine how such attitudes affect self-image and sense of worth and turn back on the person or group to engender a sense of failure, to reinforce a realization—not always exact—that their own mistakes have contributed to the ambiguity.

Moreover, intrinsic to the experience of impasse is the impression and feeling of rejection and lack of assurance from those on whom one counts. At the deepest levels of impasse, one sees the support systems on which one has depended pulled out from under one and asks if anything, if anyone, is trustworthy. Powerlessness overtakes the person or group caught in impasse and opens into the awareness that no understandable defense is possible. This is how impasse looks to those who are imprisoned within it. It is the experience of disintegration, of deprivation of worth, and it has many faces, personal and societal.

There is, however, another dimension of impasse that philosophers and psychologists, sociologists and theologians, poets and mystics, have reflected upon from their particular perspectives. Belden Lane, director of historical theology at Saint Louis University, indicates it in his article, *Spirituality and Political Commitment:*

> . . . in a genuine impasse one's accustomed way of acting and living is brought to a standstill. The left side of the brain, with its usual application of linear, analytical, conventional thinking is ground to a halt. The impasse forces us to start all over again, driving us to contemplation. On the other hand, the impasse provides a challenge and a concrete focus for contemplation . . . . It forces the right side of the brain into gear, seeking intuitive, symbolic, unconventional answers, so that action can be renewed eventually with greater purpose.[3]

The negative situation constitutes a reverse pressure on imagination so that imagination is the only way to move more deeply into the experience. It is this "imaginative shock," or striking awareness that our categories do not fit our experience, that throws the intuitive, unconscious self into gear in quest of what the possibilities really are.

Paradoxically, a situation of no potential is loaded with potential, and impasse becomes the place for the reconstitution of the intuitive self. This means the situation of being helpless can be efficacious, not merely self-denying and demanding of passivity. While nothing seems to be moving forward, one is, in fact, on a homeward exile—*if* one can yield in the right way, responding with *full consciousness* of one's suffering in the impasse yet daring to believe that new possibilities, beyond immediate vision, can be given.

It must be stressed, writes Dorothée Soelle, that insofar as the experience of impasse, or suffering, is repressed, "there is a corresponding disappearance of passion for life and of the strength and intensity of its joys" and insights.[4] The person caught in impasse must find a way to identify, face, live with, and express this suffering. If one cannot speak about one's affliction in anguish, anger, pain, lament—at least to the God within—one will be destroyed by it or swallowed up by apathy. Every attempt to humanize impasse must begin with this phenomenon of experienced, acknowledged powerlessness, which can then activate creative forces that enable one to overcome the feeling that one is without power.[5]

A genuine impasse situation is such that the more action one applies to escape it, the worse it gets. The principles of "first order change"—reason, logic, analysis, planning—do not work, as studies by three Stanford psychiatrists try to show. Thorough-going impasse forces one, therefore, to end one's habitual methods of acting by a radical breaking out of the conceptual blocks that normally limit one's thinking.

Genuine change occurs through a "second order" response, "one which rethinks the solution previously tried and suggests something altogether unexpected. The quality of paradox is at the heart of 'second order change.' "[6] It implies that the unexpected, the alternative, the new vision, is not given on demand but is beyond conscious, rational control. It is the fruit of unconscious processes in which the situation of impasse itself becomes the focus of contemplative reflection.[7]

The psychologists and the theologians, the poets and the mystics, assure us that impasse can be the condition for creative growth and transformation *if* the experience of impasse is fully appropriated within one's heart and flesh with consciousness and consent; *if* the limitations of one's humanity and human condition are squarely faced and the sorrow of finitude allowed to invade the human spirit with real, existential powerlessness; *if* the ego does not demand understanding in the name of control and predictability but is willing to admit the mystery of its own being and surrender itself to this mystery; *if* the path into the unknown, into the uncontrolled and unpredictable margins of life, is freely taken when the path of deadly clarity fades.

DARK NIGHT IN JOHN OF THE CROSS

When I am able to situate a person's experience of impasse within the interpretive framework of dark night, that person is reassured and energized to live, even though she feels she is dying. The impasse is opened to meaning precisely because it can be redescribed.

In order to understand dark night, it is important to realize that John of the Cross begins and ends with love and desire in his poems and prose writings.[8] He is intent on showing what kind of affective education is carried on by the Holy Spirit over a lifetime. He delineates, therefore, the movement from a desire, or love, that is possessive, entangled, complex, selfish, and unfree to a desire that is fulfilled with union with Jesus Christ and others. In the process of affective redemption, desire is not suppressed or destroyed but gradually transferred, purified, transformed, set on fire. We go *through* the struggles and ambiguities of human desire to integration and personal wholeness.

This means there is a dark side to human desire, and the experience of dark night is the way that desire is purified and freed.[9] What is important to realize is that it is *in* the very experience of darkness and joylessness, in the suffering and withdrawal of accustomed pleasure, that this transformation is taking place. Transfiguration does not happen at the end of the road; it is in the making now. If we could see the underside of this death, we would realize it is already resurrection. Since we are not educated for darkness, however, we see this experience, because of the shape it takes, as a sign of *death*. Dark night is instead a sign of *life*, of growth, of development in our relationship with God, in our best human relationships, and in our societal life. It is a sign to move on in hope to a new vision, a new experience.

Night in John of the Cross, which symbolically moves from twilight to midnight to dawn, is the progressive purification and transformation of the human person *through* what we cherish or desire and through what give us security and support.[10] We are affected by darkness, therefore, where we are mostly deeply involved and committed, and in what we love and care for most. Love makes us vulnerable, and it is love itself and its development that precipitate darkness in oneself and in the "other."

Only when love has grown to a certain point of depth and commitment can its limitations be experienced. Our senses are carried to deeper perception, as it were, by exhaustion. A fullness in one way of being and relating makes one touch its limits. This is not a question of disgust, as it often appears and feels like, but of a movement through sensual pleasure and joy to deeper, stronger faithfulness and to the experience of a love and a commitment, a hope and a vision, unimagined and unexpected on this side of darkness.

We all need some satisfaction of our desire in order to begin and go on in prayer, relationship, or ministry, but it is the withdrawal of pleasure and the confrontation with limitation (our own and others') that signals the transition or growth crisis of the dark night. The test is whether we can, in the last analysis, maintain the direction or momentum of our life without either glancing off permanently into another direction to escape, or succumbing to the darkness of total despair.[11]

Love (romance!) makes us hunger for the unambivalent situation. Yet it is in the very light of love that we encounter the opaqueness of our own humanness and experience the destructiveness within ourselves and the "other." Ambiguity arises, on the one hand, from human inadequacy; it arises, on the other hand, from the Spirit of God calling us beyond ourselves, beyond where we are, into transcendence. We are being challenged to make the passage from loving, serving, "being with," because of the pleasure and joy it gives us, to loving and serving regardless of the cost. We are being challenged to a reacceptance of the "other."[12]

Every God relationship, every significant human love, every marriage, every ministry, every relationship between a person and a community, and perhaps every human group and every nation will come to this point of impasse, with its intrinsic demands for and promise of a new vision, a new experience of God, a quieter, deeper, freer, more committed love. And it will come precisely when imagination seems paralyzed, when intimacy seems eroded, and when desire feels dead.

This brings us to John of the Cross' signs for discerning the genuineness of the dark night purification. Traditionally, they have been recognized as theological signs of the passage in prayer from discursive meditation to contemplation and are, therefore, descriptive of one's spiritual development, one's intrapersonal life. A careful reading of John of the Cross, integrated with concrete human experience, would seem to indicate, however, that the interpretation of these signs must be extended to one's inter-personal life as well, and perhaps even to one's societal life. I submit that a societal interpretation of these signs, and dark night in general, throws considerable light on the contemporary experience of societal impasse.

Although John seems to delineate a smooth transition, his developmental model includes breakdown and failure. This is why the signs speak to us of death, even though they are in reality signs of development and growth. There are two sets of signs, one in the second book of the *Ascent of Mount Carmel* (chap. 13, nos. 2–4); the other in the first book of the *Dark Night* (chap. 9, nos. 2–8). Although the perspective is different in each (the *Ascent* signs are given from the side of the person's faith response, the *Dark Night* signs from God's side), the signs are the same and can be correlated.

The first set of signs underlines one's powerlessness to pray with one's reason or rational mind "since God does not communicate himself through the senses as he did before, by means of the discursive analysis and synthesis of ideas, but begins to communicate himself through pure spirit by an act of simple contemplation in which there is no discursive succession of thought." The senses cannot attain to this contemplation, and dryness results.[13]

Basic to the experience of disintegration or dark night is an apparent breakdown of communication and a powerlessness to do anything about it. One's usual way of functioning, or relating, provides no satisfaction and does not work. What formerly was essential for growth and fidelity (e.g., an active choice and decision for Christ in reasoned meditation) now hinders growth.[14] Nothing happens in meditation. One cannot relate to the loved one as before. The system on which one depends breaks down. Certainty and pleasure give way to ambiguity, misunderstanding, and dryness or boredom.

It is difficult to realize, except by hindsight, that a new kind of love and deeper level of communication, transcending the former love, is developing and is already operative (contemplation). Accustomed to receiving love and insight in one way, one perceives this communication and situation as darkness. What is, in fact, a call to a new vision and to deeper, more genuine intimacy with God, with the "other," and with the world, is experienced as less commitment and less love, precisely because the call comes when intimacy seems to be falling apart and limitation looms large. There seems no possibility of movement backward or forward but only imprisonment, lack of vision, and failure of imagination. "Everything seems to be functioning in reverse," writes John, in this forced passage from rational, analytical, linear thinking to intuitive, metaphorical, symbolic consciousness.[15]

In his probing article "Atheism and Contemplation," Michael J. Buckley shows that John of the Cross, like Feuerbach, is very "sensitive to the humanization consciousness works on its God." John is acutely aware, with Freud, that the religious movement toward God can emerge either from the desire for satisfaction or from the drive for reassurance.[16] In other words, John is conscious of the tendency of religion to become projection and is always subtly asking the question What is the focus of your desire, of your religious awareness and its commitment? "He takes the theological dictum, 'Whatever is received is received according to the mode of the one receiving it,' and he applies it to a person's conceptions and images of God."[17]

> Because in the initial stages of the spiritual life, and even in the more advanced ones, the sensory part of the soul is imperfect, it frequently receives God's spirit with this very imperfection.[18]

We make our God, or gods, in our own image. "Our understanding and our loves are limited by what we are. What we grasp and what we long for is very much shaped and determined by our own nature and personality-set," writes Buckley. If this is not changed by the Spirit of Jesus gradually permeating individual experiences and influencing patterns of development and growth, "there is no possibility of [the] contemplation of anything but our own projections."[19] John of the Cross is at pains to show how our images of God are progressively and of necessity changed and shattered by life experience. The very experience of dark night does, in fact, critique our present images of God. As Buckley says,

The continual contemplative purification of the human person is a progressive hermeneutic of the nature of God. The self-disclosure of God . . . is finally only possible within the experience of the contradiction of finite concepts and human expectations. The darkness and its pain are here, but there are finely dialectical movements in which the human is purified from projection by a "no" which is most radically a "yes." The disclosures of God contradict the programs and expectations of human beings in order to fulfill human desire and human freedom at a much deeper level than subjectivity would have measured out its projections.[20]

When, in the first sign, we reflect on the breakdown of communication and relationship, therefore, we are assuming also a change and a shattering of one's images. This causes confusion and a sense of loss and meaninglessness.

This is not a defense of Christian masochism, as Dorothée Soelle calls it, nor a sadistic understanding of God, but rather a recognition of the ongoing process of self-acceptance and reacceptance of the "other" that is necessary for real, enduring love and progressive, mutual insight and creativity. This process presupposes that, in every significant relationship, we come to the experience of limitation, our own and others'. We come to the point where we must withdraw and reclaim our projections of God, of friend, of ministry, of community, and let the "others" be who and what they are: mystery.

The emphasis in the second set of signs is on emptiness in life experience and deadness of desire. Not only is prayer dry, but life is dry, relationship is dry, ministry is dry.

Souls do not get satisfaction or consolation from the things of God [and] they do not get any out of creatures either. Since God puts a soul in this dark night in order to dry up and purge its sensory appetite, he does not allow it to find sweetness or delight in anything.[21]

John assures us the time must come in our development when neither God, nor the "other," nor one's life project satisfy, but only disappoint, disillusion, and shatter one's naive hope.

Because desire seems dead, because there is no inclination to do anything about the situation, because one really ceases to care, the temptation to quit, to walk away, becomes overpowering. Hopelessness and worthlessness invade one's perception and one's psyche. It is in the throes of this crisis that people abandon God and prayer, a marriage, a friend, a ministry, a community, a church, and forfeit forever the new vision, the genuine hope, the maturity of love and loyalty, dedication and mutuality, that is on the other side of darkness and hopelessness. Darkness is the place where egoism dies and true unselfish love for the "other" is set free. Moreover, it is the birthplace of a vision and a hope that cannot be imagined this side of darkness.

John can write about self-knowledge as a primary effect of the dark night for two reasons. First, the light and development of contemplative love show up one's limitations. Second, the withdrawal of accustomed pleasure in life, and the consequent frustration of desire, trigger one's seemingly destructive tendencies and move them into action on a level that is beyond conscious control.[22]

What must be remembered at all costs is that desire is not destroyed. Rather, right in this situation of unassuaged emptiness and apparent deadness of desire, in the very area of life in which one is most involved and therefore most vulnerable, desire is being purified, transformed, and carried into deeper, more integrated passion. Dark night mediates the transfiguration of affectivity, and obstacles conceal within themselves untold, hidden energy.

Here we sense what powerful symbolism dark night is. It is an image of productivity and speaks of life buried in its opposite: life concealed, life invisible, life unseen in death.

Thus the third set of signs has two different moments, moving from painful anxiety about culpability to a new and deeper level of appreciation of God and/or the "other" in a quiet, loving attentiveness. John describes the suffering side of this experience when he writes,

> The memory ordinarily turns to God solicitously and with painful care, and the soul thinks it is not serving God but turning back, because it is aware of this distaste for the things of God.[23]

Here it is a question of being obsessed with the problem. How much easier it would be to bear the darkness were one not conscious of one's failures and mistakes. The most confusing and damnable part of the dark night is the suspicion and fear that much of the darkness is of one's own making. Since dark night is a limit experience, and since it does expose human fragility, brokenness, neurotic dependence, and lack of integration, it is understandable that it undermines a person's self-esteem and activates anxious self-analysis.

The only way to break out of this desperate circle of insoluble self-questioning is to surrender in faith and trust to the unfathomable. Mystery that beckons onward and inward beyond calculation, order, self-justification, and fear. John continues, therefore:

> The third and surest sign is that a person likes to remain alone in loving awareness of God, without particular considerations, in interior peace and quiet and repose. . . .
>
> If those in whom this occurs know how to remain quiet, without care and solicitude about any interior or exterior work, they will soon in that unconcern and idleness delicately experience the interior nourishment.[24]

It is precisely as broken, poor, and powerless that one opens oneself to the dark mystery of God in loving, peaceful waiting. When the pain of human finitude is appropriated with consciousness and consent and handed over in one's own person to the influence of Jesus' spirit in the contemplative process, the new and deeper experience gradually takes over, the new vision slowly breaks through, and the new understanding and mutuality are progressively experienced.

At the deepest levels of night, in a way one could not have imagined it could happen, one sees the withdrawal of all one has been certain of and depended upon for reassurance and affirmation. Now it is a question, not of satisfaction, but of support systems that give life meaning: concepts, systems of meaning, symbolic structures, relationships, institutions. All supports seem to fail one, and only the experience of emptiness, confusion, isolation, weakness, loneliness, and abandonment remains. In the frantic search for reassurance, one wonders if anyone—friend or spouse or God—is really "for me," is trustworthy. But no answer is given to the question.[25]

The realization that there is *no* option but faith triggers a deep, silent, overpowering panic that, like a mighty underground river, threatens chaos and collapse. This "scream of suffering contains all the despair of which a person is capable, and in this sense every scream is a scream for God," writes Soelle.[26] In this experience of the cross of Jesus, what the "soul feels most," John explains, "is that God has rejected it and with abhorrence cast it into darkness."[27] And Soelle continues:

> All extreme suffering evokes the experience of being forsaken by God. In the depth of suffering people see themselves as abandoned and forsaken by everyone. That which gave life its meaning has become empty and void: it turned out to be an error, an illusion that is shattered, a guilt that cannot be rectified, a void. The paths that lead to this experience of nothingness are diverse, but the experience of annihilation that occurs is the same.[28]

Yet it is the experience of this abandonment and rejection that is transforming the human person in love. This is a possession, a redemption, an actualizing and affirmation of the person that is not understood at the time. Its symbolic expression is dispossession and death.[29]

John seems to say that one leaves the world of rejection and worthlessness by giving away one's powerlessness and poverty to the inspiration of the Spirit and one moves into a world of self-esteem, affirmation, compassion, and solidarity. Only an experience like this, coming out of the soul's night, brings about the kind of solidarity and compassion that changes the "I" into a "we," enabling one to say, "we poor," "we oppressed," "we exploited." The poor are objects until we are poor, too. This kind of identification with God's people, with the "other," is the fruit of dark night.[30]

Some years ago it became evident to me that in our most significant human relationships we go through precisely the kind of suffering John describes concerning the soul's journey to God. In our ministries, moreover, we inevitably come to personal impasse. John's signs of passage and development, refashioned for the present time, should be a valuable tool for discernment. They relate to the breakdown of marriages, to departures from priesthood and religious life, and to the contemporary phenomenon of burnout, among other things.

SOCIETAL IMPASSE

I want to bring together dark night and societal impasse because, as I said, our experience of God and our spirituality must emerge from our concrete historical situation and because our time and place in history bring us face to face with profound societal impasse. Here God makes demands for conversion, healing, justice, love, compassion, solidarity, and communion. Here the face of God appears, a God who dies in human beings and rises in human freedom and dignity.

We close off the breaking in of God into our lives if we cannot admit into consciousness the situations of profound impasse we face personally and societally. If we deal with personal impasse only in the way our society teaches us—by illusion, minimization, repression, denial, apathy—we will deal with societal impasse in the same way. The "no way out" trials of our personal lives are but a part of the far more frightening situations of national and international impasse that have been formed by the social, economic, and political forces in our time.

We are citizens of a dominant nation, and I think that as a nation we have come to an experience of deep impasse and profound limitation. On the other side of all our technology, we have come to poverty and to dark night. We can find no escape from the world we have built, where the poor and oppressed cry out, where the earth and the environment cry out, and where the specter of nuclear waste already haunts future generations. We can find no way out of the horror of nuclear stockpiles but more sophisticated and deadly weapons systems.

As Americans we are not educated for impasse, for the experience of human limitation and darkness that will not yield to hard work, studies, statistics, rational analysis, and well-planned programs. We stand helpless, confused, and guilty before the insurmountable problems of our world. We dare not let the full import of the impasse even come to complete consciousness. It is just too painful and too destructive of national self-esteem. We cannot bear to let ourselves be totally challenged by the poor, the elderly, the unemployed, refugees, the oppressed; by the unjust, unequal situation of women in a patriarchal, sexist culture; by those tortured and imprisoned and murdered in the name of national security; by the possibility of the destruction of humanity.

We see only signs of death. Because we do not know how to read these kinds of signs in our own inner lives and interpersonal relationships, we do not understand them in our societal or national life, either. Is it possible these insoluble crises are signs of passage or transition in our national development and in the evolution of humanity? Is it possible we are going through a fundamental evolutionary change and transcendence, and crisis is the birthplace and learning process for a new consciousness and harmony?

Let us examine the signs. Our impasses do not yield to hard, generous work, to the logical solutions of the past, to the knowledge and skills acquired in our educational institutions. The most far-sighted economists said some years ago that the economic solutions of past decades do not fit the present economic crisis in the world. It is argued that the whole economic, social, and political system would collapse were we to feed the poor with surplus crops and stop the wars, the exploitation, the oppression, in which we are involved. Not only God and the loved one fail us, our institutions fail us.

We are obsessed with the problem and with the need for new insight and breakthrough; we are disillusioned with a political system that contributes to international oppression, violence, and darkness. Is it any wonder we witness the effects of impasse among us— anger, confusion, violence—since real impasse or dark night highlights destructive tendencies? Frustrated desire fights back.

Recently, a Jesuit on our local Peace and Justice Commission described the stance of a prominent Roman Catholic theologian, a layman, at a meeting of theologians, bishops, and others on the nuclear question. It was the focused awareness, the incredible logic and rationality, of this man who favored nuclear superiority and denied that a nuclear freeze was a good idea that made such a negative impression on pro-freeze participants. Reason, left to itself, moved to a basically destructive position, unrecognized and unacknowledged in the speaker.

Dark night shows up the "shadow," the dark side of desire. If we refuse to read the signs of dark night in our society and avoid appropriating the impasse, we see cold reason, devoid of imagination, heading with deadly logic toward violence, hardness in the face of misery, a sense of inevitability, war, and death. And we witness the projection of our national shadow on others, "the inevitable shadow of over-rational planning," as Irene de Castillejo calls it.[31]

Today, instead of realizing that the impasse provides a challenge and concrete focus for prayer and drives us to contemplation, we give in to a passive sense of inevitability, and imagination dies. We do not really believe that if we surrender these situations of world impasse to contemplative prayer that new solutions, new visions of peace and equality, will emerge in our world. We dare not believe that a creative re-visioning of our world is possible. Everything is just too complex, too beyond our reach. Yet it is only in the process of bringing the impasse to prayer, to the perspective of the God who loves us, that our society will be freed, healed, changed, brought to paradoxical new visions, and freed for nonviolent, selfless, liberating action, freed, therefore, for community on this planet earth. Death is involved here—a dying in order to see how to be and to act on behalf of God in the world.[32]

This development suggests two questions: Do we really expect anything at all of the contemplative process of prayer in our world today? And how does the failure of imagination and creativity in our national life relate to the breakdown of the contemplative process of prayer and transformation in people's lives? With these questions concerning the intersection of impasse and contemplation, I move into my concluding reflection, on women's religious experience today.

FEMININE IMPASSE

I submit that the feminine experience of dark night, if we read it, interpret it, understand it, and live it through, is in itself a critique of religious consciousness and, therefore, ultimately of Christianity, with its roots in a sexist, patriarchal culture. It is not my intention simply to apply a Christian theme, dark night, to a contemporary issue, women. Rather, I am probing a resource within the theological-mystical tradition in order to understand the contemporary feminist experience of God and to see if John of the Cross' dark night can function in the struggle of women for liberation and equality.[33]

Behind every new spirituality and any creative re-visioning of the world—at the root of any real theology—is an experience of God. Yet every religious experience comes from a meeting with a new and challenging face of God in one's own time and social situation. I suspect that although it is imperative, for example, for feminist theologians to develop new interpretive paradigms that function to liberate people, only women's *experience* of God can alter or renew our God images and perhaps our doctrine of God. I want, therefore, to examine the feminist experience of God in impasse, because this is where many women in the Church, and in the world, find themselves. "We have only begun to experience the depth of women's alienation from Christian belief systems and from the existing Churches," writes Elisabeth Schüssler Fiorenza.[34]

Today feminists struggle with the Judeo-Christian image of a male God and a male Church. Just as Marxism sees religion as the opiate of the people and Christianity's doctrine of God as a support of oppression and misery, so the feminists see a patriarchal system that visualizes God, and consequently Church, in almost exclusively patriarchal terms as basically destructive. The masculine image of God is experienced as unsatisfying and confusing because it serves to reinforce male domination, a patriarchal value system, and an entire male world view.

This is an impasse for women, since their past religious experience has come to them through these images and this inherited symbol system, which does not function for women now as it did before. There is no going back to what was—what gave comfort and clarity and brought feminists to their present stage of religious development and commitment—but there is no satisfactory going forward either. There seems to be no way out of this God-less situation because no genuine evolution of God images has really occurred. We touch this in Alice Walker's latest novel, *The Color Purple*, a story of a black woman, Celie, who moves from being oppressed and brutalized to self-actualization and religious transformation. What is significant is that Celie's transcendence requires or coincides with a radical redefinition of God. "The author's choice of the genre of the epistolary novel, in this case composed entirely of letters for which there is no direct response," places the whole story in a prayer context.[35] In the first fifty-five letters Celie writes the story of her life to God, because she is ashamed to talk to him about it. Abused by the man she thought to be her father and deprived by him of the children she consequently bore, dehumanized by her husband and deprived by him of any knowledge of or communication with her sister, she is loved by one woman, Shug Avery. Aware finally, under the influence of Shug's love and affirmation, of the extent of her exploitation, Celie rebels not only against men but against God and can no longer write to *him*. She writes instead to her sister:

> What God do for me? I ast. . . . He give me a lynched daddy, a crazy mama, a lowdown dog of a step pa and a sister I probably won't ever see again. Anyhow, I say, the God I been praying and writing to is a man. And act just like all the mens I know. Trifling, forgitful and lowdown. . . .
>
> All my life I never care what people thought bout nothing I did, I say. But deep in my heart I care about God. What he going to think. And come to find out, he don't think. Just sit up there glorying in being deef, I reckon. But it ain't easy, trying to do without God. Even if you know he ain't there, trying to do without him is a strain.

When Shug asks what her God looks like, Celie senses the incongruity of her image but replies:

> He big and old and tall and graybearded and white. He wear white robes and go barefooted.
>
> Blue eyes? she ast.
>
> Sort of bluish gray. Cool. Big though. White lashes, I say. . . . Ain't no way to read the bible and not think God white, she say. Then she sigh. When I found out I thought God was white, and a man, I lost interest. You mad cause he don't seem to listen to your prayers. Humph! Do the mayor listen to anything the colored say? . . . Here's the thing, say Shug. The thing I believe. God is inside you and inside everybody else. You come into the world with God. But only them that search for *it* inside find it. And sometimes it just manifest itself even if you not looking, or don't know what you looking for. Trouble do it for most folks, I think.
>
> . . . [U]s talk and talk about God, but I'm still adrift. Trying to chase that old man out of my head. I been so busy thinking bout him I never truly notice nothing God make. Not a blade of corn (how it do that?) not the color purple (where it come from?) Not the little wildflowers. Nothing.

> Man corrupt everything, say Shug. He on your box of grits, in your head and all over your radio. He try to make you think he everywhere. Soon as you think he everywhere, you think he God. But he ain't. Whenever you trying to pray, and man plop himself on the other end of it, tell him to git lost, say Shug. Conjure up flowers, wind, water, a big rock.
>
> But this is hard work, let me tell you. He been there so long, he don't want to budge. He threaten lightening, floods and earthquakes. Us fight. I hardly pray at all. Every time I conjure up a rock, I throw it. Amen.[36]

Thus feminists, unable to communicate with the God of patriarchy, are imprisoned in a night of broken symbols. They ask how the idea of God undergoes transformation.

Is it by changing our religious language? By feminizing God, uncovering feminine images and attributes of God in the Scriptures? Is it by the desexualization of God and a move toward deism? Or is it by contemplation? (A step in the criticism of Marxism is implied here. Can experience really be altered simply by changing language?) What our programs to eliminate sexist language in our theological, devotional, and liturgical life have shown us is that our solutions are unsatisfactory and confusing. We find impasse not only in the problems but even in the solutions.

So-called postpatriarchal theologians and philosophers have suspected this for some time and in consequence have moved beyond Judeo-Christian religion. These radical feminist thinkers claim feminine consciousness and Christian faith are contradictions in terms. Aware, like John of the Cross, of the tendency of religion to become projection, they have rejected the Christian God that patriarchy projects. But is this the only option? Here the advance of postpatriarchy intersects with the development of contemplation. If one admits that religious belief and desire can be analyzed into episodes of projection, does the force of this discovery indicate a movement toward the total rejection of the God of patriarchy, or can it equally indicate that faith and desire must move into contemplation, one movement of which is apophatic? Is the alternative either to deny the reality of the God of Christianity or to insist that the evolution of faith and desire must pass through the darkness and the cross, in which the meaning of the night is found? It is imperative to emphasize, as Buckley observes, that apophatic theology is not primarily one which does or does not make statements about God. It is primarily an experiential *process*, a process of entering into the infinite mystery that is God, so that gradually one is transformed by grace and this grace moves through the intense experience of darkness [impasse] into the *vision* of the incomprehensible God [the God who transcends present images and symbols]. Apophatic theology involves both interpretation and criticism, conceptualization and theological argument. But all of these are descriptive of *a process in which one is engaged*, a process in which *one must be engaged* in order to grasp its interpretation in any depth.[37]

If the impasse in which feminists find themselves *is* dark night, then a new experience of God, transformative of alienating symbols, is already breaking through even though it is not comprehensible yet, and impasse is a call to development, transcendence, new life, and understanding. Ultimately, therefore, impasse is a challenge to feminists to be mystics who, when human concepts disillusion, symbols break, and meanings fail, will let their "faith . . . relocate everything known within a new horizon in which it is radically reinterpreted and transvaluated."[38] Feminists need to realize that the gap that exists between human, patriarchal concepts of God and what is internalized by them in impasse is exactly what promises religious development and is the seed of a new experience of God, a new spirituality, and a new order—what Elizabeth Janeway calls the "Great Myth, as yet unborn," to which Madonna Kolbenschlag refers in her article, "Feminists, the Frog Princess, and the New Frontier of Spirituality."[39]

I believe there is no alternative for feminists except contemplation, if they are to avoid the trivialization of their own religious experience in dark night. The experience of God in impasse is the crucible in which our God images and language will be transformed and a feminine value system and social fabric generated. All the signs (of dark night) indicate this is the next step in any positive, creative re-visioning of the future, in any genuinely feminine generativity. Theology is dependent on this experience, which cannot be created by theological reflection alone. Dark night is, as was stated before, "a progressive hermeneutic of the nature of God." If this passage is not recognized and traversed, a certain kind of atheism and permanent cynicism are inevitable.

The contemplative love experience, which is beyond conscious control and is not given on demand, is concerned not for the image of God, as political theologians are, but with God, who does in the end transcend our images and expectations. What is critical to see is that one has to *allow* the experience to take place through a love that is gradually welling up from the ground of one's being and that serves as a basis for contemplation. Only this experience can give to theology the insight it needs "to search out a new doctrine of God which is related to the intellectual, practical, and ethical concerns of the present situation of women and which suggests transformation or emancipative possibilities for the future."[40]

Contemplation, and ultimately liberation, demand the handing over of one's powerlessness and "outsider-ness" to the inspiration and power of God's Spirit. How imperative it is that women take possession of their pain and confusion; actively appropriate their experience of domination, exploitation, and oppression; consent to their time in history; and hold this impasse in their bodies and their hearts before the inner God they reach for in the dark of shattered symbols. Although the God of the dark night seems silent, this God is not a mute God who silences human desire, pain, and feeling, and women need to realize that the experience of anger, rage, depression, and abandonment is a constitutive part of the transformation and purification of the dark night. This very rage and anger purify the "abused consciousness" of women in the sexism they have internalized.[41]

If there is, as we suggest, an incipient experience of God, this presence of God will necessarily throw light on woman's "shadow" and reveal her to herself with all the destructive power she has and all the repressed possibilities or "lost alternatives" that cry within her for a voice. It is in the experience of this kind of night, when women put all the power of their desire, not in ideology, but here before the inner God, that the real bonding of women takes place, and purified of violence, they are readied for communion with their God, for sisterhood, equality, liberation, and mutuality.

Impasse internalizes the option for the poor and effects an identification with and compassion for all "women whose cry for liberation is so basic and unmistakable that it shouts out for all of us in our common quest for equality."[42] In one's own womanhood, one holds every woman before God, women of the present and women of the past. This is an experience, not a theory! Though one lives in Baltimore or Atlanta or California or Washington, one's life is lived within the bleeding borders of El Salvador and Guatemala, Lebanon and South Africa, Afghanistan and Cambodia. Though one lives at the end of the twentieth century, the voiceless sorrow of women long dead is felt as one's own. One senses this in Alice Walker's essay "In Search of Our Mother's Gardens":

> When Jean Toomer walked through the South in the early twenties, she discovered a curious thing: Black women whose spirituality was so intense, so deep, so *unconscious*, that they themselves were unaware of the riches they held. They stumbled blindly through their lives: creatures so abused and mutilated in body, so dimmed and confused by pain, that they considered themselves unworthy even of hope. In the selfless abstractions their bodies became to the men who used them, they became more than "sexual objects," more even than mere women: they became Saints. Instead of being perceived as whole persons, their bodies became shrines: what was thought to be their minds became temples suitable for worship. These crazy "saints" stared out at the world, wildly, like lunatics—or quietly like suicides; and the "God" that was in their gaze was as mute as a great stone. . . .
>   . . . [T]hese grandmothers and mothers of ours were not "saints," but Artists: driven to a numb and bleeding madness by the springs of creativity in them for which there was no release. They were Creators who lived lives of spiritual waste, because they were so rich in spirituality—which is the basis for Art—that the strain of enduring their unused and unwanted talent drove them insane. Throwing away this spirituality was the pathetic attempt to lighten the soul to a weight the work-worn sexually abused bodies could bear.[43]

Such a time is past: the time of throwing away one's spirituality in order to survive.

It is regrettable that the possible liabilities of dark night theology cannot be dealt with in full here. Although some *interpretations* of dark night could reinforce passivity and women's internalized inferiority, subordination, lack of self-esteem and self-actualization, John of the Cross sings of the affirmation of the person by God within and of the redemption or transformation of affectivity that dark night effects. Dark contemplation is not a validation of things as they are or a ploy to keep women contented "outcasts of the [patriarchal] land"[44] but a constant questioning and restlessness that waits for and believes in the coming of a transformed vision of God; an affirmation of the self as woman that comes from deep inside and the consequent maturing to wholeness as a complete person; and a new and integrating spirituality capable of creating a new politics and generating new social structures.

Contemplation is what Dorothée Soelle calls revolutionary patience and is the epitome of passionate desire, activity, self-direction, autonomy, and bondedness.[45] It is a time bomb and will explode in new abilities and energy in women that cannot be conquered. Ultimately, it is the mystic, the contemplative woman, who will be reassured, affirmed, and loved, who will see and love, and for whose sake the world will be given sight, language, reassurance, and love. And she will understand Celie's final epistle, a letter to God: "Dear God. Dear stars, dear trees, dear sky, dear peoples. Dear Everything. Dear God."

NOTES

1. See David Tracy, *The Analogical Imagination, Christian Theology and the Culture of Pluralism* (New York: Crossroads, 1981), chap. 3, "The Classic."

2. Not only Tracy has influenced my methodology, but also Thomas H. Groome, *Christian Religious Education* (San Francisco, Harper & Row, 1980), pp. 185–222, and John Shea, *Stories of Faith* (Chicago: Thomas More Press, 1980), pp. 76–90. These three studies are helpful in dealing with the dialogue between tradition and contemporary story or issues.

3. Belden C. Lane, "Spirituality and Political Commitment: Notes on a Liberation Theology of Nonviolence," *America*, March 14, 1981; see also Urban T. Holmes III, *Ministry and Imagination* (New York: Seabury, 1981), pp. 89–93, for a good treatment of right- and left-brain thinking. Holmes works out of the contributions of Jerome S. Bruner, *On Knowing: Essays for the Left Hand* (New York: Atheneum, 1971), and Robert E. Ornstein, *The Psychology of Consciousness* (New York: Viking, 1972), pp. 57–64.

4. Dorothée Soelle, *Suffering* (Philadelphia: Fortress, 1975), p. 36.

5. See ibid., p. 76, 11.

6. Lane, "Spirituality and Political Commitment," p. 198. Lane's discussion of the theory of Paul Witzalawick, John Weakland, and Richard Fisch in *Change: Principles of Problem Formation and Problem Resolution* (New York: Norton, 1974).

7. There are other models to explain and verify this experience: e.g., the creative process as it is described by Ralph J. Hallman, "Aesthetic Pleasure and Creative Process," *Humanitas* 4 (1968), pp. 161–68, or *Journal of Humanistic Psychology* 6 (1966), pp. 141–47; the process of individuation developed by Carl Jung and described by John Welch, O. Carm., *Spiritual Pilgrims: Carl Jung and Teresa of Avila* (New York: Paulist Press, 1982), esp. pp. 136–37, 141–43, 151–62; the model of structure and anti-structure developed by Victor W. Turner, *The Forest of Symbols: Aspects of Ndembu Ritual* (Ithaca: Cornell University Press, 1967), pp. 93–101, *The Ritual Process: Structure and Anti-Structure* (Chicago: Aldine, 1969), *Dramas, Fields and Metaphors: Symbolic Action in Human Society* (Ithaca: Cornell University Press, 1974). See Holmes, *Ministry and Imagination*, pp. 119–36, for material on Turner's structure and anti-structure.

8. See John of the Cross, *The Collected Works of St. John of the Cross*, trans. Kieran Kavanaugh and Otilio Rodriguez (Washington, D.C.: Institute of Carmelite Studies, 1973), *Ascent of Mount Carmel*, Book I, chap. 13, no. 3; chap. 14, no. 2: poem, "The Dark Night," p. 296; poem, "The Spiritual Canticle," pp. 410–15; *The Dark Night*, Book II, chap. 9, no. 1; *The Living Flame*, stanza 3, nos. 1,3,7.

9. See John of the Cross, *CW, The Dark Night*, Book I, chaps. 1–8, for a view of the dark side of human desire. John calls this dark side the faults of beginners.

10. See Michael J. Buckley, "Atheism and Contemplation," *Theological Studies* 40 (1979), p. 696; see also John of the Cross, *CW, The Spiritual Canticle*, stanzas 3–7, to grasp how one moves through that which one cherishes—the self, the world, relationships—to deeper love for God.

11. See John of the Cross, *CW, The Dark Night*, Book I, chap. 7, no. 5; chap. 8, no. 3.

12. See ibid., Book I, chap. 9, no. 4.

13. For the first set of signs, see ibid., Book I, chap. 9, no. 8; *Ascent of Mount Carmel*, Book II, chap. 13, no. 2.

14. John, *CW, The Dark Night*, Book I, chap. 9, no. 7.

15. Ibid., Book I, chap. 8, no. 3.

16. Buckley, "Atheism and Contemplation," p. 694.

17. Ibid., p. 693, see also p. 690.

18. John, *CW, The Dark Night*, Book I, chap. 16, no. 2.

19. Buckley, "Atheism and Contemplation," p. 694.

20. Ibid. pp. 696–97.

21. See John, *CW*, *The Dark Night*, Book I, chap. 9, no. 2; for correlating signs, see also *Ascent of Mount Carmel*, Book II, chap. 13, no. 3.

22. See John, *CW*, *The Dark Night*, Book I, chap. 14, where he speaks of the spirit of fornication, blasphemy, and confusion *(spiritus vertiginis)*, or what I would call frustrated desire. See also Welch, *Spiritual Pilgrims*, pp. 141–46.

23 John, *CW*, *The Dark Night*, Book I, chap. 9, no. 3.

24. John, *CW*, *Ascent of Mount Carmel*, Book II, chap. 13, no. 4; *The Dark Night*, Book I, chap. 6, no. 2.

25. See Welch, *Spiritual Pilgrims*, p. 145.

26. Soelle, *Suffering*, p. 85.

27. John, *CW*, *Ascent of Mount Carmel*, Book II, chap. 6, no. 2.

28. Soelle, *Suffering*, p. 85.

29. See Buckley, "Atheism and Contemplation," p. 696.

30. See Constance FitzGerald, "Contemplative Life as Charismatic Presence," *Contemplative Review* II (1978), p. 45, or *Spiritual Life* 29 (1983), p. 28.

31. See Irene Claremont de Castillejo, *Knowing Woman: A Feminine Perspective* (New York: Harper & Row, 1974), pp. 32, 39; see also pp. 17–18 for a very interesting analysis of the different levels on which people discuss nuclear weapons.

32. See Holmes, *Ministry and Imagination*, p. 154. The entire chapter 6, "Dying to Image," pp. 137–164, is excellent supplementary reading to my development.

33. See Anne Carr, B.V.M., "Is a Christian Feminist Theology Possible?" *Theological Studies* 43 (1982), pp. 282, 292; Elisabeth Schüssler Fiorenza, "Toward a Feminist Biblical Hermeneutics: Biblical Interpretation and Liberation Theology," *The Challenge of Liberation Theology*, ed. Mahan, p. 109: "Theological interpretation must also critically reflect on the political presuppositions and implications of theological 'classics' and dogmatic or ethical systems. In other words, not only the content and traditioning process within the Bible, but the whole of Christian tradition should be scrutinized and judged as to whether or not it functions to oppress or liberate people."

34. Elisabeth Schüssler Fiorenza, "Sexism and Conversion," *Network* (May-June 1981), p. 21.

35. Sue E. Houchins, "I Found God in Myself/And I Loved Her/I Loved Her Fiercely: A Study of Suffering in the Archetypal Journey of Alice Walker's Female Heroes," a chapter of a dissertation in progress. p. 15.

36. Alice Walker, *The Color Purple* (New York: Harcourt Brace Jovanovich, 1982), 164–168.

37. Buckley, "Atheism and Contemplation," p. 690. (italics mine).

38. Ibid. p. 695.

39. Quoted by Madonna Kolbenschlag, "Feminists, The Frog Princess, and the New Frontier of Spirituality," *New Catholic World*, July-August 1982.

40. Carr, "Is a Christian Feminist Theology Possible?" p. 293.

41. Here I am addressing the call of Fiorenza for "a spirituality that understands anger, persecution, defamation, violence and suffering in political-theological terms." See "Sexism and Conversion," pp. 20–21.

42. Maureen Fiedler, "The Equal Rights Amendment and the Bonding of Women," *LCWR Newsletter* 8 (1980), p. 5.

43. Alice Walker, "In Search of Our Mother's Gardens," in *Working It Out*, ed. Sara Rudick and Pamela Daniels (New York: Pantheon 1977), p. 93.

44. Houchins, "I Found God in Myself," quoted from Anne Pratt, *Archetypal Patterns in Women's Fiction* (Bloomington, Ind.: Indiana University Press, 1981), 5.

45. Dorothée Soelle, *Revolutionary Patience* (Maryknoll, N.Y.: Orbis, 1977): see also Marianne Katoppo, *Compassionate and Free: An Asian Woman's Theology* (Maryknoll, N.Y.: Orbis, 1980), p. 21.

Revisioning the Ignatian Rules for Discernment

Joann Wolski Conn

Discernment ranks high on the list of central themes in Christian spirituality. In Catholic circles, it is often identified with Ignatius of Loyola because his *Spiritual Exercises* (1951) contain extended guidelines on this subject. I am interested in the general characteristics of Ignatian discernment and their usefulness for women today.

HISTORICAL CONTEXT

Any contemporary use of classical material must begin by understanding its historical context. For hundreds of years Jesuit scholars insisted that their founder, Ignatius of Loyola, wrote the *Spiritual Exercises* because of direct mystical experience ten years earlier and not as a result of an historical process of studying the literature of his day. Recent scholarship (Boyle), however, shows the precise parallels between Ignatius' discussion of discernment and the ascetical literature of early Christianity as well as sixteenth century Reformation debates about who is Spirit-led. One can now appreciate Ignatius' treatment of discernment of spirits as a creative distillation and application of the wisdom of earlier tradition (Lienhard). Absent from Ignatius' writing are earlier assumptions that the gift of discernment was given only to clerics or advanced ascetics. Present everywhere are those strands of the tradition which see the "spirits" less as multiple personifications of good and evil and more as emotions and reasoning within each person, as these are influenced by God and by evil that is both within and beyond the scope of individual human acts.

CHARACTERISTICS OF THE
IGNATIAN RULES FOR DISCERNMENT

The goal of Ignatian discernment is arriving at a choice of the authentic Christian response to God's presence in each concrete situation of our life. It is not a matter of choosing between good and evil. Rather, it is choosing among possible good actions under the influence of grace, presuming God's providential presence and obscurity in the way that presence manifests itself (Futrell:47).

Summarizing the rules omits nuance but suffices for my purpose here. There are two short sets of rules or guidelines (Loyola:#314–336)—one for those in the initial stage of conversion from sin and beginning a serious relationship with God, and another for those more advanced. The term "evil spirit" is often used synonymously with the phrase "the enemy of our human nature," showing a positive view of nature itself and a view of evil as that which is inimical to our basic human capacity for friendship with God. Clues to the influence of the good or evil spirit are emotions. What we must attend to above all are feelings and affective judgments. Anxiety and sadness characteristically prevent advancement toward God; courage, consolation, tears, and peace are God's way of assisting us.

Ignatius defines "consolation" and "desolation" differently from other spiritual writers and uses them in his own way (Buckley). Consolation is any interior movement that invites and attracts the person to God, that directs a person ultimately to the Creator. Often consolation is a peaceful feeling but it is definitely not identified with comfortable, pleasant feelings. Desolation, on the other hand, is any feelings and thoughts that incline a person away from God. Restlessness may be an example of either consolation or desolation depending on the direction in which it leads one. Ignatius does not use these terms to mean God's rewards or punishments, but as affective states that are indicators of our life-direction. Ignatius gives advice about how to understand and combat desolation, how to benefit from consolation, and how to test for genuine consolation. The latter is surely from God if it is consolation "without previous cause," that is, if it is a non-conceptual experience of complete openness to God (Rahner; Egan). For persons more advanced in their spiritual life, evil characteristically assumes the guise of an "angel of light," attacking their weakest point. Thus, one must learn from previous experience by examining the whole course of her or his thoughts and emotions to see where and why one was led astray. One must be sure to distinguish the original genuine consolation from the period that follows. At such time a fervent person may form plans that are not necessarily inspired by God. Thus, basic directives for discernment must be reintroduced and the process begun again.

SIGNIFICANCE FOR WOMEN

How can Ignatian guidelines assist women's process of self-transcendence? What does a feminist revisioning of Christian spirituality notice about this approach to discernment?

Ignatian discernment presumes that Christian life decisions are not logical applications of revealed or self-evident principles. They do not look to external authority. Therefore, they are pertinent for today when the collapse of traditional religious structures forces women to interiorize religious values in light of new experience and new theology. Christian feminism is causing women to rethink models of holiness and styles of ministry. In this atmosphere discernment is often their primary task.

Unlike monastic traditions of discretion or discernment, Ignatius' guidelines arise from an apostolic spirituality involved in the public sphere. Now that women are as much in the public sphere as in the private, they want to respond to God's presence and call in every situation.

Moving against mainstream American culture which reinforces conformity to dependent roles for women, these directives confirm the value of self-direction. Our freedom is what God values and affirms.

Discernment promotes nuanced self-understanding and alerts women to subtleties of self-deception. The scrutiny of this process could disclose the "feminine mystique," for example, as really a shield against the rigors of intellectual creativity or the struggles involved in working out an egalitarian marriage. Discernment could confirm women's knowledge that their affinity for relationships is a healthy corrective to exaggerated autonomy. It promotes candor about vulnerability—a human quality women specialize in—without using it as an excuse. Women are beginning to see many more ways in which "evil assume[s] the appearance of an angel of light." Under the guise of "self-sacrifice" women have repressed many talents or looked the other way when patriarchal structures oppressed women and men.

Consolation, as Ignatius defines it, is a trustworthy measure for women's self-transcendence. What actually leads one toward God— not merely what feels comfortable, secure, or "consoling"—is the consolation characteristic of God's spirit. If women's awkwardness in learning to care for their own interests results in a freer relationship with God, then this discomfort is not desolation. It need not be the "pangs of conscience" due to selfishness. The direction it manifests—a mature relationship to God—shows it is consolation. If women's frustration expressed in anger and resentment, even anger at God, can result in a more candid, adult response to God, then its direction reveals it to be consolation. It brings the deeper peace which springs from "gut level" honesty before God in all times and places.

Distinguishing rules for discernment appropriate to beginners and to the more advanced might be applied to the case of women reconciling patriarchal Christian tradition with feminist values. Those newly converted to a struggle against sexism in the Church and to insistence on equal discipleship might be tempted to romanticize the easier times when clergy and laity, men and women, knew "their place." The secure gratification of aesthetic worship, using a common source, could tempt them to abandon the tedious task of rooting out hymns and prayers that reflect militarism and sexism. Those more experienced in the way feminist values witness gospel values might discern more subtle temptations. Ignatius advises these women to examine the full course of their emotions and thoughts to see when and why they went astray. When, for example, did their adult assertiveness and healthy anger turn rigid and become intolerance of women and men less feminist than they? Or why have they lately given less time to focused prayer? Is the justification presented as a need to devote more time to important ministries? Could the deeper reason be discouragement or boredom? When prayer is now dry instead of filled with the joy that came when first using feminine God-images, is movement away from God appearing as an "angel of light" in the guise of devotion to duty?

These are just some of the ways a feminist perspective can revision this traditional Christian theme of discernment.

REFERENCES CONSULTED

Boyle, Marjorie O'Rourke
   1983 "Angels Black and White: Loyola's Spiritual Discernment in Historical Perspective." *Theological Studies* 44:241–257.
Buckley, Michael
   1973 "The Structure of the Rules for Discernment of Spirits." *The Way* Supplement 20:19–37.
Egan, Harvey E.
   1976 *The Spiritual Exercises and the Ignatian Mystical Horizon.* St. Louis: Institute of Jesuit Sources.
Futrell, J. C.
   1970 "Ignatian Discernment." *Studies in the Spirituality of Jesuits.* Number 2.
Ignatius of Loyola
   1951 *The Spiritual Exercises of St. Ignatius.* Translated by Louis J. Puhl, S.J. Westminster: Newman.
Lienhard, Joseph T.
   1980 "On Discernment of Spirits in the Early Church." *Theological Studies* 41:505–529.
Rahner, Karl
   1964 *The Dynamic Element in the Church.* New York: Herder and Herder.

Thérèse of Lisieux from a Feminist Perspective

Joann Wolski Conn

Authors who examine the history of Christian spirituality from a feminist perspective (i.e., affirming and promoting women's mature autonomy and equality in society and in the Church) have, by now, given us some excellent studies of the spirituality of Julian of Norwich, Catherine of Siena, Mechtilde of Magdeburg, Teresa of Avila. I would like to add to this list a brief study of a woman who is seldom even mentioned in connection with explicitly feminist issues: Thérèse of Lisieux.

Most persons with whom I begin to discuss Thérèse will say that they learned about her when they were school children or when they were novices in a religious community. What they remember about her, now that they are sensitized to feminist issues or to the characteristics of adult faith, makes them quite uncomfortable with Thérèse. She is remembered as the epitome of the simple, unquestioning, pious, sentimental, accepting "child-woman." They cannot envision Thérèse dealing with the struggle for adult autonomy as an integral aspect of her "little way" to holiness. They can imagine Teresa of Avila as "the first man of Spain" (as Teresa's contemporaries called her) but they can only imagine Thérèse of Lisieux as the Pollyanna-type "good little Sister" who picked up pins for the love of God and let filthy laundry water splash in her face.

The Thérèse I have discovered is quite a different woman from the "little flower" I, too, knew and loved years ago. In studying Thérèse from the perspective of feminist concerns, I have discov-

317

ered that Thérèse's deep holiness was the opposite of conventional conformity to the ideals of her family and her Lisieux Carmelite monastery. Thérèse demonstrates a consistently developing appropriation of her own original vision of life. That women become their own authority, that is, the author of their own distinctive life-vision, is a central feminist value.

How did she acquire this original vision? Principally, she trusts her own experience of God and her own insight. That women affirm their own experience is also a feminist concern. Thérèse calls herself an "explorer" into Scripture, discovering new insights that she is drawn to because they support her own prior experience of God. She strengthens her original vision by attempts at expressing and sharing it with her sisters—three of whom are in the same Carmel. When she realizes that they most often misunderstand her, she makes a basic effort to clarify her ideas but does not pursue the explanation. She does, however, peacefully persevere in her own original vision. Her originality demonstrates Thérèse's growth beyond the conventional to an autonomous, adult personality who can freely give a mature self to God.

In what ways is Thérèse original? There is one way that is already commonly associated with her: in a Catholic milieu permeated by fear and rigorism Thérèse proclaims her experience and convictions about a God who is full of tenderness, mercy, and love. However, there are many other aspects of her originality that could only recently be recognized with the help of critical editions of her autobiography and letters, more thorough studies of nineteenth century French popular religion in general, and of French Carmels in particular.[1] This essay will explore three aspects of Thérèse's perspective: the originality of her vision of spiritual development, of the Church, and of heaven.

THE NATURE OF SPIRITUAL DEVELOPMENT

For several reasons Thérèse thought especially carefully about the nature of spiritual development. First of all, for the first seven years of her religious life she wanted to share with her dearly-loved sister, Celine, (who also wanted to be a Carmelite, but stayed home to care for their sick father) all that she, Thérèse, was discovering about the spiritual life. She did this in letters which gradually reveal the younger sister, Thérèse, as the spiritual director of the older. These letters (1888–1894) cease when Celine enters the Lisieux Carmel where Thérèse is, by now, the acting directress of novices. Thérèse's involvement with the religious formation of the novices from 1893 onward of course prompted special focus on what is at the core of Christian spirituality. Then, in the last three years of her life, Thérèse is told to write about her life, a task she decides to accept as an opportunity to review "the mercies of the Lord" in her life. These sources show that Thérèse is quite well aware of the fact that the vision of life she has developed is uncommon and even goes directly against habitual methods of spiritual direction in her day.

After seven years in Carmel—from the beginning, trusting in Jesus as her spiritual director—Thérèse confides to Celine that she is not following the most basic pattern of advice followed by other religious (and laity) in her day. As late as the 1950s, this same pattern was a common method of spiritual formation and direction.

> Directors do in fact bring souls forward in the way of perfection by having them make a great many acts of virtue, and they are right; but my director, Jesus, does not teach me to count my acts, but to do *everything* for love . . .—but all this in peace, in *abandonment*, Jesus does everything, I nothing.[2]

Thérèse desires spiritual liberty, not counting acts and avoiding stain to her Baptismal robe. She trusts her desires, her inspirations. She trusts that a way of freedom rather than careful self-supervision could be inspired by Jesus.

Another common presentation of the spiritual life assumed that perfection automatically meant the search for the "more difficult." Thérèse breaks with this perspective also. To her sister Leonie, whose worries and scruples were partly generated by an all too common image of God as really satisfied or pleased only when we are unhappy, Thérèse writes:

> I assure you that God is even kinder than you think. He is satisfied with a look, a sigh of love. . . . Personally, I find perfection quite easy to practice because I have realized that all one has to do is *take Jesus by the heart*.[3]

Another original insight into the nature of spiritual development is evident in this same letter. It is actually Thérèse's own "little way" written in summary fashion for the first time here in a letter to the Martin sister whom the family considered backward and almost a misfit since she was in and out of different convents four times. For this "poor soul" Thérèse took the initiative to explain her central message, before she gave it to her Carmelite sister, Marie. For Thérèse, there are not two classes of souls: on the one side, the aristocrats, the great souls capable of heroic abnegation and, on the other, the lesser souls who can do ordinary things. Rooted in hope, Thérèse trusts that the "poor souls" are the first who can believe in Love and allow themselves to be invaded by Love.

Ironically, though Thérèse's canonization process was designed—like all canonizations—to prove she practiced "heroic virtue," Thérèse rejected that ideal of holiness: the extraordinary; what others could observe and testify about. Only once in Thérèse's autobiography does she use the word heroic. There it refers to her burning desires to do every courageous daring deed to make Jesus loved. Her thoughts move, however, immediately to declare that she was not satisfied to identify herself with any visible organ of the mystical body (i.e., which did heroic deeds), but could only rest in identity with the heart (love). Thérèse always chooses what is HIDDEN. This term (caché) appears forty-six times in her autobiography and represents her ideal of holiness. A common misinterpretation of Thérèse's hiddenness—perhaps partly due to the way canonization testimony is a priori fitted into certain categories—is the portrayal of her as practicing a "little heroism" rather than great heroism, as being heroic in doing little things (e.g., picking up pins). This influences some people to see her as preoccupied with little things, since she is in a cloistered milieu where small things take on a disproportionately larger significance. On the contrary, in context, Thérèse speaks of these small acts with ironic humor, genuinely viewing them as small and candidly admitting that she "often . . . allow(s) these little sacrifices . . . to slip by."[4] For example, she does not see herself as heroically standing silent to receive the reprimands of a Sister who was upset when Thérèse caused a racket which awoke the sick Prioress. Knowing she could not take this reprimand in peace, Thérèse describes her flight and the "heroic oration" of the angry Sister: "I left without fuss, allowing the Sister to continue her discourse which resembled the imprecations of Camillus against the city of Rome."[5]

Lastly, Thérèse's final manuscript shows that she clearly departs from the ascetic ideal of the nineteenth century Carmel: "the rough stairway of perfection." Rather than use this classical metaphor (which some have associated with a Platonic hierarchy of being which has levels to which not everyone can aspire) Thérèse's central image is very modern (for 1897): an elevator. Trusting her own experience of desire for a straight, short way to God, Thérèse searches the Scriptures and finds a reinforcing maternal God-image (Isaias 66:13, 12) which she immediately associates with Jesus. For her, the "elevator" is Jesus' maternal embrace into which she abandons herself and is content to be little and to be lifted up to God.[6] There is a touch of humor associated with her image because now it is not the rich but the poor, the little ones, who have this elevator.

THEOLOGY OF THE CHURCH

Thérèse formulates an original theology of the Church, especially for a twenty-three-year-old Carmelite with no theological training. Again, trusting her experience of great desires she describes her search in the Scriptures until she found what confirmed her prayerful intuitions about ministry in the wider community. Finding this, she says, "I finally had rest."

What she did was take two chapters from First Corinthians, each with a different tone and theme, and make her own original connection. If in chapter XII Paul speaks of the Church as a "body" with different ministries symbolized as different members of a body, chapter XIII has a quite different tone. Here Paul speaks in the first person: "If I speak in tongues . . . and do not have love, I am nothing." Thérèse's genius is to join the two texts.[7] For her, the comparison with members of a body does not go far enough. If the essential for a Christian is love, so must it also be for the Church. From there the body comparison is enlarged to include a heart "burning with love" which "*alone* made the Church members act." Thérèse identifies herself with this love. Note that, true to her ideal of holiness, this member of the body (the Church) is hidden. Essentially, then, for Thérèse the Church is not works but love.

That this vision is original is supported by the kind of response that Thérèse received when she shared it with her Carmelite sister, Marie. In a letter written back to Thérèse on the day after Thérèse shared her own vision with Marie, Marie shows her inability to comprehend Thérèse.

> I have read your pages, with their burning love for Jesus. . . .
> Ah, you say that you do nothing . . . but what about your desires? How do you reckon them? The good God certainly regards them as works.[8]

Marie's viewpoint was the common concern with progress in the spiritual life measured by counting one's acts of virtue, one's good works. Thérèse replies to Marie with another letter to say that she is content to see herself without desires or virtues which could be clung to as riches which, in a pharisaical way, make us count on ourselves instead of trusting in God's transforming love.[9]

Equally original is Thérèse's insight which links this vision of the Church as burning love with a new perspective on her Carmelite vocation to be a mother of souls. Thérèse sees the Church first as Spouse and only then as Mother. Nineteenth century missionary work was often described as carrying the true message to those living in darkness, as freeing miserable pagans from their ignorance. Thérèse inserts a new perspective. The Church, first of all, *is* love. Thus, missionary zeal for souls must be an expression of genuine love. If the Church is first Spouse and only then Mother, she will not be an instrument of maternalism which can be condescending or patronizing toward "poor sinners."[10] This vision of the Church as Spouse who is love supports Thérèse's own vision of herself which is one of a sister to sinners. In her last eighteen months of life Thérèse experiences a profound trial of faith in which she can speak of herself as in sisterly union with those who are without any faith.[11]

HEAVEN

One of the words used most often by Thérèse—145 times—is "heaven." Tracing its use through her autobiographical manuscripts and letters, the originality of her understanding becomes gradually more evident.

Her early understanding was very common to her era: heaven is an eternal Sunday afternoon with one's family. Gradually the image represents a more mature understanding, especially as a result of her original use of some ideas from a popular nineteenth century book, *Fin du monde présent et mystère de la vie future*, which she read very carefully the year before she entered Carmel.

What Thérèse omits from her use of *Fin du monde* is as significant as what she finds inspiring. Written by a scripture professor, this book used Old and New Testament texts, in the method typical of its day, without any sense of literary genre. Thérèse does not retain any of the theological propositions which fill it. For example, it declares as "of divine faith and theologically certain that souls in purgatory are submitted to the action of real fire." Nor does she retain the blatant antisemitism in the book: "the Anti-Christ will be a Jew; the Jews are the great social peril." Rather, Thérèse retains what she sees as essential: the theme of our "divinization." God will transform us so that we become gods ourselves. This forms the theme of a letter to Celine a few months after Thérèse is in Carmel. Our divinization in heaven is repose but not inactivity, she learns. Gradually she makes her own original application. Becoming convinced that God's first love is for sinners and outcasts and that heaven will mean she is totally absorbed into this love, she begins to view heaven not as flight from the exile of this life but, rather, an opportunity to continue doing what God is doing: caring for humanity on earth.

From Easter 1896 until her death (30 Sept. 1897), Thérèse is plunged into a severe trial of faith. At the center of her darkness is precisely the question of heaven. Earlier, in 1891, the great interior trials she experienced during her retreat culminate in the question of heaven.

> At that time I was having great interior trials of all kinds, even to the point of asking myself whether heaven really existed.[12]

In subsequent years the thought of heaven returns to console her. However, in 1896, heaven becomes the focus of the deep struggle which lasts up to Thérèse's death in 1897.

During those very joyful days of the Easter season . . . He permitted my soul to be invaded by the thickest darkness, and that the thought of heaven, up until then so sweet to me, be no longer anything but the cause of struggle and torment.[13]

When one realizes what heaven had come to mean for Thérèse: continued opportunity for loving care for humanity, her crisis of faith in heaven, in life after death, takes on its full dimension. Thérèse continues to speak of heaven, especially as a place of hope, and her words bear special poignancy knowing she is speaking out of an experience of darkness and profound struggle.

CONCLUSION

These three examples of Thérèse's adherence to a remarkably original vision support, I believe, an evaluation of her as a woman who was involved with feminist concerns: growth beyond conventional roles; striving for an autonomous, adult personality. Thérèse definitely struggled with issues of intellectual independence and mature autonomy as intrinsic aspects of her life's process of completely giving herself in mature surrender to God's love.

Women whose vision of ministry and of themselves is often misunderstood or even rejected can take courage and legitimate pride in this young woman who is popularly and commonly seen as the model of traditional femininity: sweet, pliable, childlike, living only to please others. However, a closer look at the evidence can reveal quite the contrary model. Thérèse is a strong, creative, mature young woman who thought independently and originally, who could thus give a genuine self in a free loving relationship to God.

NOTES

1. English language editions of Thérèse's autobiography and letters are: *The Autobiography of St. Thérèse of Lisieux,* trans. by John Clarke, o.c.d. (Washington, D.C.: Institute of Carmelite Studies, 1975); *Collected Letters of St. Thérèse of Lisieux,* ed. by Abbé Combes, trans. by F.J. Sheed (N.Y.: Sheed and Ward, 1949). Regarding needed caution when considering what are called Thérèse's last words as a source for authentic There-

sian spirituality, see my review of *St. Thérèse of Lisieux: Her Last Conversations* in *Horizons* 6 (Fall 1979), 308–309. On popular religion see, for example, A. Latreille, "Pratique, piété et foi populaire dans la France moderne au XIXème et XXème siècles," *Popular Belief and Practice*, ed. by G.J. Cuming and Derek Baker (Cambridge, 1972).

2. *Collected Letters*, entry for 6 July 1893.

3. *Ibid.*, entry for 12 July 1896.

4. *Autobiography*, 250.

5. *Ibid.*, 224.

6. *Ibid.*,208.

7. Jean-François Six, *Thérèse de Lisieux au Carmel* (Paris: Editions du Seuil, 1972), 272.

8. *Collected Letters*, entry for 16 September 1896.

9. *Ibid.*, entry for 17 September 1896.

10. Six, *Thérèse au Carmel*, 272–273.

11. This theme is developed in my article "Conversion in Thérèse of Lisieux," *Spiritual Life* (Fall 1978), 154–163.

12. *Autobiography*, 173.

13. *Ibid.*, 211.

Authors

ANNE CARR, professor in the Divinity School of the University of Chicago, is the author of studies in feminist theology and *The Theological Method of Karl Rahner.*

CATHERINE OF SIENA (1347–1380), mystic and religious reformer, is a Doctor of the Church.

JOANN WOLSKI CONN, professor of religious studies at Neumann College, and the Neumann Graduate Program in Pastoral Counseling, has published articles in *Cross Currents, Spirituality Today, Horizons,* and *Human Development.*

BERNARD COOKE, professor of religious studies at College of the Holy Cross, Worcester, Massachusetts, is the author of many articles and books, including *Ministry to Word and Sacraments.*

LUISE EICHENBAUM is co-director of The Women's Therapy Centre Institute in New York and co-founder of The Women's Therapy Centre in London.

ELISABETH SCHÜSSLER FIORENZA, professor of New Testament at the Episcopal Divinity School, has recently written *In Memory of Her: A Feminist Theological Reconstruction of Christian Origins,* and *Reclaiming the Center.*

CONSTANCE FITZGERALD, contemplative nun, author, and spiritual director, is a member of the Carmel of Baltimore, Maryland.

JAMES FOWLER, professor of theology and human development at Emory University, Atlanta, Georgia, is the author of *Stages of Faith,* and, most recently, *Becoming Adult, Becoming Christian.*

CAROL GILLIGAN, professor of education in the Harvard Graduate School of Education, Cambridge, Massachusetts, is the author of *In a Different Voice: Psychological Theory and Women's Development.*

NAOMI GOLDENBERG, professor in the religious studies

department of the University of Ottawa, is the author of *Changing of the Gods: Feminism and the End of Traditional Religion.*

ROSEMARY HAUGHTON, lecturer and author of many books on religious experience, most recently published *The Passionate God.*

IGNATIUS OF LOYOLA (1491–1556), mystic and religious reformer, founded the Society of Jesus.

JOHN OF THE CROSS (1542–1591), mystic, and one of the greatest Spanish poets, also wrote commentaries on his poetic texts such as *The Spiritual Canticle* and *Dark Night of the Soul.*

ELIZABETH JOHNSON, professor at the Catholic University of America, has published articles in many journals including *Theological Studies, Heythrop Journal,* and *Horizons.*

ROBERT KEGAN, lecturer on education at the Harvard Graduate School of Education, and a member of the core faculty at the Massachusetts School of Professional Psychology, is the author of *The Evolving Self: Problem and Process in Human Development.*

JEAN BAKER MILLER is a psychiatrist practicing in Boston, Massachusetts.

SUSIE ORBACH is co-director of The Women's Therapy Centre Institute in New York and co-founder of The Women's Therapy Centre in London.

SANDRA M. SCHNEIDERS, professor of New Testament and spirituality at the Jesuit School of Theology and the Graduate Theological Union in Berkeley, California, is a lecturer, spiritual director and author of articles in journals such as *Theological Studies, Horizons,* and *The Catholic Biblical Quarterly.*

TERESA OF AVILA (1515–1582), mystic and religious reformer, is a Doctor of the Church.

ELISABETH M. TETLOW, an attorney practicing in New Orleans, Louisiana, is the author of *Women and Ministry in the New Testament* and *An Inclusive Language Translation of the Spiritual Exercises of Saint Ignatius of Loyola.*

DEMARIS WEHR, professor of religious studies at Swarthmore College, Swarthmore, Pennsylvania, has taught feminist perspectives on Jungian psychology at the Harvard Divinity School.